Oldacre

A Gloucestershire Family and Business
1881–1986

OLDACRE
A Gloucestershire Family and Business 1881–1986

Denys Charnock

The Book Guild Ltd

Sussex, England

To
My grandchildren Matthew, Sally,
Timothy, Thomas and Henry part of whose
heritage this story covers.

The history of British Family Surnames gives the name
Oldacre as coming from 'one who lives by the old ploughed
field'.

The Book Guild Ltd.
25 High Street,
Lewes, Sussex.

First published 1990
© Denys Charnock 1990
Set in Baskerville
Typesetting by Kudos Graphics
Slinfold, Sussex.

Printed in Great Britain by
Antony Rowe Ltd.,
Chippenham, Wiltshire.

British Library Cataloguing in Publication Data
Charnock, Denys
    Oldacre: a Gloucestershire family and business 1881–1986.
    1. England. Entrepreneurship. Oldacre (Family), history
    I. Title
    338.04092242

ISBN 0 86332 481 9

CONTENTS

AUTHOR'S NOTE

William John Oldacre was a man of immense stature. He was born on 9 May 1889, eight years after his father Walter John Oldacre Senior had started trading as a carrier and hay merchant. Over the next one hundred years, three generations of the family were totally dedicated to the business, all were brought up under a stern discipline and taught that hard work and thrift were the basis of a true and happy life. When William John died on 21 January 1983, Oldacres was the largest manufacturer of animal feed compounds in private ownership.

After William John's death, his son Walter John Junior, agreed that I could tell the story of the family and the business based largely on the life of his father.

The early part of the story follows from the recollections of William John and older members of the family, supplemented by information readily available in records such as those of Bishops Cleeve Parish Church, St Catherine's House, the Probate Register at Gloucester, and Gloucestershire Records Office. I am indebted to the Rev John Mead, Rector of Bishops Cleeve for his help.

The history of the business comes from the records of W J Oldacre Ltd, and its successor companies, to which I was given free access by Walter John Oldacre Junior. I received help from Walter John Oldacre Junior, Henry Shouler, Freda Wise and Leslie Aston.

All the members of William John's immediate family, his daughters Mary, Catherine, Hilda and June, and his son recalled events from their busy lives whenever I asked them. I am also indebted to Dorothy Irons, Lucy Pears, Ethel Minett and Doris Burnett for information about the family.

I have attempted to be objective in putting together the information which I have collected but a certain amount of licence has been necessary to make the narrative more readable. Some may feel that the facts are not recorded exactly as they remember them; I ask that they make allowance for any flaws which they may find.

Finally I thank Susan Sinnott (the younger daughter of Walter John Oldacre Junior), for reading and advising on the early drafts of the manuscript, without whose help and

encouragement the story would never have been finished,
and Eric Watterson (the family solicitor), for reading through
the final draft.
Denys Charnock
1989

SOURCES

'A few memoirs of William John Oldacre (1896–1979)
The Victoria History of Gloucestershire
The Victoria History of Lancashire
Diaries of Thomas Beckingsale (1833–1869)
Notes on the History of the Beckingsale Family
Diaries of Gladys Mary Oldacre
St Michael and All Angels Church, Bishops Cleeve
   Baptismal, Marriage and Burial Registers
   Parish Magazines and other Records
General Register Office, London
   Birth, Marriage and Death Certificates
Probate Office, Gloucester
   The 'Wills' of William John Oldacre (1839–1898), Eliza
Oldacre (1843–1910), Henry Minett (1813–1881), Maria Minett
(1814–1909), Walter John Oldacre (1862–1933), and Lucy
Oldacre (1853–1942)
W J Oldacre Ltd, and Successor Companies
   Annual Reports
   Minutes of Board Meetings
   Minutes of Management Meetings
   Staff Journals and other Company Records
   Private Papers of Walter John Oldacre Junior
Gloucestershire Echo
The Royal Gloucestershire Hussars Museum
Collins and Hart – 'Principles of Road Engineering'

PHOTOGRAPHS

Family Albums
Company Records
Gloucestershire Echo
Tim Curr, Teddington, Gloucestershire

THE OLDACRE FAMILY
(1839–1989)

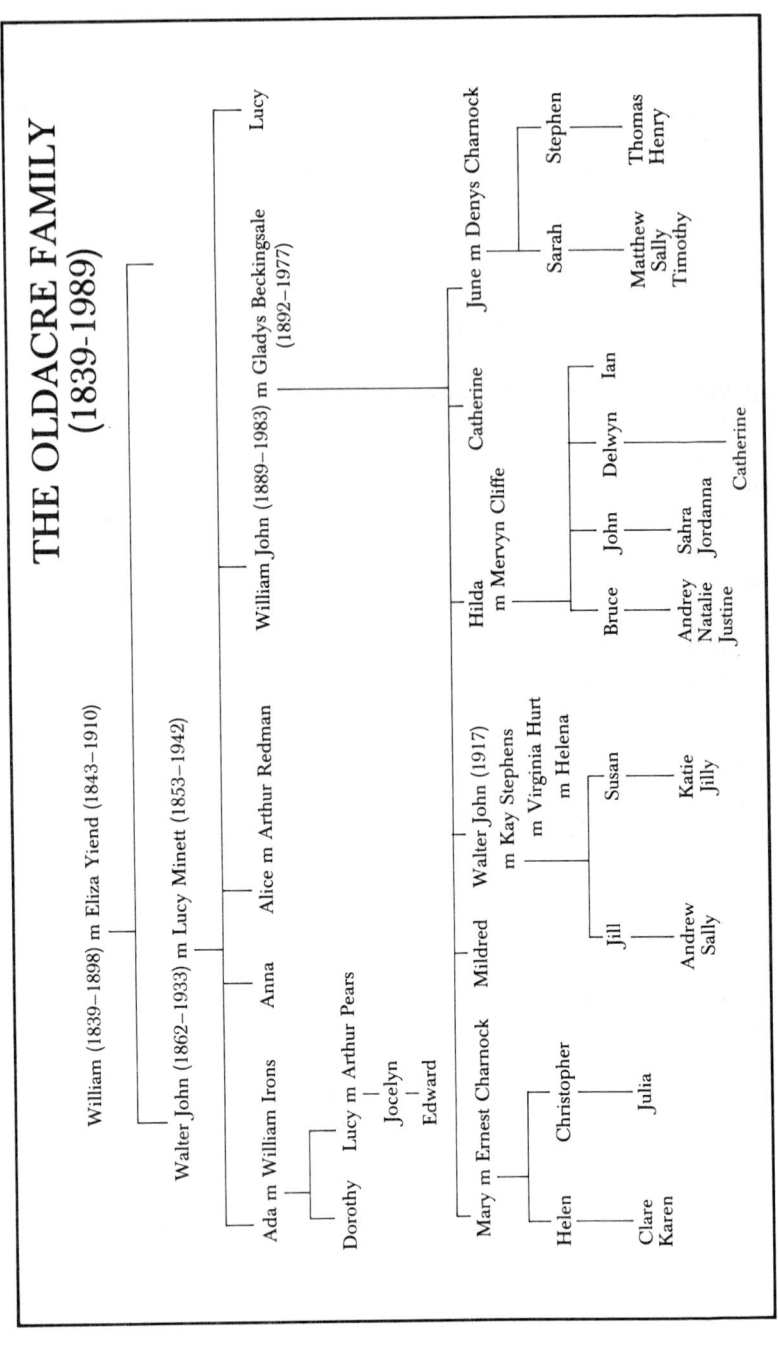

1

ARRIVAL IN BISHOPS CLEEVE

(i) William Oldacre leaves home

William Oldacre closed the door of the cottage behind him. He did not look back but set off at a brisk pace in the direction of Whittington, a village near Andoversford in Gloucestershire. All his possssions were carried on a stout blackthorn stick angled across his left shoulder, and the few sovereigns which he had managed to save for just such an eventuality were contained in a pouch securely fixed around his waist. William was 20 years old, tall, blond and sturdy. He could read and write, was capable of undertaking any job on a farm and prepared to work as a general labourer if the need arose.

Dawn was breaking as he passed through Whittington. The sky was clear and the morning air was fresh with the scent of new mown hay, the hedgerows glistened with the early morning dew and the song of the birds was a joy to hear. But William's heart was heavy. He had warned his mother of his impending departure from the family home and was sad to be leaving behind him someone he loved so much.

William was taking this drastic step because he could no longer tolerate his father's attitude towards him, nor his violent temper. As he strode briskly along he tried once again to analyse the root cause of the breakdown in their relationship. He had been close to his father when he was young but as he grew to manhood his father had continued to demand total subservience. John Oldacre had very firm ideas about how life should be lived and how each task on his farm should be performed. William accepted that he had rebelled against such strict and harsh discipline, but his father's reactions were always illogical and violent. The young man

11

was convinced that his father was losing his reason and that the fierce arguments which had become commonplace, would ultimately end in physical violence. Perhaps his father was jealous of the love which William showed towards his mother although there was little evidence of this being the case. Or did his father's state of mind stem from the hardships which he had endured in his own youth? William knew that the Oldacres came from yeomen stock and that in 1839 when he was born, his father was a labourer. By 1847, as a direct result of hard work and extreme thrift, his father had acquired the small parcel of land which he now farmed in his own right. William could only think it was these early struggles which had turned him into such an aggressive and intolerant man.

Once William had passed through Whittington, his thoughts changed to the more immediate problem of finding work. Long before he left home he had decided that as he moved northwards towards the industrial Midlands, the farms in the Severn Valley or the Vale of Evesham would be likely to employ a strong, healthy and willing young worker on haymaking and harvesting. If all else failed, he was sure that he could find work in one of the many quarries on Cleeve Hill.

It is not difficult to imagine the wonder with which this young man gazed down on the Severn Valley from Cleeve Hill in the summer of 1859. His childhood had been spent in the closer landscape of a Cotswold hill village and now he had before him a birdseye view of a vast expanse of valley stretching from Gloucester in the south, almost as far to the north as Worcester. He will have seen the towers of Gloucester Cathedral and Tewkesbury Abbey, the spires of the churches at Bredon and Upton-on-Severn, as well as the tower of Bishops Cleeve church in the foreground. Across the valley a patchwork of fields spread out before him, interspersed with high elm trees, the urban growth of Cheltenham, the racecourse at Prestbury and in the far distance a background of the Black Mountains, May Hill, the Malverns and the Clee Hills. Is it any wonder that he was happy for his journeyings to end at this place?

Southam and Woodmancote were hamlets lying on the lower wooded slopes of Cleeve Hill, the highest in the

Cotswolds. The civil administration of them, together with the villages of Bishops Cleeve, Stoke Orchard, Gotherington and Brockhampton, came under the town of Winchcombe, but they were much influenced by the larger parish of Bishops Cleeve on the level ground at the foot of the hill.

Bishops Cleeve grew up in Saxon times around a church and a manor house. The name Cleeve comes from its position below the escarpment and the prefix 'Bishops' was added after a monastery was granted to the Bishop of Worcester in the ninth century. The monastery only survived for a short period and the Saxon church was replaced early in the 12th century by a fine Norman church built in stone. The old rectory dating from the 13th century and a 15th century tithe barn are also stone buildings. The village was almost totally destroyed by fire in the 15th century, and the houses built on the ashes were mainly of timber frame construction with thatched or stone-tiled roofs, but among them were houses of good oolitic limestone, again with stone-tiled roofs.

Bishops Cleeve had been as large as Cheltenham in the eighteenth century, but the industrial revolution had passed it by and when William arrived, much of the population of the village had drifted away to the prosperous Midlands. Mercifully for the beautiful Cotswold countryside coal had not been found there although some survey work had been done. The only damage to the face of the escarpment had come from quarrying which was an important industry.

In addition to quarrying, employment in Woodmancote and Bishops Cleeve was centred around the small farms, the gravel pits, the training of race horses and the racecourse itself which had been sited on Cleeve Common in 1830 before it was moved to the present site at Prestbury. The farms in the area were small indeed. Fields in Bishops Cleeve, Southam, Brockhampton and Woodmancote were enclosed by a single enclosure award in 1847 when only the Earl of Ellenbury and the Rector of Bishops Cleeve were granted more than 200 acres. Three landowners had 100 to 200 acres, four land-owners 50 to 100 acres, 10 landowners 10 to 50 acres and 110 had smallholdings. In the mid-19th century, almost one third of the working population of the area were involved in a craft or trade of some sort. They were carpenters and joiners, wheelwrights and wainwrights, coop-

Where the footpath begins for Bushcomb
Woodmancote stores

ers, blacksmiths and farriers, weavers and tailors, bakers and the like. They were craftsmen who had been prepared to spend many years of their youth in apprenticeships and the men were proud of the skills which they learned.

We do not know if William came down immediately from the hill along Gambles Lane or Stockwell Lane, or whether he worked for a time in one of the quarries on the hill. We do know that he met members of the Yiend family who were masons and quarrymen and that he was soon welcomed into their home. In the warmth and comfort of the Yiend kitchen he enjoyed home cooked farm meals for the first time since he left his mother's kitchen and he also found a comradeship which had been missing from his relatively short life. The change must have been a rare pleasure for him after his gruelling tramp over the Cotswolds, and the nights which he had spent sleeping rough.

Eliza, the daughter of the Yiend family, was hard working and intelligent. Unlike her brothers, she could read and write and William Oldacre was attracted by her. He felt they had much in common and it was not long before William proposed marriage. The Yiend family were delighted with this turn of events and William and Eliza were married at Saint Michael and All Angels Church, Bishops Cleeve on 13 April 1861. He was 21 years of age and she was 18.

The young couple had few worldly goods but they did have a roof over their heads, warmth and plenty of food. They lived in a small timber framed and thatched cottage at Horses Green, Woodmancote, where Eliza ran the general store. William continued to work as a farm labourer, and in the quarries, but he also helped his wife in the shop.

On 25 January the following year, Eliza gave birth to a boy. Shortly afterwards the child was christened Walter John in the parish church. A few years later, after his parents had lost an infant daughter, Walter John's sister Anna Maria was born. Their father was by then farming a few acres of land and like many other mid-nineteenth century country folk, striving hard to give his children a good start in life.

William's own father John Oldacre, died at Hampton Shipton on 8 July 1873. The death certificate gives the cause of death as 'diseased brain', so William was right about his father's state of mind when he left the family home in 1859.

Birthplace of Walter John Oldacre

His mother Ann Oldacre moved in with William and Eliza some months before her husband's death and survived him by six years. Ann is buried near to the east wall of Bishops Cleeve churchyard.

(ii) Walter John's early life

Walter John was subjected to firm discipline and a strict religious upbringing. He attended the village school and proved to be an apt pupil. At an early age he was expected to carry out such simple duties as collecting and chopping wood; fetching logs and coal for the fire; filling and trimming oil lamps; pumping water from the well deep down in the gravel beds and carrying it to the house for his mother. By the time he left school, he was used to digging, planting, hoeing and harvesting, looking after the dogs and cats, and feeding the pigs and poultry. His father had taught him how to fodder, groom and harness a horse and how to look after cattle and sheep. He had little enough leisure time and there were few recreational pursuits open to him. His pleasures were restricted to reading, playing draughts and chess in the winter, and to walking, shooting and ferreting in the summer.

He was a strong tall youth with eyes that were always alert. When he left school he worked on local farms and helped his parents with their daily tasks in the village store. He drove his parents' horse and carriers' cart the four miles into Cheltenham to collect goods for his mother's shop and he made deliveries in the village. This work brought him into contact with the villagers, and he soon made a place for himself in the local community and the parish and it was not long before this personable young man was looking for ways of establishing himself in a business venture in his own right. He realised that he could easily give a carrier service from Cheltenham to the village without interfering unduly with his other activities. The local people were pleased to accept the rates which he offered and he was soon carrying their surplus eggs, butter, cheese, vegetables, poultry and preserves to markets in Cheltenham. For the return journey he picked up their shopping, pig and poultry foods and any other commodity which they required from the town. He worked long hours at these tasks for six days each week. Sunday was a day of rest; he attended morning and evening prayer at the parish church, and walked over the hills in the afternoon.

The Reverend W L Townshend, who had been Rector of Bishops Cleeve since 1830, was probably the most influential person in the village. He was a stern man but he gathered into his church all the farmers, craftsmen and tradespeople of importance. He regarded Walter John Oldacre highly for his diligence at school and the work which he did at home. He considered that the boy was a credit to his parents and set a good example to the other boys in the parish. Walter John was unaffected by mockery from people of his own age and he was physically strong enough to deter any attempts at violence against him. He helped with the organisation of harvest suppers, the flower shows and other activities in the parish and in so doing he became friendly with the Minett family.

Henry Minett was a carpenter and cooper who lived and worked at St Margaret's, now called Owls End, in Station Road. The property belonged to his wife, Maria, and it seems more than likely that he had taken over the business of his father-in-law James Yeend, who is described as a carpenter in the baptismal records of his children. The Minett family was large and some of Henry's relations farmed a considerable acreage of land in Bishops Cleeve and the surrounding villages, and most of that land was in their ownership.

Henry and Maria had a family of at least five sons and four daughters, of whom Lucy, born on 12 September 1853, was the youngest. One of Lucy's brothers was an accountant with the Cheltenham Borough Council, others, including Henry, her immediate senior in the family, were farmers at Stoke Orchard and Elmstone Hardwick. Her youngest brother worked with his father as a cooper, before marrying and later emigrating to farm in Canada. There is little doubt that the Minett and Yeend families were people of some substance in Bishops Cleeve where their ancestors had been farmers and craftsmen for many generations.

A carpenter and cooper was an important member of a rural community, most of the members of which lived in timber framed buildings on small areas of land where they tended their vegetables, kept a few fowls, a few pigs and a house cow, and turned the apples which they grew in their orchards and gardens into cider. The cooper not only made barrels for the cider but also fashioned furniture, wooden buckets, wooden yokes, butter churns and milking stools – all essential items for the villagers in those days.

In addition to their cooperage business, the Minetts had a cider press in their outbuildings, and here they crushed their own and their neighbours' apples into pulp in a stone mill. The pomace so formed was then wrapped in hessian and pressed into 'cheeses' to release the apple juice which was then stored in timber barrels made in their own workshop. It took time to ferment into cider and the pomace cheese was used as fertiliser along with the pig manure and their garden and domestic compost.

Henry Minett's wife and his daughter Lucy, who was unmarried and lived with her parents, sold both locally and in Cheltenham, the vegetables, fruit, cream, butter, cheese, pickles, chutneys and preserves, which they harvested on their own property. They regularly used the carrier service provided by Walter John Oldacre.

It is clear that by the second half of the nineteenth century the family of Henry Minett was well educated and that with the backing of their parents' strong financial position, the children were able to move out into the professional classes, or to become farmers on their own land.

Walter John's ancestors were farmers whose daily lives were spent working with nature, but he was now associating with craftsmen whose lives were made happy by their skills and who believed that the use of natural materials in the execution of their craft, brought them nearer to the original purpose of life and nearer to their maker. Neither farmers nor craftsmen searched for idleness nor did they look to recreation to find happiness. They were truly happy. Walter John's early training in the home, the people with whom he associated during his youth, together with his inborn verve and zeal were invaluable to him throughout his life, and formed a firm foundation for his business.

In 1881 there were two events which had a profound effect upon Walter John. Henry Minett died in January that year at the age of 68. His widow, Maria, now found herself living at St Margaret's with her 27 year old daughter Lucy, as all her other children had left home. The property occupied some four acres and there were good workshop buildings for which she hoped to find a tenant.

It was at about this time that Walter John's father was offered the tenancy of a farm of more than 50 acres at Badgeworth, near Gloucester. He accepted it and wanted both his son and his daughter to move to Badgeworth with him. But Walter John had built up a good carrier business at Bishops Cleeve and wished to make his own way in life so he offered to buy his parents' horse and carriers cart; arranged to take lodgings with Mrs Minett at St Margaret's; and offered to rent the workshop and outbuildings formerly used by Henry Minett in his cooperage business.

At first William was upset at his son's refusal to accompany the family to Badgeworth, but he had no intention of behaving as his own father had done when he was Walter John's age. He tried to dissuade Walter John by logical argument, pointing out that the acreage at Badgeworth was sufficient for them both to farm the land, that the tenancy would eventually pass to him and that the situation at St Margaret's was not ideal.

'The Minett family tend to be tight fisted when it comes to dealing with money,' he argued. 'They will expect a great deal from you in return for your lodgings and the tenancy.

And you will have to watch that Mrs Minett isn't after you for a son-in-law. Lucy is well on the way to being an old maid.'

'I love Lucy and I want to marry her,' the young man replied. 'But I don't expect she will have me . . . '

His father knew when he was beaten. 'She won't find a better husband anywhere around,' he said. 'She's too old for you, but if you have made up your mind I won't stand in your way.'

So Walter John bought his parents' horse and cart and moved into St Margaret's. He ran the carriers' business from the workshop and outbuildings formerly used by Henry Minett. Under contract to the London, Midland and Scottish Railway and to local councils, he hauled stone and gravel from the quarries in which his mother's Yiend relations worked and continued to make regular carrier journeys into Cheltenham, often accompanied by Lucy Minett who took produce from St Margaret's to customers in the town and the surplus to Cheltenham market.

Before the end of 1881, Walter John was in a position to make a bid for a rick of hay which a local farmer was offering for sale. It was the first such deal he had attempted so he was feeling more than a little apprehensive as he walked the short distance to the farm and knocked boldly on the door. It was opened by the farmer's wife.

'G'morning missus. Is the boss at home?' he inquired, trying to sound confident and business-like.

'He's just come in for his dinner,' she replied. 'Come along inside and I'll call him.'

Walter John entered the kitchen where bread and cheese was set out on the table, together with a jar of cider. Soon he was joined by the farmer.

'What can I do for you then?' he asked.

'I am looking for a good quality rick of hay and I understand that you have one for sale', said Walter John.

'Happen I have,' said the farmer. 'You had better come along with me and have a look at it.'

They walked together towards the rick-yard and the farmer pointed out the rick that was for sale. Walter John paced out the length and width of it and estimated the average height.

Taking a new rick probe out of its leather case he carefully screwed the sections together. When it was long enough he thrust it into the heart of the rick, judging the density of the hay by the resistance against the probe, so estimating the weight of hay in the rick. When he pulled the probe out he carefully examined the hay that had been retained on the hook, lifted it to his nose and inhaled deeply. The hay was cool and the scent was sweet. He repeated the procedure twice and then thanked the farmer.

The two men returned to the farm kitchen and sat in front of the fire. They talked about everything except the rick – the state of farming, the market for beef and the price of grain. At length, Walter John returned to the purpose of his visit.

'I know what the rick's worth to me. Will you take £35, which I believe to be a fair price?' he asked. 'But I shall want to cut and truss the hay in your rick yard and to do the work as and when I have a market for the hay.'

The farmer held out his hand. 'It's a pleasure to do business with you Mr Oldacre, you can have my hand on it.'

The two men shook hands and the deal was sealed. When Walter John had left, the farmer turned to his wife.

'Young Oldacre knows his job, his figure was fair but it will give him a tidy profit. I would not be a bit surprised if he made a go of things. We shall be seeing more of that young man.'

Walter John was delighted with his purchase and the arrangements which he had made for cutting and trussing the hay. He needed some hay for his own animals but the bulk of the rick could be sold at a profit.

Back at St Margaret's, Walter John passed on his good news to Lucy.

'I've made a real start as a trader,' he told her. 'I'm sure that I can build up a good business if you will help me.' Then very quietly he said, 'Will you wed me, Lucy?'

'I don't know about that John.' She hesitated. 'I'm very fond of you and would like to be your wife, but you are still very young and you may regret it later.'

'I know my own mind,' he insisted. 'I don't want anyone else and I never will.'

'We will see then.' There was another pause before Lucy continued. 'I do want a family of my own but I must have time to think, you must give me time to think.'

Walter John was deeply disappointed that Lucy would not accept his offer of marriage immediately but he knew what he wanted. Lucy Minett was the only woman for him and he was determined to have her for his wife.

2

THE FOUNDATIONS ARE LAID
1881–1923

(i) Walter John Oldacre, business and family man

Walter John always considered that his business really began when he moved to St Margaret's in 1881. Ethel Minett, Lucy's grand niece by her brother Henry, remembered her favourite uncle saying:

> 'I started from scratch and bought one rick of hay which I cut into trusses and then sold the trusses around the district.'

After buying the rick, Walter John continued with his carrier business and built up a reputation for service and fair dealing with local farmers and through his contacts at the village church. He was good at selecting the best hayricks and assessing the quality and the quantity. When completing a purchase he always offered a fair price but one on which he could profitably cut and truss the hay for sale. He also knew the requirements of his farming customers and the more rigorous demands of the race horse trainers. He soon realised that he would increase his profit on animal feed if he bought the pig and poultry foods in bulk, stored them at St Margaret's, and then repacked and sold them to his customers in the village.

This change in his method of trading meant that his carriers' cart was not adequate for the job in hand so he talked the matter over with his friend James Tarling of J. Tarling and Company, wainwrights, wheelwrights and black-smiths, Tarlings Yard, Church Road, Bishops Cleeve. The two men decided that an all purpose dray was needed – one with a flat bed, shallow sills on the two sides and at the rear and with removeable side-boards. The front-board would need to be 24 inches high, to display the owner's name and the nature of his business and also act as support for a carter's seat. A ladder would have to be fixed to the rear of the waggon to extend the bed when hay or straw was being carried. The four wheels would have to be of uniform diameter, small enough to pass under the chassis and to allow the front swivel axle the maximum amount of movement. A dray designed in this way would be highly manoeuvrable, and would operate well on winding lanes, in the hills, in restricted farm-yards and in town conditions.

As his business developed, so did Walter John Oldacre's love for Lucy Minett. Impressed by his faithfulness, determination and devotion, Lucy agreed to marry him in the autumn of 1884. Walter John and Lucy were married at Cheltenham Registry Office. He was 23 and she was 31 and they gave their address as the George Inn Tap, Albion Street, Cheltenham. The marriage proved to be a happy match in every way, and soon they had a family around them.

Walter John's business reputation was further enhanced by his marriage to Lucy Minett and his customers increased in number. He purchased a small vertical steam engine and mill so that he could grind his own feeds and also offer a grinding service to the small farmers in the district. Fetching coal in his carts from the LMS railway yard at Ashchurch and stoking and maintaining the steam engine was a very heavy and time consuming burden, and it was important for him to undertake the maximum amount of work whilst he had 'steam up'. The mills were driven by crossed belts which passed over pulley wheels located on a long shaft. The belt drive arrangement was used in mills with a shaft drive until the middle of the 20th century.

It seems likely that the brick extension to the house and the brick outbuildings at St Margaret's were built at about this time. Walter John was then renting 30 acres of land which he used as pasture for his horses and from which he harvested a crop of hay. There was a limited amount of storage space still available at St Margaret's, the equally limited haulage capacity and the general lack of mobility beyond the

St Margaret's – Birthplace of William John Oldacre 1889–1983

immediate environs of Bishops Cleeve, had a controlling influence upon the speed of growth of the business.

Life was not easy for the young couple. They worked long hours, lived frugally and ploughed back any profits which were made into the business. Their first child Ada Ellen, born shortly after the marriage, was followed in 1886 by twin daughters, Anna Louise and Lucy Louise, the latter dying in infancy, and in the following year Alice Emily. Much as they loved their daughters both Walter and Lucy longed for a son and on 9 May 1889 their prayers were answered.

Early that morning, Lucy went into labour and Walter John rushed off to fetch the midwife. On his return, there was little that he could do to help except ensure that the kitchen fire was burning brightly, and that there was plenty of boiling water on the hob. So he went to work in the stables. Soon his mother-in-law Maria Minett came rushing across the yard.

'John, it's a boy,' she shouted.

Walter John did not need to be summoned more than once. He ran into the house, up the stairs two at a time and into the bedroom. Lucy was holding their son. He bent down and kissed her and then gently took the baby into his arms.

He noticed the child's head was covered in soft blond down and that his eyes were bright blue. His tiny hands opened and closed, grasping Walter's finger quite firmly.

'He's a fine boy, my love,' he said bending down to kiss his wife again. 'Thank you from the bottom of my heart.'

'Isn't he beautiful?' said Maria as she came into the room. 'A lovely nine pound baby boy. What will you call him?'

Husband and wife smiled at each other. 'William John', they said in unison.

Six years after their marriage and within a year of William John's birth, the couple had saved sufficient capital to purchase, in Lucy's name, The Pollards, a property at the junction of the main Evesham to Cheltenham road and the main street of the village. The property, which is still the site of the Bishops Cleeve mill, included a fine family house, about four and a half acres of garden, paddock and orchard, and out buildings suitable for use as an engine house, mill, warehouse, coach house, and for stabling.

Along the road frontage the property was flanked by a stone wall. The house itself faced towards the west, and between the front garden and the yard there was another stone wall in front of which was a line of pollarded lime trees. The other boundaries of the property were made up of hedges and fences. The house was not built of dressed stone but had a white rendered finish surmounted by a stone tile roof.

The site was ideal for Walter John's business because it was opposite the village smithy. It was quite normal for as many as 40 horses to be shod there on weekdays and many of the owners were his customers. He could talk to them over his own gate as they waited.

The interior of the house was simple. To the left of the front door was a sitting room occupying the full width of the northern end of the house; immediately opposite the front door was the dining room which also served as Walter John's office, and next to that was a kitchen with a large black range. Beyond the kitchen and at a slightly lower level was a scullery, the dairy, and other domestic outbuildings. Upstairs on two floors there were seven bedrooms.

The furnishing at The Pollards was substantial and functional, matching the lives of the owners. The large sitting room had a cottage piano on one side and a chest of drawers on the other side of the fireplace which stood opposite to the door; a china cabinet and a chiffonier were against the right hand wall; a grandfather clock and a round table stood between the two windows on the left hand side of the room; in the centre of the room there was a round dining table and six dining chairs. The dining room was again furnished with a round dining table and six dining chairs, in addition there was a mahogany bureau, a blanket chest, a high backed Windsor chair and a wicker arm chair. The main furniture in the kitchen included a dresser, and a substantial deal table and chairs.

The yard with its farm buildings occupied the remainder of the road frontage, the stables were against the wall. The buildings used for the warehouse and mill lay beyond the line of the south wall of the house, and the coach house was situated between the mill and the domestic outbuildings. Behind the yard there was a paddock and further to the south, orchards and pasture fields.

The family now numbered five children; Lucy Elizabeth being born shortly after the move to The Pollards. During the years the children were growing up, the business progress of Walter John can be followed in the baptismal records of the parish. He is referred to as a 'carrier' when Ada was born, later as a 'farmer' and by the time of the birth of Lucy Elizabeth, as a 'corn dealer'.

In the 1890s Walter John was a respected member of the community. He was a sidesman at the church and helped with various village activities including the celebrations for the golden and diamond jubilees of Queen Victoria in 1887 and 1897. He was now a recognised corn merchant, a miller of animal feeds and an experienced trader in hay, straw, and other goods which he knew he could sell to the local farmers and villagers at a profit. In order to increase his output of animal feed and to offer a better grinding service to the farmers, he purchased a portable steam engine and horizontal stone mill, and shortly afterwards a cider scratter mill, to ensure that the activities in his mills were extended over the longest possible season.

The shaft of the mill which was driven by the engine was about 30 feet long and as much as three hundredweights of

A Bishop Cleve Committee c 1890
Minett, Ballinger, Rev Hemmings, ?, Walter John?
Edgington, Tarling, Edgington, Shipway, Minett, ?

coal was burnt each day to keep all this machinery moving, but fortunately, Bishops Cleeve was served by the LMS railway line which ran from Birmingham to Gloucester, and there were stations at Stoke Road and at Ashchurch. He hauled coal from both stations for his own use, and soon realised that there was a profit to be made retailing coal to his farm customers and other villagers.

The capacity of his mill and his warehouse space was now sufficient to cope with the requirements of farmers who worked as much as 30 to 50 acres and also the larger racing stables. But the majority of his customers were still men with between two and ten acres, perhaps just a pasture field and an orchard on which the family kept a milking cow, a few pigs, sheep, and some chickens.

At the turn of the century Walter John took the tenancy of Dean Farm which was situated on the west side of the Evesham road and a mile distant from The Pollards. This meant an increase in the quantity of pasture available for his own horses; the quantity of hay which he could make for himself and at the same time he would have room to keep cows and start selling milk, butter and cheese.

No sooner had he signed the lease for Dean Farm than he was involved in a serious accident. There were, of course, no health and safety at work regulations in those days and the pulleys, belts and other machinery at the mill were not equipped with wooden or metal guards. Although he was experienced at handling the machinery in the mill and well aware of the dangers, he caught his right hand in the crossed belts and, as a result, lost his little finger and the top half of his middle finger. He was rushed to Winchcombe Hospital for treatment but fortunately there were no complications and he was soon back at work.

In spite of the accident his business continued to grow, but if it was to be successful then it was important to keep production costs to an absolute minimum and this meant that the whole of his family must be committed, in one way or another, to it.

The children were all tall, physically strong and mentally alert and as they grew up they were obliged, like their father before them, to undertake any task suitable to their age and physical capabilities. There was no line of demarcation in their lives between the family, the home and the business. They lived in an era when hard work was a virtue. William John gardened, sawed logs, chopped wood, mended sacks, and was expected to milk the cows and carry two four-gallon buckets of milk on a yoke across his shoulders from Dean Farm to The Pollards before setting out for school at Cheltenham. He had no transport, not even a bicycle, and so he often had to run all or part of the four miles if he was to get to school on time.

Meanwhile his sisters were engaged with the usual domestic duties because their mother had no other help in the house. They looked after the poultry and dairy products, collected eggs, skimmed cream, made butter, preserved and bottled fruits and vegetables, and made pickles. Everything they made was used in the home and the surplus sold to customers in Cheltenham.

As she reached school leaving age, Ada showed exceptional academic and musical abilities and Mr Cox, headmaster of the local school, persuaded her parents, against quite strong opposition from them, to allow her to stay on as a pupil teacher until she could get in to a training college in Cheltenham. But she still had to help her father in the business. She would do a day's work at the school or at college, walk home, and would then be expected to harness the horse and take the cart out with a load of feeding stuff to a customer. Even when she was studying in the evenings she was always likely to be interrupted by her father with – 'Its time we had a look at the ledgers' but, in spite of these distractions she passed her exams and her first job as a certificated teacher was at Kempsey near Worcester. Later she became head mistress of Corse Lawn School and an organist at Eldersfield Church.

Anna, the most attractive of the sisters although she never married, was happy helping her mother in the home. She cooked and sewed, washed and ironed and cleaned and scrubbed. She it was who made the jams, preserves and pickles, she bottled fruits and made excellent wines from dandelions, parsnips, elderberries and rhubarb.

Alice soon showed that of the sisters she was the one interested in the business. When she left school she was trained as a book-keeper and soon took over the accounts of the business much to the delight of Ada who had never particularly enjoyed the work.

The family ran on patriarchal lines and so it was William John, the son and heir, who was expected to succeed Walter John. However, the automatic assumption that William John would succeed his father in the management of the business led to difficulties between William John and his sister Alice.

William John was a strong and self-willed boy. He was spoilt by his mother and to some extent by his eldest sister although strongly disciplined by his father. Nevertheless, after he had walked out of Winchcombe Grammar School following a heated exchange with one of the school masters, his father allowed him to move to Cheltenham Grammar School, where he showed considerable ability particularly with figures. But school learning irritated him and he was happiest when helping his father.

William John's harsh upbringing did not detract from the love, admiration and respect which he felt towards his father; the boy had sharp eyes and watched and learned from him.

He noted the ease with which his father used gardening and carpentry tools, lifted and carried sacks and handled farm implements; he recorded in his mind everything which he witnessed. He learned to distinguish between good and poor quality farm land and the art of hedging, ditching, drainage, ploughing and cultivating. Walking through the crops with his father, he would pluck the ripening ears of corn, rub them between his palms, blow off the chaff and test the grain between his teeth.

'Is it ready for the scythe?' his father would ask.

He mastered the skills of building hay and corn ricks at an early age and it was not long before he could thatch. He learned animal husbandry, the preparation of feeds, and the skills of a butcher. He became an expert at selecting and handling horses, and also took careful account of the skills which his father used when selecting, buying and selling any farm commodity in the market place. He was untried in trading but he gained valuable experience by making a few coppers from his own working hobbies.

William John watched with the utmost care when his father harnessed a horse. He knew that the collar had to be made to fit snugly on the neck so that the pull of the load was taken on the shoulders and not on the windpipe of the horse. The collar was followed by the hames which carried the reins and traces. The saddle and girths came next. The saddle carried a trace which passed from one shaft of the waggon to the other and transferred the weight of the shaft of the waggon to the horse. The girths prevented the saddle from leaving the horse's back in the event of the load lifting upwards. The front of the collar was steadied by a strap which passed between the horse's legs and was then attached to the girths. The breech bands came next, this part of the harness prevented the waggon from overtaking the horse. Lastly the bridle was placed over the head of the horse.

His father was not William John's only teacher. His grandfather, William Oldacre, enjoyed the company of his only grandson and loved to be questioned about the workings of the farm. Interspersed with answers to the boy's questions, William told him tales of his own youth and how he had left home, but these reminiscences soon ended. William Oldacre died in his sixtieth year when the boy was only nine. His grandmother now went to live with her daughter Anna Maria at Hardwick Hay Farm, Eldersfield, where Anna's husband George Charles Smith farmed, her nieces and nephew now became regular visitors at the farm.

(ii) William John joins his father in business

By the time William John was 15 years old, he was ready and eager to take his place in the business. His sister Alice had already spent more than two years working in the office and had become a competent book-keeper. Walter John was determined that his son should undertake any task that came along as soon as he started full time work, be it heavy manual work or office routine, and he continued that practice for many years thereafter.

The construction by the Great Western Railway of a new line between Honeybourne and Cheltenham started at about the time that William John left school. The line passed though the village and a new station was built just above St Margaret's in Station Road. Oldacres were employed to carry stone from the quarries on the hill to form the railway embankments and the station yard. William John spent many months as a carter on that work. In good weather and bad he trudged up the hill and experienced the difficulties of handling a horse which was being pushed by a fully loaded waggon down a steeply sloping road. When the waggon was on level ground the problems were still not over. He then had the tricky task of negotiating the muddy tracks which gave access to the embankment itself. The line was opened in 1906 and William John never forgot the location of wet areas under the embankment.

It was not long after starting work that William John was sent out on foot canvassing for business from farmers in the locality. He was surprised to be entrusted with the job but his nature was such that he accepted the challenge with relish. His confidence and determination proved to be invaluable. When he was 90 years old, he still remembered his earliest attempts at selling goods to local farmers:

'I was only sixteen when my father sent me out on foot looking for business. I was nervous of approaching the farmers but knew that I must do as my father had ordered. It was tiring and at first I was not successful. I was promised orders but didn't take any. One winter evening at about half-past-four I did not know what to do, whether to go home without a firm order or to go on to Southam. Eventually I decided to try at one more farm. I knocked on the door. The farmer's wife came and invited me into the kitchen where it was warm. The farmer was having his tea of home-made bread, butter and jam and invited me to join him. I felt much better. After we had finished tea I explained the reason for my visit. He expressed surprise that such a young man was calling on farmers for feed orders, but I boldly told him that everyone had to start at some time. Then he asked me about the goods I was offering and my prices. About one hour after entering the kitchen, I was given an order for a ten ton truck of coal and two tons of wheatfeed. It was after seven when I arrived home and I was dog-tired.'

This episode early in his working life is typical of the man. He would never be beaten by adversity and could use his natural charm to further his cause. Clearly his father was pleased with his son's efforts because he then bought a bicycle, and set William John to extending the range of their business to Oxenton, Teddington, Alderton and Gretton.

The need to expand was fully accepted by Walter John, but the pace at which he was prepared to move was somewhat slower than his son demanded. It seems clear that William John was critical of some methods which his father used in running the mill and the business generally, and was anxious for change. Also, that he felt that his sister Alice was interfering on the accountancy side of the business and he was sure that she continually dissuaded her father from investing in any of the ideas which he put forward.

In an attempt to overcome some of his frustrations, he joined the Cheltenham Troop of the Royal Gloucester Hussars. The troop was formed in 1795 during the reign of George III, when the country was under threat of an invasion by the French. William John enjoyed the horsemanship and the comradeship with his colleagues who were mostly farmers' sons, and therefore men who might prove useful

William John Oldacre
Royal Gloucestershire Hussars

contacts for the future. All were volunteers and had to provide their own horses.

His association with the Hussars enabled him to develop a new social life, and one which offered him a wider scope than was available in his home village. Although he had little time, he did some hunting and shooting with his new friends and also attended social functions and dances, usually accompanied by his sister Anna. He was not slow to notice that his friends found her attractive and that she enjoyed their company. It was a very different world for them both. William John was over six foot tall and looked handsome in his dark blue dress uniform, with its five rows of brass buttons on the 18 looped braids across the front of the short jacket. Sparkling spurs were fixed to his highly polished boots, and they made a clinking noise as he walked. Anna enjoyed the ritual of filling in dance cards and both learned the etiquette of such functions. Many years later, William John would tell his family that Anna was prepared to flirt with his friends but if any man began to take a real interest in her, then she became very timid. He gave this as the reason why his attractive sister never married. For her part, Anna told the

40 Winchcombe Street
William John, Lucy

family that her brother was always flirting with the girls.

His father, realising that his son was becoming restless and that there was increasing antagonism between him and Alice, decided to offer his son a challenge. In 1907, he rented a shop in Winchcombe Street, Cheltenham, which he opened as a hay, corn and coal merchants. He changed the name of the firm to W J Oldacre and Son and made William John manager of the Cheltenham branch.

The challenge proved to be a heavy one. William John, helped by his youngest sister Lucy, found himself up against a neighbour who was the largest of a number of corn merchants in the town. While Oldacres were able to attract the smaller type of customer into their shop, it was difficult to persuade the larger farmers to change their allegiance from W Ride and Company. It was an uphill task. Meanwhile, the original business in Bishops Cleeve continued to prosper and Alice's hold on the purse strings grew ever tighter.

(iii) Seven difficult years for William John

Between 1907 and 1914 William John had to chart his way through the first of a number of critical periods in his personal and business life. During these same years two people came into his life, both of whom had a major impact upon the family and the business. They were Gladys Mary Beckingsale and John Ernest 'Jack' Charnock.

In 1907, Arthur Robert Beckingsale bought the post office and general store which had been founded as a bakery and store in Bishops Cleeve in 1754. He came from an educated family, as can be seen from diaries written in the 1840s by his father Thomas Beckingsale (1833–1869). The history of the family is also well recorded. Their ancestors came from Denmark and had probably settled in England before William the Conqueror landed. By the end of the 14th century they were landowners and during the reign of Charles II they lived in Brizenorton, Oxfordshire. Later there were arguments about property and the family split, one brother moved across the hills to Wiltshire, and the branch of the family to which Gladys belonged settled near to Stow-on-the-Wold. The family at Stow still had property but William Beckingsale (1753–1829) was not in any profession or business, he was of a nervous temperament and he feared that he would lose what money he had instead of gaining more. In 1823, a few years before William died in the same room in which he had been born seventy six years earlier, his son Thomas (1800–1850) founded a grocery and butcher's business at 426 High Street, Cheltenham, and that business was inherited by Thomas the diarist.

Arthur Robert, by his own choice, became a pupil on a farm at Hay in South Wales. By the time he was 23 years old, it was clear that he had neither the stamina nor the capital to succeed in farming. In 1888 he opened a grocery and butchers shop in Wotton-under-Edge, and shortly afterwards married Mary Kate Hanks. The business was a success but he was still set on farming. He sold the business with the full agreement of his wife, and invested all his capital in Seymour Farm at Corse, with disastrous results. By 1907 he had lost most of his money and moved to Bishops Cleeve to become the postmaster and run the general stores. The Beckingsale family included two boys and four girls, of whom Gladys was the eldest, and they made a bare living from the village store. At first Gladys helped her father in the post office before being apprenticed to the drapery trade in Cheltenham at Shirers, later called Shirer and Lances.

When the Beckingsales arrived in Bishops Cleeve, Gladys was a good-looking and capable 15 year old. She was five feet seven inches tall, blonde, with delicate skin and a good complexion. She held her head high and her fine figure was accentuated by an 18 inch waist. She was a happy and lively girl who preferred the company of her elder brother Hanks and his friends, to that of her studious sister Ida and other girls. Gladys joined the boys in their games of football and cricket, and their other lively activities, she always aimed to show that she was as good or better than the boys. Hanks had left home to train in gentlemen's outfitting before the family moved to Bishops Cleeve and Gladys had turned to her younger brother, Reg, for friendship. The presence of a pretty and vivacious young girl at the post office was noted with pleasure by the young men in Bishops Cleeve and not least by William John Oldacre.

William John was then 18 years old. He was friendly with the daughters of a number of local farmers, but in his eyes none of them could compare with Gladys Beckingsale. On a Sunday morning he walked to church with his father and sisters in the hope of catching a glimpse of Gladys as he passed the shop, his eyes searched longingly for her. He heard little of the sermon, his mind was filled with Gladys' beauty.

Gladys was not unaware of the obvious interest which she aroused in William John Oldacre and was more than happy to encourage it. She was attracted to the smartly dressed, tall broad-shouldered youth.

Mrs Beckingsale was a staunch Baptist and kept a close watch on any boy who attempted to pay court to her daughter. William John found that it was difficult to be alone with Gladys without her parents being present, but kept trying to puzzle out how he could avoid their constant surveillance. Eventually he noticed that Gladys and Reg were allowed to go for walks without their parents. He traced their routes carefully and decided that he could make contact with them when they were out of sight of the village shop. Soon he was joining them regularly on those walks.

It was not long before Mr and Mrs Beckingsale and Mr and Mrs Oldacre noticed William John's sudden interest in walking. They then became aware of the looks which he exchanged with Gladys, looks which were returned with a coy smile. The couple were forbidden to see one another by both sets of parents and every obstacle was placed in the way of the relationship.

The concensus view at The Pollards was that a fine young man like William John, with excellent prospects, should be courting the daughter of a local farmer who would have land and property as her dowry. His sister Alice considered her brother to be a fine catch and was appalled to see him throwing himself away on a pretty and flighty blonde whose father was hardly able to keep a roof over the head of his family. The truculent attitude which William John displayed over the matter of Gladys Mary Beckingsale did little to reduce the concern of the family at The Pollards.

Meanwhile at the shop, Gladys was forbidden to see this rather wild and aggressive young man. It was Mrs Beckingsale who was particularly anxious about her daughter's infatuation with William John Oldacre, and her anxiety was passed on to her second daughter Ida. Ida was a student at Pate's Grammar School, gaining an Arts Degree from Bristol University, but she lived in the shadow of her elder sister. Gladys' interest in William John was encouraged by both her brothers and they were a source of strength and support to her. The twins, Alice and Enid, were far too young to know much about what was going on.

The strong opposition to William John and Gladys walking out together came from both families, but it did not stop them from meeting. They arranged a signalling system using lighted candles in the windows of The Pollards and the post office, to indicate when the coast was clear and they could safely spend time together. They were together whenever they could get away from their work and dodge the family surveillance. One of their favourite walks was through the fields from Bishops Cleeve to Gotherington and this stretch of countryside remained a favourite throughout their long lives.

Whatever his feeling may have been about Gladys Beckingsale, William John still had to make a success of the shop and build up the business in Cheltenham. He recalled in his memoirs that the cash takings in the first week after opening in 1907, had been 19 shillings and 10½d and that throughout the first two years of trading takings were bad. Business was so difficult that there was every likelihood that Oldacres would have to withdraw from the town, but William John was not a man to admit defeat and just as things looked very bleak indeed, he took a calculated risk with tenders for the supply of hay, straw and oats for the Corporation stables, without the knowledge of his father and his sister Alice.

This tender and one to supply pig food, flour and coal to the workhouse, was accepted and almost immediately the price of the commodities went firmly in his favour, allowing him to make a substantial profit. Shortly after this Oldacres were able to take new premises in Winchcombe Street, nearer to their main competitor, and thereafter they were able to put more pressure on Ride's business.

Jack Charnock came on the scene in 1909 when he was appointed by Hutchinsons, flour millers of Liverpool as their area manager in Gloucestershire and South Wales. He was 24 years old, five foot ten-and-a-half inches tall, slim and muscular, with dark brown eyes. He had been educated at Merchant Taylors School, Great Crosby, Lancashire, and on leaving school he joined Waterloo Rugby Football Club and gymnastic and swimming clubs. Like William John, he was in the Volunteers, serving with the Kings Liverpool Regiment until taking up his appointment in the south. One of his first problems was to find a local storage depot for his firm's goods and eventually he called at Oldacres new shop in Winchcombe Street, Cheltenham.

The first conversation between these two contrasting men was about flour milling and the animal feed business. They soon learned to respect the knowledge and understanding which the other exhibited about their common trade, and before the meeting ended they were talking freely about their problems. Jack had gained an order from Oldacres and they had reached an agreement whereby Hutchinsons would rent part of Oldacres new warehouse premises in Winchcombe Street.

'The next time you call, you must meet my father and see our mill at Bishops Cleeve, which is our business headquarters,' William John said as they parted.

'I'd like that, thank you.'

'I'll expect you in two weeks time,' William John continued, 'And I'll tell the family that you will stay for supper.'

So started a lasting friendship and one that was welcomed by Walter John and Lucy Oldacre immediately they met Jack Charnock. They saw in Jack, a calm and quiet man who had great strength of character and one who might help restrain their rather volatile and impetuous son.

Jack had lost his own father, a baker and provender dealer with three businesses in Liverpool, when he was only eleven years old. Although close to his mother he missed the help and advice which a father would have been able to offer him and in Walter John Oldacre he found a valuable father figure.

The Charnocks originally came from Astley Hall, Charnock Richard, Lancashire, but they were Royalists and lost all their lands between the Civil War and the time when William and Mary ascended the throne. The branch of the family to which Jack belonged were Protestants and they were farmers, farriers, wheelwrights, and veterinary surgeons centred at Melling, near to Aintree racecourse.

Jack had wanted to follow in the footsteps of his grand-father, who was a horse doctor, and his uncle who was amongst the first to be registered as a Member of the Royal College of Veterinary Surgeons, but his mother had not agreed to this, even though her in-laws had offered to pay the fees at the University of Liverpool. Although she had been unable to continue with her husband's businesses, she advised her son to enter the flour trade, arguing that bread was the staple diet of the people, and therefore, the flour millers and bakers would always have an important role to play in the life of the community and the economy of the country.

Jack had been trained at Vernons of Liverpool, before joining Hutchinsons. After his first meeting with William John, he became a regular visitor at The Pollards – visits which continued until the outbreak of the First World War in 1914. He always remembered the help which he received from Walter John Oldacre and the wonderful meals which they all enjoyed together. The great joints of rare beef, whole home cured hams, collared head eaten with home grown vegetables or salads and homebaked bread, followed by apple or plum pie and cream, and all washed down with home-brewed cider and piping hot coffee. It reminded Jack of his own childhood and the visits which he used to make with his father to his grandfather Charnock's farm at Melling, or to his mother's family farm at Fazakerley in Liverpool.

William John's success with the public tenders and the agreement which he had reached with Hutchinsons over the tenancy of part of the Winchcombe Street warehous, ensured the continued presence of Oldacres in Cheltenham. William John and Jack were both making their way successfully in business. At their regular meetings they compared notes about markets and prices, and generally helped one another.

The Oldacre family was by now highly respected in Bishops Cleeve. Walter John was one of the main employers of labour in the village and he continued as a sidesman at the church. By village standards they were prosperous, well-housed, well-clothed and well-fed. In the traditional Vic-torian way, everyone in the family was still called upon to play his or her part in ensuring the well-being of the family enterprise. The property in which they all lived and from which they ran the family business was owned by Mrs Oldacre; the milling and other machinery, livestock, transport, and the stores belonged to the father, Walter John; Anna ran the home; Alice did the book-keeping; William John worked for the business and on the farm; and Lucy helped with the shop and the book-keeping at Cheltenham. The family were a unit, the young people were kept rent free and they were allowed a small wage for their services, but this amounted to little more than pocket money. The total endeavour was that every penny made and every action taken was invested in the furtherance of the business and their status and position in the community.

On 26 November 1909, Lucy Oldacre's mother Maria Minett died at the age of ninety five. In her will she left her house, garden and orchard to Lucy (provisions were made regarding her other children), and in so doing she took into consideration 'the help she has been to me and the services she has rendered to me'. A few months later, Eliza Oldacre died at Hardwick Hay Farm, Eldersfield. After a life of hard work she left the few hundred pounds which she and her husband had saved, to her daughter Anna Maria Smith.

During the last years of her grandmother Oldacre's life, Ada Oldacre the only member of the family to have found independence, was teaching close by at Corse Lawn. She enjoyed calling at her Auntie Smith's farm, visiting her grandmother regularly. In 1911, Ada married William Irons, a farmer from Corse Lawn, and their wedding at Bishops Cleeve parish church, was a very grand affair organised, of course, by the parents of the bride. Ada wore a full length white lawn dress trimmed with lace, with a tight waist, and a high neck edged with velvet. A long white veil was held in place by a coronet of orange blossom, and she wore long white gloves. There were four bridesmaids, three of whom were her sisters Anna, Alice, and Lucy and they wore dresses similar to the bride's and white picture hats with gay satin sashes decorated with flowers, and trimmed in velvet. Ada was given away by her father and her brother, William John, was best man. All the men were dressed in morning suits, with flowered waistcoats, and had stiff white collars on their shirts, white carnations in their button-holes and carried

Wedding of Ada Oldacre and William Irons
Walter John   William John
Lucy, Anna, The Couple, Alice, ?

bowler hats. The photograph of the 30 principal guests included Oldacres, Minetts, Irons and Tarlings, and the elaborate menu at the reception was completed with a tiered wedding cake and champagne.

The run up to the First World War saw considerable growth in Oldacres trade both in Bishops Cleeve and in Cheltenham, and this meant that the output from the mill was not enough to meet demand. The village had been connected to the gas supply from Cheltenham a few years earlier, and so Walter John was able to install a new 25 horse-power gas engine to run the mill. This increased the output but it was not long before the engine size had to be doubled again to 50 horse-power. Mr Oldacre was now able to employ a full time mill man and this released both himself and his son for other duties. At about the same time they employed a cousin of the family to canvass in the Hatherley, Reddings and Badgeworth areas to the south of Cheltenham. The new man picked up a number of good clients, some of whom were Yeomanry colleagues of William John, but it was not long before there were discrepancies in the accounts of his customers and the cousin disappeared. The disappearance of their representative meant more work for father and son who had to put the losses which they had sustained out of mind, and restore the confidence of their new customers.

During the first decade of the 20th century, a high proportion of their trade was concerned with the supply of fodder for the horses which were still being used for ploughing, sowing and reaping on the farms, and which provided the main power used for the movement of people and goods over short and medium distances. But the transport scene was changing. Steam traction was in use on the farm, and as early as 1831 steam engines had been used to transport passengers between Gloucester and Cheltenham for a short period. In spite of the fact that these and other similar journeys were being made without accident, the development of mechanical transport was held back by the introduction of the 'Man and Flag Act' in 1864, when speeds were restricted to four miles per hour in the country and two miles per hour in the town; and of course a man with a red flag had to walk in front of such vehicles. The Act was repealed in 1896 and by 1908 young William John Oldacre was aware that, in the next few years, the emergence of the motor car could have a profound effect upon that part of his Cheltenham trade which came from customers who bought fodder for their trap horses. The significance of the coming changes were not so acutely apparent to his father who thought that the old ways would continue for the foreseeable future, a view not surprising since the newspapers were questioning whether or not motor vehicles should be allowed to use the public highway and if they did, whether or not they should be allowed to exceed a speed of 10 miles per hour.

Jack Charnock, who had a motor vehicle licence dating from 1905, always arrived at The Pollards on a motorcycle, but William John was still required to walk, cycle or use a horse and cart. He and his young sister Lucy continued to make their daily journeys to Cheltenham by horse and cart, which was used during the day to deliver goods in the town. On these journeys they saw more and more motor vehicles and also became aware of how dangerous they were. The extent of that danger was made plain to them one afternoon in 1912. It was early closing day and they had left the shop at about 1.30 pm when a car travelling from North Street into Warwick Road drove straight into the horse, broke the shafts and Lucy was thrown off the cart and onto her head in the road. She was never able to work again. She went blind and was nursed devotedly by her sister Anna until she died in 1920. This was a severe blow to William John because he felt that she was the only sister who really understood and supported his vision for the future of the business.

Walter John now began to understand his son's point of view much more clearly, and was willing to consider the impact of the internal combustion engine upon their lives. However, William John was so devastated by the loss of Lucy's support that, despite the change of attitude of his father to mechanical transport, he began to feel even more isolated in his views on how the business should progress.

It was to Gladys Beckingsale that he turned for solace. They were both working in Cheltenham and their relationship blossomed in spite of the continued opposition from both families. William John was concerned to find that there was another suitor for Gladys' hand and he confided in Jack Charnock who was himself engaged to be married. Jack was trying to save enough money to put down a marriage settlement and to furnish a home for his fiance Elfrida Burrell who came from a well-to-do family in Prenton, Wirral, but he was prepared to listen and do his best to advise his friend.

In 1913, William John decided he would wait no longer. Gladys accepted his proposal of marriage knowing full-well that the match would hardly be welcomed by either household. The wedding took place at Bishops Cleeve parish church in September 1913. William John was 24 years old and Gladys 21. Anna and Alice later told the family that the wedding of their brother was very different from that of their eldest sister. The Oldacre family did not attend and the only witnesses were the bride's father and James Tarling, the friend of the family who stood with William John.

The wedding did not end the troubles of William John and Gladys. They were so poor that they were forced to live with and look after an elderly relative in Cheltenham, where they stayed for about two years. William John worked hard for the business during these years and his wages remained low. When he looked back at the standard of life at The Pollards he was angry. His friend Jack was married in October 1913 and he and his wife lived in Cardiff.

(iv) The Great War brings many changes

The war came as no surprise to Walter John Oldacre. He had expressed his concern about increasing German rivalry on international, colonial and commercial matters on many occasions, he disliked the arrogance of the German Kaiser and his henchmen. Nor did he subscribe to the generally held view that 'it will be over by Christmas'. The initial German advance may have been foiled at the battle of Marne in September 1914, but within a few weeks of that battle both sides were dug-in for a protracted conflict.

Early in 1915, Walter John advised his son that The Laurels in Stoke Road, Bishops Cleeve was vacant and suggested that he should rent the property for his wife and his one year old daughter Helen Mary. By the time the move was made Gladys was pregnant again and William John had volunteered for service in the Royal Artillery. Their second daughter, Alice Mildred, was born in October 1915 and Gladys was faced with the task of bringing up their two small daughters on a soldier's marriage allowance plus a small pension from the business.

When William John enlisted billboards in every town were carrying the grim faced poster of Kitchener pointing his finger directly at all the young men, with the caption 'Your Country needs YOU'. Young men from Bishops Cleeve answered the nation's call, accepted the king's shilling and flocked into the army. They were given a basic infantry training in England, transported to France spending as little as two weeks learning methods of trench warfare before experiencing the horrors of the Western Front. Hanks Beckingsale was among those enlisting, in the Army Veterinary Corps. Reg Beckingsale was lumbering in Canada at the outbreak of war but he returned to England to volunteer for the Gloucestershire Regiment.

News of the progress of the war came to Bishops Cleeve from official communiques and from the casualty lists in the papers. In the summer of 1915 the war dominated conversations between Walter John and his friends whether he was leaning over his gate at The Pollards, or strolling around the village after evensong on a Sunday. Walter John could not tolerate defeatist talk but he was deeply moved by the sadness which the war brought to the village and the hardships which many families were suffering.

Walter John kept a close eye on the family at The Laurels while his son was away from home. He soon realised that he had been wrong to think that Gladys Beckingsale was an unsuitable wife for William John. Clearly, she had not been a dumb and flighty blonde looking to make a good match with the most eligible bachelor in the village. Her character and personality mirrored that of Jack Charnock, the young man whom he had accepted so readily into his home at the same time that he had rejected Gladys. Like Jack she too was calm and able to subdue William John's impulsive manner with calm reasoning and warm support. Gladys had a strong and determined character and was an ideal partner for William John. The life which she led was far from tranquil, but her father-in-law now saw that she could move through the troubled waters with a calm serenity and strength of purpose which could hardly have been matched. Walter John also became aware of the role which she had already played and was continuing to play, as a prop for the whole of the Beckingsale family, with the exception of her sister Ida: who after graduating from Bristol University had taught in Shanghai. Then she married Gerald Hummel a stockbroker; they retired to Victoria, Canada in the mid-1930s and she never lived in England again.

During the war years life at The Laurels was far from easy. There was no running water, no indoor sanitation, and her only means of cooking was on the open range in the kitchen. She did receive some help with the children from the families at The Pollards and the post office. When the children were ill, Grandfather Beckingsale was prepared to walk down to The Laurels after a hard day's work in the shop, and spend the night with his daughter helping to comfort her little ones and Grandpa and Granny Oldacre were always happy to have Mary with them as often as possible, for she was their great favourite.

The German attack against the French lines at Verdun early in 1916 put considerable pressure upon the British to open an offensive. In June an attack was launched on the Somme, the battle raged for the remainder of the year resulting in nearly 500,000 British casualties. Sergeant William John Oldacre was perhaps fortunate that his hearing was badly damaged in training by the noise and blast of the heavy guns. After a long spell in hospital, he was posted to a training battalion in England and never served in France. Gladys' two brothers were less fortunate. They experienced the mud, filth, depravation and the sight of death and mutilation at the front. When Hanks and Reg returned home on leave they were exhausted and lice ridden. In that condition they were not welcome at the village shop, but at The Laurels, Gladys was always ready to welcome them. She boiled water for them to take a hipbath in front of the kitchen fire, and washed their lice ridden clothes. All too soon their leave was over and they were sent back to France. Her twin sisters Alice and Enid, were only seven years older than Mary, and they were regular visitors to The Laurels whether or not their brothers were on leave. The children enjoyed the freedom of their sister's home and the chance of taking their young nieces for walks in the countryside.

British families in wartime suffered many hardships at home and the Oldacres were no exception, but William John blamed his sister Alice for added strain placed upon his wife. Alice was living rent free at The Pollards but drawing twice the salary that his wife was receiving as a pension, and this aggravated even further the relationships between brother and sister.

Meanwhile, business during the war was far from easy. There was a shortage of good grain and much of the available hay and straw was being comandeered by the army. In spite of these hardships, the government did not take any action to increase grain production at home until 1917, when the German U-boat campaign began to bite. The farmers were then called upon to increase their productivity in order to help feed the nation. They were encouraged to this end by the Corn Production Act of 1917 which guaranteed the price of grain until the end of 1922. When the war was over, the government no longer needed the farmer to keep up production, and so contrary to their promises the Act was repealed in 1921, with the result that the price of grain was halved overnight. Labour was also in short supply during the war and Walter John who was now in his mid-50s, was once again involved in hard manual labour on the farm, in the mill and in his garden. Nevertheless he was determined to preserve the business which was his life's work, and to keep it in a sufficiently strong state to ensure that there would be a reasonably good base for his son to build upon when hostilities ceased.

Alice was invaluable to her father during this period and, in addition to working for the business, she and her sister Anna served in the Red Cross. They attended the military hospital based on the racecourse and helped men who were convalescing from wounds by pushing their wheelchairs, writing letters and reading to those who had been blinded. In spite of the excellent work which his two daughters were doing, Walter John like many of his generation, never came to terms with the new role which women were now playing.

Country folk of course did fare better in wartime than those living in the industrial towns. They could, if they were willing to work, supplement their meagre rations from their own land or garden, from their own pigs and poultry and find brushwood and logs to cut up for their own warmth. Thus the Oldacres managed to keep a reasonably good table in spite of their other difficulties.

Even as men were dying in their thousands on the Western Front, new life was being born each day. Gladys was pregnant again and the family hoped that the child would be a boy. William John was equally as anxious for his wife to give him a son as his father had been in the 1880s. On 28 August 1917, while her husband was away from home and her two children were in the care of Anna Oldacre, Gladys gave birth to a boy. William John came home on compassionate leave and there was great rejoicing as Walter John Junior was welcomed into the world by the whole family.

Meanwhile, Reg Beckingsale was in the salient where the third battle of Ypres had been in progress since June 1917. The attack on the Messines Ridge had been successful but the battle raged on for another five months. Reg was amongst the 300,000 British casualties, he received a serious knee wound which kept him in hospital for an extended period and left him with a permanently stiff leg.

The war finally came to an end on 11 November 1918 with the signing of the Armistice. Gladys' husband and her two brothers survived but 55 young men who had marched off to war from Bishops Cleeve did not return, a dreadful toll for a small village.

William John had been released from the army early in 1918 to return to the family business: this was because of his hearing disability and the importance being attached to farming. Once the war was over, re-establishing the position of Oldacres as hay, straw, corn and coal merchants was an uphill task. The family attacked the rebuilding with their usual vigour. Personal differences were an aggravation but did not divert the family from their main goal which was to build a successful business. William John found that for much of his time he was back to a life of manual work. He was often seen driving a horse and dray around the district dressed in his old army uniform. Any load was acceptable to Oldacres who again hauled considerable quantities of stone and gravel from the hill quarries, as well as hay, straw, coal and animal feed which came from their main milling activity. By that time coal could be picked up at the GWR station yard in the village itself.

The Cheltenham shop had been closed during the war and re-establishing the town trade was particularly difficult, not least because the landlord attempted to double the rent on the premises. William John appealed to the ex-servicemen's association against the unreasonable attitude of the owner, as a result the rent was raised by only 50 percent. Hay was still in short supply but the army was anxious to reduce its stocks, and offered Oldacres three ricks within 25 miles of Bishops Cleeve. The distance of the ricks from Bishops Cleeve meant that the hay trussers could only cut and truss the hay efficiently if they were accommodated near to the ricks. William John supervised the work and became involved in the haulage operations, making at least 12 journeys of almost 50 miles, each journey taking six hours to complete with a horse and dray. Straw was also difficult to find and long distances had to be travelled by train and bicycle to locate supplies and William John went as far as Bourton-on-the-Water, Naunton and Charlton Abbot in search of it.

As William John trudged around the district with the horse

and dray his mind was active. The business would need new policies if it was to prosper and grow once supplies of raw materials became easier. The mill was under his father's control and capable of increasing output. William John decided that it was the office routine and the working of the sales staff that needed the most urgent reorganisation.

Eventually business did stabilise by which time Oldacres employed three sales representatives, four office workers and a labour force of seven men. William John's new sales policy was to canvass within a ten mile radius of Bishops Cleeve, working outwards from the centre and saturating each concentric ring before moving further away from headquarters. The honest and straightforward purchasing policy, plus the controlled development of the market and the high ethical standards demanded from the sales staff by Walter John, finally began to show good results and Oldacres was once again a force to be reckoned with in the market place.

Increased trade and profits did nothing to improve the relationship between William John and Alice. Alice had been at her father's side during the difficult war years and did not take kindly to the return of her brother. She resented his forceful attitude and his interference with office procedure. On the other hand William John could not forget the manner in which he believed his wife and young family had been treated by his sister while he was away. Nor could he accept that her wages were almost the same as his own and he was managing much of the business and having to keep a family. However, although he was strong willed and volatile, the love which he felt for his father and the respect in which he held him was such that he could not make a head-on challenge to the parental authority. Also he found difficulty in expressing his views in a clear and temperate manner.

A number of the young men had found great difficulty in settling down to civilian life after their wartime experiences. They did not find that England was a land fit for heroes as they had been promised and many were disillusioned. Friends of William John had packed their bags and gone in search of a better life in Canada, Australia or New Zealand and he thought of following their example. Gladys sensed his frustration and one day he burst out:

'I can't go on like this Gladys, that woman balks my every

proposal. I don't know why Dad takes so much notice of her.'

'What do you want to do, then?' she asked.

'I don't want to hurt Dad but I've a good mind to get right out of it all. I've always fancied farming in New Zealand. Would you risk it with me?' he asked.

'You must do what you think best. I will support you whatever you decide,' she replied.

A few days later he burst into the kitchen. 'We're going to New Zealand, I've booked a passage for us all,' he announced.

When William John told his father, he was immediately questioned about the reason for such an unexpected and drastic step. Once William John had been invited to air his grievances, he was able to explain his worries and frustrations without appearing to challenge his father's authority. He pointed out that he could no longer accept being an underpaid employee expected to give his whole life to an organisation over which he apparently had less controlling influence than his sister Alice. He wanted a position in the firm, a proper wage, a share of the profits and a clear definition of his duties and of the duties and responsibilities of Alice in the office.

In the hope of reducing the tension between brother and sister and in order to keep his son with him, Walter John decided that he would turn the business into a limited company. He would make William John, Anna and Alice his co-directors and clearly define their duties and responsibilities. William John agreed to the proposals and cancelled his passage to New Zealand. Although Alice was strongly opposed to the changes and to any action that would increase the power of her brother, W J Oldacre Limited was formed on 20 April 1923.

3

THE YOUNG COMPANY

1923–33

(i) The first years of the company

It was just before ten o'clock on the morning of 4 June 1923 that Walter John and his two daughters Anna and Alice assembled in the dining room of The Pollards which also served as the company office of W J Oldacre Ltd. The weather was warm and there was no fire in the black-leaded grate which was partly hidden by a decorated fire screen. Walter John closed the mahogany bureau at which he had been working and moved to his place at the round table in the centre of the room where Alice had placed the agenda for the meeting.

The atmosphere was tense as they awaited the arrival of William John who entered the sitting room just as the grandfather clock was striking the hour.

The group now settled down ready for the task in hand. The hostility between William John and Alice was clear to see from their faces and the looks which they exchanged. Anna tended to shrink away from the impending onslaught, but Walter John was very much in charge of the situation. In his usual calm and positive manner he opened the meeting.

'Let's settle down and get on with the work we have to do,' he ordered. 'You have the agenda in front of you, the matters with which we are dealing are of a general and routine nature. First of all we must elect a chairman.'

It was a foregone conclusion that he would be the chairman, but the formal procedures were adopted and the same discipline was extended throughout the meeting. All of those present were apointed directors with Walter John as chairman and managing director, and Alice as company secretary. The directors then approved The Pollards, Bishops Cleeve as the address of the registered office; the design of the company seal; Barclays Bank Cheltenham as their bankers; and they appointed auditors and solicitors. They authorised the memorandum and articles of association of the company and the allotment of ordinary shares. Each director was required to pay £1 for each of the 20 shares in respect of which they had signed the memorandum and articles of association and Walter John allotted the 3,920 fully paid one pound ordinary shares due to him under the sale and purchase agreement to be divided equally between the four directors. Walter John did not allow any opportunity for contentious items to be raised, even under any other business, and the meeting closed in a remarkably amicable manner.

On 23 June 1923 the authorised share capital of the company was £30,000 divided into 8,000 ordinary shares of £1 each and 22,000 five percent preference shares of £1 each. The fully paid and issued ordinary share capital was £4,000.

The minute book shows no evidence of any serious disagreement between the directors in the first two years of the company's existence. One of the reasons behind the formation of the company had been to establish clear lines of responsibility for the family members, and it seems likely that William John was anxious to show that the decision had been a correct one. Alice, on the other hand, had been against the idea of forming the company and did not wish to appear petty minded once the decision had been taken.

During these first two years, the directors agreed the salaries which they would be paid always provided that the company was in a position to make such payments.

Walter John was to receive £200 per annum, for services other than those of managing director. It is not clear what these services included or what Walter John was to be paid as managing director. He lived with his wife and two daughters at The Pollards which was owned by his wife Lucy, she still sold eggs, butter, vegetables and poultry both locally and at Cheltenham market. In addition the couple's income was further enhanced by dividends received on their ordinary and preference shares and by rents from the properties which they owned; including those properties used by W J Oldacre Ltd.

Alice as secretary of the company was to receive £200 per annum. Anna received no salary from the company but did receive a small sum from her mother in respect of the domestic work which she did. Both daughters lived rent free and neither were asked to make any contribution towards day-to-day expenses in the home.

By contrast, William John as manager of the company was to receive £300 per annum. Unless the company made a profit and was in a position to pay a dividend on his ordinary shares, his salary represented his total income. Out of this sum, he had to keep his wife and five children and pay rent for The Laurels. The standard of living of the family at The Laurels was considerably lower than that of his sisters at The Pollards and yet William John was making the major contribution to the management of the family business. This disparity sowed the seeds of frustration and jealousy.

William John known as 'Governor' by the men, was now very much in control of the day to day running of the business, the whole structure and scale of which began to change after the company was formed. This was partly due to the renewed drive which he put into his activities and partly due to the changing attitudes and requirements of the farming community and of the town customers, who no longer depended solely upon the horse.

William John began to work with the Gloucestershire County Agricultural Commission on new formulae for poultry foods, such as layers mash and chick mash, and on improved pig meals for a market which was calling for leaner pork and bacon.

At the mill, the work was being done by a gang of men including Fred Cresswell and Bill Cook. Fred had been in the trenches during the war and was lucky to be alive. He carried the scars of a bullet which had passed through his cheek and his mouth, before leaving through the other cheek. Fred was a strong man, and he had a spirit which over the years led him into many skirmishes with the Governor. Bill Cook was the engine man and someone who could coax life into the most stubborn engine. They were both employed to run the mill and the warehousing operations. During the 1920s, the mill was engaged in cleaning corn of all sorts; grinding barley, wheat, and oat meal; kibbling maize, wheat and oats; and cutting chaff. Maize was brought into the country from the Americas by boat and was then transported by rail to Bishops Cleeve GWR station in 2 cwt sacks. Wheat, barley and oats were all purchased from local farms and transported to the mill in four bushel sacks, the bushel being a liquid or dry measure equal to eight Imperial gallons. The weight of each sack depended upon the density of the grain; one bushel of wheat weighed 63 lbs, one bushel of oats 43 lbs, and one bushel of barley 56 lbs. Oil cake was being kibbled and mixed with chaff, pulped roots (mainly sugar beet), and meal and this was the forerunner of the modern complete diet feeding for cattle, sheep and pigs. The company was also starting to market compound animal feeds in meal or cube form, for which they acted as agents for Albion Cakes of Liverpool and Thames Milling of London. These compound feeds contained a high molasses content. However, provender milling was to be continued for many more years.

William John also set about expanding even further the area over which his representatives canvassed for farming business. He had earlier acquired a belt driven motorcycle and sidecar, which enabled them to go further afield. Later the board of directors hired a Calthorpe car for business purposes, in particular for the conveyance of directors to and from the Cheltenham branch. William John used this car to visit customers and was able personally to observe the changes taking place in farming.

The company were still selling large quantities of hay. Ricks were being sought after and selected by both William John and his father. Expert hay trussers like Bill Little, then broke down the ricks into tidy and manageable sized trusses for sale direct to the customers. Bill Little was a freelance worker employed by many of the farmers in the district as well as by Oldacres. He did not work on one rick until it was completely cut and trussed, but always cut the hay as and when it was needed by his various employers. Some of the ricks which Oldacres bought, were bulk loaded and then carted directly to the mill where the hay, together with straw and grain husk was chopped into chaff. The chaff was sold as dry fodder to farmers, haulage contractors, livery stables and to individual horse owners.

Hay and fodder was fed to horses and cattle in their mangers. Fodder was also carried by the carters in the horses' nosebag which the carter hung at the rear of the cart until it was time for the horse to have a feed, or until a time when the carter wished to keep a lively horse occupied while he himself made up or delivered his load. It was quite usual to see a horse standing at the side of the road or in a farmyard stamping its foot, the horse's face deep in a nosebag. A lift and a shake of the horse's head would bring more of the fodder in the bag into the reach of the horse's mouth, this would be followed by a munching sound and a blowing from the nostrils to clear the air passages, to be followed by a blast of chaff coming out of the edges of the nosebag.

In the mid-1920s Oldacres had a fleet of ten drays and waggons for coal hauling, farm delivery, the collection of grain from the station and from their customers' farms and for use on their own farm. They had 25 horses, which were either kept in the stables at the mill yard, or on the pasture fields which went to make up the farm which Walter John either owned or rented in various parts of the village. The larger drays carried three and a half ton loads and were drawn by two horses in separate shafts side by side. The smaller drays carried one and a half ton and could be managed by one horse. On the hills, or on difficult ground, a trace or chain horse was used. The trace horse was harnessed in front of the shaft horses when the waggon was loaded and extra power was needed. However, when the waggon was travelling on easy ground or unloaded, the trace horse was attached to the rear of the waggon and the horse was allowed to follow behind without doing any work. The trace horse was usually one of the strongest animals from the stable. When the trace horse was harnessed up, the carter had to be careful and watch that the other horses did not rest on the shafts, or the trace horse would be doing all the work.

Ted Aston and Fred Weaver were two of the men who worked as carters for Oldacres in the 1920s. Fred Weaver worked from the Winchcombe Street branch and kept his horse in Trinity Lane, Cheltenham during the week, but at weekends he took the animal back to Bishops Cleeve so that it could be put out to pasture before Fred himself cycled back to the town and home. Ted Aston looked after the coal hauling work with his horse Sailor. Some carters travelled as far afield as Toddington, Stanway, Bredon, Westmancote and Gretton with loads of farm feed. One grey horse called Captain was much a one-man horse and a change of carter meant weeks of coaxing before he gave of his best. If the carters were to make deliveries up in the hills they looked for short striding horses, on flat ground they preferred the longer striding horses.

The loads and the journeys which the carter and his horse made varied each day, but they would try to reach a farm at dinner time where the farmer and his wife expected them and were ready with a bucket of water for the horse, and a pot of hot tea for the carter. At Christmas and on other special occasions, a stronger drink might be waiting, but any sign of drunkenness on their return to the yard was likely to be severely punished. So also was any sign that the carter had been slack at his job and allowed the harness to rub the horse and make him sore. This was sure to arouse the wrath of the Oldacres. By and large the horses were well looked after while they were at work, and on his return to the yard the carter could quietly remove the harness, water, bed down and feed the horse, and then return to his home for a hot meal.

Ted Aston on the coal round was able to organise his own working day. Oldacres now owned four railway trucks which carried eight to ten tons of coal. These trucks were brought into the siding at Bishops Cleeve GWR station and the company were allowed three days to empty any truck before demurrage had to be paid. As much as possible of the truck load of coal was weighed and bagged by Ted for direct delivery to the customers. He had to judge the time when he must off-load the coal onto his waggon in bulk and take it to the stockpile in the yard at The Pollards, in order to ensure that the company did not incur demurrage.

The coaling job was dirty and heavy work, and the coarse sacks filled with lumps of coal were uncomfortable to handle and carry. Ted, like other coalmen, covered his head and shoulders with an empty sack and this eased the position somewhat, keeping a little of the dust and dirt out of his hair and from going down his back.

The coal was usually loaded onto the dray or into sacks using a coal-fork rather than a shovel. The fork was lighter than a shovel and was made up of strong thin prongs which were shaped into concave form so that each time the fork was dug into the pile of coal, the maximum quantity was held on the face. On the back of the coal dray there was a pair of balance scales which were used when filling the sacks at the station. When the sacks were filled at the mill yard, a heavier weighing machine was used.

The working day started at 6 am and there was a great deal of freedom for a man once he left the mill yard. The pace of the horse was slow and on a fine summer day the carter could enjoy the warmth of the sun on his back and the beauty of the countryside. In winter the job could be a very cold and wet one.

The men took their recreation out of working hours at the local pubs. Oldacres men were to be seen every evening and on Saturday dinner time, at Dick Chandler's pub, the Old Elm Tree. There they played darts and crib, and made up teams for games of skittles and dominoes. The teams were often captained by Nobby Clark the church sexton, and a man named Ern Townsend who, if he became upset with the run of the game, would pick up his stick and bang the table soundly. During the weekday evenings, the men drank cider at 3d a pint. All was well if the cider in the glass was clear, but if there cobwebs over the top of the drink, then they had to watch out or they suffered badly from the after effects. On Friday evenings and on Saturdays, after they had been paid, beer was their favourite drink and was sold at 5d a pint. The pubs closed at 10 pm and the men were back home and in bed shortly after this, ready for an early start next morning.

Ted Aston's son Leslie remembered that at weekends his father and a friend often went out on their bicycles ostensibly to work on their allotments. In reality they parked their bikes against the allotment shed and were off up to the Old Elm Tree to drink 'stunem', a cider made from grape pulp. No one knows how they ever found their way back to their bikes again, let alone how they managed to get home, but clearly they were worn out with their gardening, because they went straight to sleep immediately they were inside their own cottages.

The men took home a wage of between 25s and 30s each week and had no holidays. In the summer at hay making and harvest time, many of them worked on their boss's farm during the working day, in the evenings and at weekends. For this work they were paid only their normal wage without overtime, but they did get wages in kind – potatoes, corn for their fowls and so on. However, the boss did provide cider in the fields and when necessary food and tea. The men enjoyed this taste of outdoor farm life, since it gave them a welcome change from the dusty mill or life on the road.

The day to day running of the business kept William John fully occupied and extended both mentally and physically. He was involved in purchasing the commodities and raw materials which were needed for the successful running of the business, and he dealt with the local farmers on their own ground and at the local corn and cattle markets. He negotiated with the large port millers, and he met the representatives from the firms who provided the more domestic goods for his shop in Winchcombe Street. He was responsible for organising and motivating the sales force and establishing the needs of his customers. He had to ensure that the products turned out at the mill came in the right quantities, at the right time and that the mixtures of fodder, grain, meal and cubes, were manufactured to meet the needs of the farmers. He had to achieve all this and at the same time make a profit against growing competition. In Cheltenham alone, he had to contend not only with Ride's, Bloodworth's, Cheltenham Agricultural Traders and others, but also with strong marketing by the port millers, some of whom were beginning to sell directly to the farmers, while others were using agents like Oldacres. William John could tackle any task which he was likely to ask his employees to undertake and he could do that task well. Perhaps his most important asset was the excellent relationships which had been established between management and the workforce by his father over the 40 years he had been in business. The people employed, or in any way involved with the company, felt that he or she was a vital cog in the smooth running of the enterprise, and that it was the business which provided them all with a roof over their head, food, warmth and a generally satisfactory life.

In March 1925 the board of directors gave Alice Oldacre
six months leave of absence so that she could visit her Minett
relations in Canada. This decision to leave the family
business for such a long period may well have been one
which Alice lived to regret. Up until that time she had been
constantly at her father's side throughout her business life, but
on returning home she was never again able to re-establish
her position and exert the same level of influence upon her
father or upon the business.

The relative peace and tranquility of the board room and
in the management of the business was shattered when Alice
finally returned from her Canadian holiday. William John
had enjoyed the months without interference from his sister
and he now found her attempts to regain her position in the
management of the company profoundly irritating. In an
attempt to clear the air and resolve conflicts of responsibility,
he asked for a meeting of the board directors. It took place on
2 February 1926. William John said that he could not carry
out his duties properly unless he was given full power and
authority as managing director, with the company secretary
being answerable to him. He pointed out that at present the
company secretary openly opposed his management position
in the company. But, Walter John did not feel that the time
was right for him to relinquish his own management position
in the company and insisted that he had to be consulted on
any matters of major consequence to the company; both
William John and Alice must remain directly answerable to
him on the activities for which they carried responsibility.
Alice expressed her total disagreement with her brother and
made it clear that she expected him to recognise her position
as company secretary, answerable only to her father who was
chairman and chief managing director. The exchange did
nothing to improve relationships between brother and sister.
These were further strained when Walter John supported
Alice in a request that the Calthorpe car 'presently being used
daily by the manager', should be free for use by the other
directors on at least one day each week.

Later that year, on 2 August, an attempt was made to hold
an annual general meeting of the company, but William John
failed to attend. Alice, rubbing further salt into the wound
which her brother had sustained, referred in the minutes to

the request for the annual general meeting having come from 'the Chief Managing Director'. The three directors present passed the accounts, but all other business had to be left in abeyance.

Shortly afterwards Alice gave up her job as company secretary when she married Arthur Redman. Arthur came from one of the old village families and had recently left the Brigade of Guards with which he had served for a number of years. The couple moved to a farm at Twinning near Tewkesbury which was given to them by the bride's father. It was a great source of aggravation to William John that although he now became company secretary, his father allowed Alice to continue looking after the private ledger of the company, assisting the office clerks in any way she felt able, and taking the minutes at the board meetings.

Nevertheless as manager and company secretary William John was very much in the driving seat and his concern for the wellbeing of the employees can be seen clearly in the company records. He fought for bonus payments to be made to the men on performance levels and for men to be given one week's holiday with pay each year. But he was still dissatisfied with the manner in which Alice was interfering with and handling the accounts. On 27 July 1927, Alice complained that a rough balance sheet showed unfavourably towards the shareholders and this resulted in the board taking decisions to cut expenses and expenditure incurred by the manager. The clear inference was that William John was making questionable decisions. He believed that those who did the work and generated the profit should benefit before the shareholders. This difference in emphasis between management and shareholders was to recur on many occasions in later years.

The situation reached crisis point at the annual general meeting held on 7 September 1927:

'William John Oldacre would not enter into the discussion on any part of the accounts. He showed a marked displeasure that Mrs Redman had assisted in the preparation of the accounts, and suggested that she should not have played any part in the compilation of those accounts. Thereupon Mrs Redman requested that her shares in the business should be sold and other monies due should be paid to her. The meeting did not wish to comply with Mrs Redman's request but offered to pay her seven and a half per cent per annum on her money if she would leave it in the hands of the company'.

Before the meeting closed William John questioned the lack of any reference to the farm account. He was reminded by Alice that the farm was not a part of the company and the accounts were solely the concern of Walter John Oldacre. The formal minutes hardly reflect the atmosphere at the meeting, which apparently ended with William John throwing an inkwell at his sister Alice.

The farming activities on which Walter John had been engaged for more than 40 years had always required the same degree of help and commitment from the family as had been called for by the business itself, and so it is understandable that William John considered that the farm should be an integral part of the whole business enterprise. Walter John now had land at The Pollards and was renting other arable land known as Wardstones, Tobysfield, and Wingmoor. Most of the farm was used as pasture and to provide hay crops for the horses, a few cows were grazed and some potatoes and oats were grown. Although the matter of the farm accounts was raised in September 1927, no action was taken at that time about William John's complaint.

Throughout the history of the business, those involved in management had taken small salaries and had reinvested their share of the profit, or the majority of that money in the business as unsecured loan. Walter John had converted £5,000 of his unsecured loan into debenture shares. Anna and Alice had large sums of unsecured loan in the business as well as their ordinary shares, and could make no changes to their investment without the authority of the board of directors. The question of rate of return on ordinary capital in the company and the family policy of investing all money which was due, but not needed for day-to-day living, back into the business was to cause disquiet amongst the family members on many later occasions.

Walter John Oldacre 1862–1933

(ii) Walter John Oldacre

When the limited liability company was formed, Walter
John still maintained overall control, but he was 61 years of
age and he was ready to enjoy the hard-earned fruits of his
labours, and to leave his son to deal with day-to-day matters.
He was now wealthy by village standards and was considered
by many to fulfill the role of squire of Bishops Cleeve. He was
the largest employer in the area and he and his family were
particularly friendly with the new rector, the Rev Morgan-
Brown and his curate the Rev E C Hanson, later to be vicar of
Emmanuel Church, Leckhampton, Cheltenham.

Leslie Aston, who was a child in the 1920s and whose father
and other relations worked for Oldacres, remembered the
'Boss' with affection.

'He was a very tall and big man in every way, he had a
long white beard and sparkling blue eyes. Many of the lads in
the village, who did not really know him, were frightened by
his size and his loud and booming voice, but they all
respected him.

At Christmas, us boys used to go to the mill yard, and we
all received a present and a mince pie. He was kind and free
with his money when any of the families of his men were in
any trouble.'

Leslie recalled that the Boss used to ride his horse Bowler
around the farm and drive a pony and trap around the
village, and that these horses were lively beasts and his pride
and joy. Leslie would watch the Boss harness up the spring
trap with longing eyes and would often hear a shout 'Jump up
then, boy', and away he would go alongside the big man for a
drive around the village and the Boss's farm.

Leslie thought that the Boss was a very different man from
the Governor, but he was careful to add, 'I got on well with
the Governor because he liked people who were not afraid of
him and could stand up for themselves.'

Walter John's day started early. He was up and about the
place by 6 am and when the men started work in the mill and
on the farm, he was there to set them about their tasks. The
fact that he lived next to the mill yard made it easy for him to
move between his business activities and the tasks which he
did about the home. He would breakfast after the mill was

Garden tea at the Pollards

working and then return to the yard, perhaps to stand at the gate to see which of his friends or customers were ready for a chat, or ready to give an order as they waited for their horses to be shod at the blacksmith's forge. He might see his grandchildren on their way to school and call a cheery 'Good morning'. The children were always prepared to meet him but hoped that their shoes were clean and that they were turned out in a manner befitting an Oldacre, otherwise they would be sent home to 'get yourself tidy'.

Cattle markets were held each Monday and Friday in Gloucester, each Tuesday in Evesham, each Wednesday in Tewkesbury and there was the Cheltenham corn market on a Thursday. Walter John would set off for one or more of these markets each week and perhaps fit in a visit to a horse fair at Stow-on-the-Wold, or Tewkesbury. He would harness up his big grey horse Billy to the trap and go off at a cracking pace. Many of his grand-daughters still remember the spring-trap with terror in their hearts, particularly from when they were young and their legs were not long enough to allow them to wedge themselves into the seat. A slight touch on the reins and Billy would go flying past the tramcars in Cheltenham and the passengers had to make sure that they were not left behind on the road.

The visits to Cheltenham corn market held at the Crown Hotel in Albion Street were, of course, an important part of Walter John's business life. These journeys were often made in company with his wife Lucy. The couple made a fine picture. They were well dressed, handsome, and they sat up high and proud on the seat of the trap. Summer or winter, the Boss's heavy top coat covered a suit tailored from thorn-proof or tweed cloth. His striped shirt was made of flannel and around his neck he wore a stiff white collar and sombre tie. A dark homburg hat was firmly set on his head and his brown ankleboots were highly polished. His wife wore a threequarter length coat over her long high-necked black frock. Lucy Oldacre's face was shaded by the wide brim of her dark hat which in turn was firmly fixed to her head by large hat-pins pushed deep into her hair-bun. Her feet were safely encased in gleaming black buttoned boots. When they arrived in Cheltenham, Billy would be stabled in Albion Street for the day and the couple would perhaps, dine at the Crown, or across the High Street at the Plough, the old coaching inn. Mrs Oldacre would then spend the afternoon shopping in the town before returning home.

Lucy Irons, Ada's younger daughter, particularly dreaded accompanying her grandparents on these Cheltenham outings. She would plead with her mother to be left behind because of her fear of a journey on the back seat of the trap, on that seat you faced to the rear.

Lucy's fear was understandable. She and her mother had been involved in an accident when travelling in the trap. On the return journey from Cheltenham, Billy slipped on some ice in Albion Street, Mr and Mrs Oldacre fell off the front seat, Lucy was thrown over the horse's head, and her mother was trapped between the horse's back legs and the shafts. Her grandfather hurriedly picked himself up and with his great strength held onto the frightened horse to protect his daughter, while passersby righted the trap. Fortunately no one was seriously hurt and they were able to mount up and return home to Bishops Cleeve.

After a normal journey from Cheltenham, Mr and Mrs Oldacre would arrive back at The Pollards in time to see the men as they finished work in the mill at 6 pm. Walter John would check that all the horses were properly fed, watered and stabled. He would then go back to the farm to check on the livestock and the crops, before returning home for supper.

Walter John spent much time discussing the management of the business with his son and also in making calls on important customers. He had a high regard for the business acumen of William John, who was indeed a brilliant trader. His son always seemed able to buy commodities at the bottom of the market and then sell them at a considerable profit. However, his son was headstrong and sometimes needed to be bridled. Walter John would listen to the ideas which flooded from the active brain of his son. Most of these ideas he accepted with the comment 'Now John, you do that!' However, sometimes he thought an idea to be too wild, and then he would only need to say 'No John!' to hold his son in check. He did have trouble on one or two occasions when he stopped his son in his tracks, but no one else involved with the business was ever able to control William John in such a simple but direct manner and without any violent repercussions.

One person who remembered his grandfather making calls on important customers was Walter John Junior. He had no fear of journeys in the trap and recalled the thrill of sitting high up in front beside his grandfather and behind a high stepping grey horse. The faster Billy cantered the better the boy liked it. On arrival at a farm with hay or corn to sell, it seemed to the child that endless time was spent haggling before a bargain was struck and then sealed with a potion in the parlour. The purchase having been made, it was off and away with Billy, and a matter of searching out likely buyers requiring that particular quality of forage or corn. It was in this way that the boy learned about quality in the horse feed business and the many grades in quality of the simple oat. Thoroughbreds and racing stables required the best, bright plump kernels, nicely clipped and polished, while the working horse had to get along with plainer fare. The boy adored his grandfather and modelled his later business life on the lessons which he learnt from him.

Sunday for Walter John was a different day in every

respect. He was a Christian man with rigid ideas about churchmanship and correct behaviour. Like many of his contemporaries he frowned on Popish practices in worship and was an avowed Protestant. The only work which he would allow to be done on a Sunday related to keeping the horses and farm stock fed and watered. His daughters were not allowed to knit or sew and games of any sort were totally prohibited. He took his place on the north side of the nave of St Michael and All Angels Church at morning and evening prayer, with his family alongside him. Some joined him in the morning and some in the evening. His grandchildren made every effort to avoid those seats in the family row which were behind the large Norman pillar, or they could see nothing of the service. As they took their places, they carefully passed grandfather's hat down the row to rest on any vacant seat and were careful not to drop it. After church he would return home for Sunday dinner and in the afternoon walk in the village or over the hill. Sunday tea was an important occasion and groups of the children would join their grandparents for home bottled fruit and cream, home made bread and butter, home made jam and home made cakes. In the summer, the

Walter John and Billy

children and possibly their grandfather would picnic in the garden and those were memorable times for the children.

There were many occasions during the year when Lucy and Walter John invited Ada and Will Irons and their two daughters Dorothy and Lucy, or Alice and Arthur Redman, or William John and his family to meals at The Pollards. Everyone had to be on their best behaviour, but they very much enjoyed these visits. The children were able to take turns in sitting on grandfather's knee and it was on these occasions when grandmother really relaxed. Mary recalled her grandmother laughing at the antics of the children or some simple remark from one of them until the tears ran down her face. Once or twice a year Mr and Mrs Oldacre had a real party when they provided mountains of food and parlour games were played. On these occasions the sideboard in the sitting room would be groaning under the weight of sides of beef, hams, chickens, collared head, brawn, salads, pickles, crusty bread, cheeses, fruit cakes, sponge cakes and fruit of all kinds. The children had only one complaint about these parties. They found themselves, from time to time, sitting on the horse hair sofa or the horse hair arm chairs in the sitting room, where the horse hair prickled and scratched their bare legs.

The children did not always find that picnic tea in the garden of The Pollards enjoyable, particularly if their grandfather was not present. Lucy Oldacre had been brought up to be careful, thrifty, and to waste nothing and on occasions she would give the children stale bread cut thickly with butter spread thinly. This soon became known as 'Grandma's bread and scrape', and was surreptitiously fed to the dog. Once, faced with some particularly unappetising fare, Lucy Irons, much to the embarrassment of her mother, marched into the house at tea time and asked for more bread and butter.

'Have you finished the whole plateful I gave you already?' her grandmother inquired.

'No' said Lucy with a pretty, appealing grin. 'We can't eat that stale bread. We want fresh bread cut from the same loaf which you are eating' – and much to the other children's surprise and delight they got it.

It seems that Lucy was often in trouble with one or other of her grandparents. When she was older and a student at St Mary's Teacher Training College, Cheltenham, she was in the habit of using a little lipstick and powder. If this brazen behaviour was noticed by her grandfather when she was staying at The Pollards, grandfather would send her upstairs to clean herself up. Mary and Mildred Oldacre suffered similar treatment from both their father and their grandfather if they were seen to be wearing make-up.

Walter John watched over the health of his workforce and of their families and encouraged the development of any children who showed particular aptitude for learning, or who showed dexterity of hand, and he offered work to as many of the youngsters as possible as they left school. If any of his employees fell upon hard times he visited and comforted them and ensured that they did not go cold or hungry. He made regular gifts of free coal and food to many of them.

After a life of hard work, Walter John Oldacre was able to live comfortably and to give meaning to the Christian way of life which he had so steadfastly followed.

(iii) William John's family move to Fieldgate

By 1926, relationships with all the family had improved and Gladys was accepted at last. The family of William John and Gladys had increased to four girls and a boy – Catherine Elizabeth was born in 1919, and Hilda Frances in 1923. Gladys could now afford help in the house but there was not enough room at The Laurels for the girl to live in. William John managed to persuade his father to buy Fieldgate Farm at the top of the village for him. It was half way up Pecked Lane past the former chapel of St Anne's, and on the corner of what is now Fieldgate Road. In those days it was an overgrown track known locally as Lovers Lane. Pecked Lane itself continued beyond Fieldgate as far as Pecked Piece Farm and Hyatts Mead where it became a footpath and passed over the railway line and eventually joined with a small lane coming down from Woodmancote Green. The property was generally rectangular in shape, about 270 yards long by seventy yards wide, a total area of four acres, it included the house and outbuildings, a garden, and an orchard. On the north side of the orchard there were two paddocks adding a further two acres of ground, one of these was purchased by Walter John, whilst the other was rented by him.

The Cotswold stone farmhouse was on three storeys and was roofed with blue slate.

The kitchen had a stone flagged floor, deeply worn by the passage of feet over many generations, and the cooking range was built into the chimney of a former bake oven and there were store cupboards on both sides of it. The stone walls of the building were sufficiently thick to house a window seat in the wall opposite the door. There was a dairy with a blue and white tiled floor, and beyond it a sitting room which was used on a Sunday and for piano practice by the children. The family lived in the kitchen for most of the time during the week.

On the first floor there were four bedrooms and on the top floor two bedrooms with dormer windows and a single window in each gable end, and two boxrooms with fan lights. The house had no main services. Drinking water was provided by a pump and a well sunk deep into the underlying gravel beds and roof water was retained in a large galvanised iron water butt. Both the pump and the water butt were housed under a lean-to outside the back door. A two seater privy down the garden and a further privy in the paddock provided the only sanitation, and waste water from the house was discharged into a soakaway. Oil lamps and candles were used for lighting.

The lack of mains services to the house meant that Gladys still had a great deal of hard work to do and her husband was anxious to lighten her load as soon as he could reasonably do so. Gas had been brought to the village in the early part of the century and was laid on to the mill. Winchcombe Rural District Council provided mains water and sewerage, and the Cheltenham Borough Council provided electricity to the centre of the village. William John asked his father if he could extend the services up to Fieldgate at his own expense, but was told firmly that he could not. This refusal meant that all William John could do was to turn one of the bedrooms into a bathroom and to install a hand pump which would lift the well water up into a storage tank situated in one of the boxrooms on the top floor of the house. Even after that work was done, hot water still had to be heated in the copper in the wash house and it then had to be carried into the kitchen, or up into the bathroom.

The wash house and outbuildings were across the gravel yard and were reached over a series of large stepping stones. The wash house included two large furnaces and a copper, and in addition a further black leaded kitchen range and a shallow stone sink. Beyond the wash house there was a wood and coal store and beyond that a large pig sty. All these buildings fronted Fieldgate Road. A number of barns and stables were located on the opposite side of the yard to the house and there were further stables, a harness room and other outbuildings in a small paddock.

Shortly after they arrived at Fieldgate, Doris Little, who was about the same age as their eldest daughter Mary, came to live in with the family and to help with the housework. Women from the village came in on wash day and a man looked after the pigs and tended the garden.

The Monday wash involved a lot of hard work. Water had to be pumped from the well and carried to the copper, under which a fire had to be lighted by six o'clock in the morning. The water was boiling by nine o'clock and it took three hours to complete the wash. Each load had to be left in the copper for three quarters of an hour before being rinsed in a large galvanised bath. White linen was then rinsed again in Reckitts Blue to preserve its whiteness, and was then hand-mangled between wooden rollers. The clothes were hung out to dry on the garden line which stretched from the house to the orchard gate.

The warm soapy water was then used to bath the younger children and was finally taken out into the garden to be used as an insecticide on the roses. Tuesday was ironing day and this activity took place in the kitchen. Flat irons were heated on the hob of the kitchen range and the ironing was done on a board, covered with a blanket and sheet, and laid between the window sill and the kitchen table.

All the cooking was done by Gladys and much of the food was home grown. The vegetable garden covered one third of an acre and potatoes, carrots, parsnips, suedes, turnips, cabbages, sprouts, peas, broad and runner beans, onions, tomatoes, lettuces and cucumbers were grown. Gladys was often to be seen, sitting on the window seat in the kitchen with a bucket full of broad beans or peas to shell, or runner beans to slice. Potato peeling was an enormous task. The vegetable trimmings were taken to the barn where they were dropped into a large vat of pig meal so that there was no waste.

There were four poultry houses in the orchard and Rhode Island Red hens were scratching about everywhere. There would also be a pen of cockerels being fattened for the table. If there were any eggs surplus to requirements they were laid down in waterglass for when the hens were off lay. This viscous syrupy solution of sodium silicate in water sets like jelly around eggs and helps to preserve them.

The pigs also had the run of the orchard which was planted with apple trees of different varieties and a number of pear trees. Soon after he took possession of the property William John planted Pershore and Victoria plum trees along the edge of the vegetable garden and he had as many as 20 hives of bees.

The pig was, of course, an animal from which there was no waste, all parts could be eaten. Sides of bacon were salted by the family. Pig meat was used as joints. Trotters were boiled and eaten as a delicacy by the older members of the family. The pig's head and any parts not otherwise used were boiled and then allowed to stand so that the fat content solidified on the top as it cooled. The fat was then skimmed off for lard and the meat was put into a pot and pressed into a meat mould; this was used either as collared head or as brawn, depending on the part of the pig that was used. Any residue which was left after these operations had been completed was again rendered down, any further fat content was added to the lard and the remaining pieces of meat, known as 'scratchings', were eaten as 'nibbles' in today's terms. Offal such as the heart, liver and kidneys were used, and the last delicacies from the pig came from the intestines. The intestines were placed in brine, taken out of the brine every day for a fortnight and turned inside out before being re-immersed. Finally they were eaten as chitterlings. The bees fended for themselves in the summer when there was plenty of pollen about, but in the winter they were fed with sugar. Some of the honey was eaten on the comb, but the majority was extracted and put into jars. This job was done by hand. The delicate wax skin was gently removed from the comb before it was put in the extractor and the machine was turned by hand and the honey was collected in the jars. If the feeding of the bees had been correct, then the honey remained smooth, but if too much sugar had been given to them the resulting honey crystallised.

The produce from the orchard and garden kept the family self-sufficient in English fruit and vegetables. Cropping was plentiful enough to allow Gladys to turn the surpluses into preserves of various kinds; jams were made; apples were pulped and bottled; plums, pears, rhubarb, gooseberries and currants were preserved in sugar solution in vacuum clip bottles; tomatoes were bottled in brine; runner beans were salted; and pickles and chutneys were made. The tightly sealed bottles and jars were then stored in the two boxrooms on the top floor at Fieldgate.

At that time William John did not keep a cow at Fieldgate. The large quantity of milk which was consumed by the family came from his father's farm or a neighbour's farm. Some cream was separated from the milk and used directly, but the bulk of the cream was made into butter.

The ear trouble that was a legacy of the war caused William John constant pain which made it difficult for him to show outward affection towards his children. He was always a happy man, but his ear trouble, coupled with pressures of the working day, could bring out a quite violent temper and the children would occasionally feel a sting from the cane which he kept hanging in the kitchen. This ear trouble became so severe in 1927 that specialist advice was sought and acute mastoid inflammation was diagnosed. William John was taken into hospital for surgery which fortunately proved to be successful. His father suggested that he should take a long holiday in Canada to convalesce and after an enjoyable crossing of the Atlantic and a cruise up the St Lawrence River and through the canal into Lake Ontario, he finally arrived at Toronto. He retained happy memories of the five weeks which he spent with his mother's relations at their home on the shores of Lake Musckoko in Ontario. He spent hours riding across the prairies and the vast open space and the scale of the farming fascinated him. He was enchanted by the colour and the beauty of the Algonquin

Park in the fall, and by the view across Lake Musckoko which seemed to vary hour by hour. William John took his wife to the home of this branch of the Minett family on a number of occasions in later years and he remained in contact with them throughout his life. On his return to England he was relaxed, free from mastoid pain and more readily able to enjoy the company of his children.

On Saturday 2 June 1928 Gladys Oldacre, who was eight months pregnant, was busily papering the walls in her bedroom when her labour pains began. The doctor was summoned and William John set off with haste for Bishops Cleeve station where he hoped to find Doris Little waiting for the Cheltenham train for she had left Fieldgate only a few minutes earlier. He and Doris arrived back home just as the doctor's car was pulling into the yard and they were all too late to witness the birth of June Lucy, the fifth daughter and sixth child in the family. The 6 lb 4 oz baby girl was soon lying in the cot beside her mother's bed in the half-papered bedroom.

Gladys was soon up and about again. She was, as always, high spirited and full of fun and the whole atmosphere at Fieldgate was relaxed and happy. It was a wonderful environment for children, most of whom attended the village school, where the eldest ones stayed until they were 11 years old, before transferring to various schools in Cheltenham. June only stayed at the village school until she was six. The older children travelled to Cheltenham by train, but by the time Hilda and June had to travel, Mary or John could take them to the town in the car as they drove to work at Winchcombe Street. Perhaps the only drawback for the children came from the fact that there was little incentive or opportunity for quiet study, but some of the children did find time for reading and all were encouraged to play the piano or the violin.

(iv) William John becomes more relaxed after Anna and Alice resign

Early in 1928 and shortly after William John had returned to the business, Walter John realised that the unsecured monies which Anna and Alice had in the business must be safeguarded. He arranged for both daughters to invest £1,000 of their unsecured loan, together with any balance standing to their credit at the end of the financial year 1927–28, in six percent debenture shares. By November of that year Anna and Alice had resigned from the board of directors of the company. Walter John bought the one thousand ordinary shares in the company formerly held by Anna; William John the thousand ordinary shares formerly held by Alice and 38 debenture shares of £100 each were created bearing an interest at six percent per annum. Twenty of these shares were issued to Anna and eighteen to Alice. Even this reduced investment and involvement in the company by his sisters was later to prove a major problem for William John.

The resignation of Anna and Alice from their directorships in the company was welcomed by William John and eased some of the tension in his business life. But Walter John was sad to think that his family could not continue working together for the good of the company and of the family as a whole.

Although Alice was the youngest of Walter John's surviving daughters, she was the only one who was really interested in the business. It seems clear that she would have liked to have had the opportunity of accepting the challenge of the top management post in W J Oldacre Ltd, but she had been born at the wrong time even though she had proved her worth during the Great War. If she wished to stay in the business, she had no alternative but to be subservient to her brother and this she was not prepared to do. And William John had a large family while she was childless. Anna, on the other hand, was a follower rather than a leader. She was content in the home and influenced by Alice.

The board was reduced to two directors, the elderly Walter John as chairman and William John as managing director and company secretary. Fortunately, Gladys was a great help to her husband and Mary, their eldest daughter, was about to leave school and was showing a marked interest in the business and an appreciation of figures. She was sent to college to learn book-keeping and business practice and proved to be an able pupil. At the same time she was also working in the Cheltenham office.

The company now expanded and in 1929 Walker's bakery

and corn merchant business of Charlton Kings, Cheltenham was acquired. In the following year, 70 acres of meadow land known as Withy Farm and owned by Mrs Togwell was rented and the company also took over the tenancy of the lands known as Wardstone, Tobysfield, Wingmoor and the Pollards from Walter John, and so W J Oldacre Ltd now farmed more than one hundred acres.

Responsibility for the new acquisitions was passed to William John, who decided to co-ordinate the management of the corn merchant side with the Winchcombe Street operations. The bakery was in poor shape, only nine sacks of flour were used each week, and the whole enterprise would have amounted to nothing if it had not been for a reasonable confectionery trade. William John set about reorganising the bakehouse and gaining the confidence of the foreman baker.

Mildred, the second daughter of William John and Gladys, began work at Charlton Kings shortly after it became a part of Oldacres. Mildred was an independent girl and was soon asking to be allowed to leave the family firm so that she could train for the drapery trade at Cavendish House, Cheltenham. This was agreed and she worked at Cavendish House before moving to posts in Harrogate and Bath and by the time she was in her early twenties she was a fashion buyer.

Freda Wise also started with Oldacres as an accounts clerk shortly after Walker's was taken over. She gave invaluable service to the company throughout the whole of the time that they were involved in the bakery trade and she remembered that business was at first slow and that it was not unusual to take as little as £8 on a Saturday. Bread was only 5d for a two pound loaf.

The corn business in Cheltenham and the surrounding countryside was increasing in spite of the general recession in farming, and more staff were needed. In particular two new representatives were appointed: Howard Counsell, who later became sales director was a most loyal member of the company until his retirement some 40 years later.

In the late summer of 1929, Jack Charnock once again called at Winchcombe Street. Jack's eldest son, Ernest, had just matriculated and, as a reward for his examination success, had been given a trip up to London with his father and two of Jack's farming uncles from Lancashire were also

with them. On the return journey to his home in Prenton, on
the Wirral in Cheshire, Jack decided to take his passengers
through Oxfordshire and Gloucestershire, to show them the
countryside and the local farming practices. It was a sudden
impulse which led Jack back to Oldacres shop. Jack was 43
years old, white haired and very thin. He ran his own
business in Liverpool under the name of Thomson and
Charnock, trading as a corn merchant and specialising in the
manufacture of high quality racing pigeon foods with the
registered trade name of 'Goldwing'. As he drove down the
A40 and into Charlton Kings, he saw the name Oldacres over
the bakery shop.

'I used to do a lot of business with that firm before the war'
he said. 'the son was a friend of mine. I thought they were
finished. I am sure John was killed. I must stop for a minute
and ask after the family.'

He parked outside 40 Winchcombe Street and walked into
the shop. At the same moment his friend William John
Oldacre walked out of the office at the back of the shop.

'Chrimes,' Jack cried, using his favourite expletive. 'It is
John. I thought you were dead.'

'I don't believe it – Jack? How wonderful', was all that
William John could say.

Neither had a great deal of time on that day to tell of the
lives which they had led since they last saw one another in
1914, but each vowed to meet again as soon as possible. The
promised reunion did not prove difficult to arrange. Shortly
after Jack's visit to Winchcombe Street, he had to dismiss his
South Wales and Gloucestershire representative and decided
to undertake that work himself. He now called once every
five weeks on his old friend, and before returning home to
Prenton, spent Thursday night with the family at Fieldgate.
The two men talked late into the night exchanging business
ideas and generally helping one another in overcoming the
difficult trading conditions.

In spite of the national depression, the year 1931 began
with Oldacres showing a good balance sheet. The annual
sales when the company was formed in 1923 were valued at
£31,413, and that figure was approaching £40,000 by 1931
but disaster was about to strike. . . .

(v) Fire at the mill is followed by Walter John's death

It was at about 3 o'clock on an April morning in 1931 and after a lengthy chaff cutting operation on the previous day, that Lucy Irons, who was staying at The Pollards with her grandparents, was awakened by the frenzied barkings of Carlo, the black Labrador dog. She could smell burning and saw a red glow through the bedroom window. She jumped out of bed and saw that her grandfather's mill was ablaze.

'Grandpa, grandpa,' she screamed. 'The mill's on fire.'

Walter John rushed to the telephone by the back door, but it was not working. He ran towards the blazing mill, broke open the door and grabbed the mill telephone which thankfully was still functioning, and called the Cheltenham Fire Brigade. At first, they declined the call because the fire was outside the town area so he summoned the engine from Tewkesbury and they were first on the scene, closely followed by the one from Evesham. Both brigades had water playing on the blaze before the Cheltenham brigade arrived. Meanwhile, Lucy Irons had alerted the families in the thatched cottages on the opposite side of the road to the mill. The village men pulled the old parish engine out of the firehouse in Trapp's yard next to The Pollards. It was a machine dating from the 19th century, hand-pumped and quite incapable of handling a blaze on the scale of a mill fire, but the men did their best to contain the fire to the mill building before the brigades arrived.

Lucy next ran to fetch her uncle from Fieldgate. One or two horses which had escaped from the paddock behind the mill yard came galloping up the village towards her and in her shocked state made her think that Lucifer himself was after her. Eventually, she arrived at the house and began shouting, in the hope that the family would hear her.

'Uncle John, Uncle John, FIRE, FIRE, FIRE' she shouted. 'The mill's on fire.'

Gladys heard her cries and started to shake her deaf husband.

'Quick John. The mill's on fire.'

William John jumped out of bed and was at the open window straining hard to hear his niece's anxious voice. He was dressed and out of the house in seconds, and speeding down the village on his bicycle so that he could be at his father's side without further delay.

Walter John's main concern was his horses. At least four animals were stabled in a building attached to the burning mill and another six were close by in the stable alongside the village street. The horses were stamping, whinnying, and screaming loudly, their eyes wide open, rolling and looking like balls of fire but he managed to release them and brought them through the flames and smoke to safety by covering their heads with damp sacks and leading each one to the relative safety of the mill yard. He was helped in this task by his son who had opened the yard gates and was helping to lead the frantic horses to safety. The two men then turned their attention to the horses in the stable alongside the road which, when released, galloped out of the yard gates and down to their pasture in Stoke Road.

By the time that the horses were released and on their way to the safety of the pasture, Walter John's beard was burned so that half of his face was almost bare of it's former fine white beard. But there was more for father and son to do. Picking up the shafts of one of the drays which was loaded with 40 sacks of maize, Walter John and his son dragged it out of danger from the fire, with such physical strength, that even in men of their stature is possible only at times of great stress. At least two drays were badly burnt, but not one of the horses suffered any serious injury.

The fire had a good hold on the mill building before any of the powerful water jets from the fire brigades were played upon it. The building and machinery was destroyed and the stock severely damaged. There was nothing more that father and son could do but wait for the smouldering embers to die down and then make an assessment of the damage.

The effort which Walter John had put into the rescue operations, and the shock which he had suffered now took hold of him and left him drained of all strength. He sank down and had to be helped gently back to his own peaceful fireside by William John. His wife and daughter Anna provided hot sweet coffee and comfort, but Walter John had seriously strained his courageous heart, and was never to recover fully his old strength and vitality.

The minutes of the board meeting on the 29 October 1931

record the fire:

> 'It has to be recorded that a disastrous fire occured at the Bishops Cleeve premises of the firm in April of this year, destroying completely all the working plant and stock and practically the whole of the building rented from Mrs Lucy Oldacre.
>
> The Gresham Insurance Company paid a sum of £1,339.4s.0d. in respect of damages, loss of dead stock and machinery (a sum of £800 being paid over by the firm to W J Oldacre Snr in respect of the mill and other machinery and engine whose property it was). It was resolved that as soon as the building could be re-erected Mr W J Oldacre Snr should re-equip it with a new engine, mills and chaff cutter etc., and have the two trolleys which had been burnt in the fire repaired for future use.
>
> Some difficulty was experienced in getting Mrs Oldacre's claim for damages done by the fire recognised by the Eagle Star and Dominions Insurance Co, but eventually the latter named paid over an agreed sum which is being spent back upon the property together with further sums by Mr W J Oldacre Snr for Mrs Oldacre and at this date the building is well under way'.

The aftermath of the fire could have spelt increased hardship for the villagers in Bishops Cleeve at that time of recession, had it not been for the resolve with which William John tackled the rebuilding and re-equipping of the mill. The old gas engine was replaced with a 50 horse power single cylinder horizontal diesel engine, and a new and larger stone mill was installed which was capable of an output of five hundredweights of hot steaming barley meal each hour. Bill Cook nursed this engine like a baby, and was to be seen each morning gently warming up the new engine with a blow lamp. Only Bill and the Governor seemed to have the ability to bring the engine to life on a cold morning.

The hire agreement for the engine, mill and machinery which the company had had with Walter John since 1923 was terminated, the company buying it out for £1,000. The only outstanding matter affecting the mill which was not yet directly in the hands of the company related to the tenancy agreement with Mrs Oldacre on The Pollards, which included the land and buildings of the mill and yard. That agreement was to remain in force for another ten years. However, Walter John did retain ownership of all his properties in the village and in Cheltenham.

The fire occurred just before the end of the financial year which had always been 30 April. The directors now changed the end of the financial year to 31 May, and, not surprisingly, the year which ended in May 1932 showed disappointing figures. But the jobs of the employees, who had been so loyal during this difficult period, had been safeguarded and Oldacres looked forward to a better year in 1932–33.

Rebuilding operations made such good progress that Jack Charnock persuaded William John and Gladys to take a short holiday and to spend Easter 1932 at his home in Prenton for he had long wanted to introduce his friend to his wife and his three sons. I was six years of age in 1932.

A brass bedstead in one of the attic bedrooms had been made up for my mother and father to sleep on as their bed was to be used by our guests and the house was even more highly polished than usual. A fire burned in the dining room which was only used on special occasions, and the table was set for seven people. The smell of cooking coming from the kitchen made it seem like a Sunday morning, because a joint was roasting in the oven and pastry had been made. I had been told by my mother how I was to behave and that I must eat everything that was put in front of me.

'Daddy says that Mr Oldacre does not like waste!' she warned me. My father's Ford V8 came into view at the window, closely followed by a maroon Austin 16 and both vehicles stopped outside our house. I scampered down the stairs.

'Mum, Mum, they are here!' I shouted.

My mother removed her apron, wiped her hands and smoothed her hair before joining me and we waited in the hall for our guests to arrive. My brother John, was 12 years old and a shy boy so he stood behind us in the hall. Ernest my eldest brother, had not yet returned from school in West Kirby. He was almost 18 and working hard for his Higher School Certificate.

Moments later the door opened and a white haired lady

walked into the house, followed by the biggest man I had ever seen.

'John, – Mrs Oldacre', my father announced as he introduced them to us. 'My wife Freda, my son John and the little one is Denys.'

Mr and Mrs. Oldacre shook hands with my mother and a few words were exchanged before they turned their attention to my brother and me.

'Hello, young man!' said the big man as he took my hand.

At least that is what I thought he had said, but I could hardly understand his broad Gloucestershire accent which was unfamiliar to me. But, he was my father's friend, and so he was my friend. I had loved him from the moment he entered the house.

William John and his wife stayed with us until Easter Monday, during which time I hardly left his side. When he sat in an easy chair in front of the fire, I immediately climbed onto his knee. When my father and mother took their friends for a walk, I accompanied them. I joined the men on their visit to my father's mill in Liverpool, We went by car to Woodside ferry and crossed the River Mersey on the luggage boat and I led Mr Oldacre up to the ticket office to show him where to pay the fare. At home I showed him my prize possessions of Dinky cars and lead soldiers. I took him out shopping, and he bought me three Dinky lorries.

'I have lorries like those back at my home!', he told me. 'You will have to come and see them.'

On Easter Sunday morning I attended morning service at Liverpool Cathedral with my father and our guests, while my mother prepared lunch. After lunch Mr Oldacre handed me the biggest Easter egg that I had ever seen. It was certainly a memorable weekend for me, but I little knew that this big man and his family would play such a dominant role throughout the remainder of my life. I did, however, believe that I was ready to go to the end of the earth with him. The strange thing is that at that time I was hardly aware of his wife, who later became a second mother to me.

This further development of the friendship between William John and Jack Charnock could not have come at a more opportune time. Soon after his return to Bishops Cleeve, William John found that the strain which his father had suffered at the time of the fire was sapping his former strength. Walter John Oldacre was now an ailing man and could only play a minor role in the running of the family business. But his concern for the wellbeing of the villagers was undiminished and he still attended church regularly.

Towards the end of March 1933, Walter John was taken ill with pneumonia. Anna nursed him with love and devotion but he became weaker and weaker and on Easter Day, Sunday 4 April, he passed peacefully away. He was 71.

St Michael and All Angels, Bishops Cleeve, was packed for the funeral service after which Walter John Oldacre was buried with his daughter Lucy, in the grave alongside that of his father and mother.

4

DIFFICULT TIMES

1933–39

(i) The aftermath of Walter John's death

William John was deeply upset by the death of his father. He and Alice were nominated executors under the 'Will', and he suffered a further body blow when the will was read.

The fully paid and issued ordinary share capital of the company was still £4,000, of which Walter John and his son each owned half. Walter John's 2,000 ordinary shares were now to be divided equally between his daughters Anna and Alice, his grand-daughter Mary, and his grandson John (once the boy had reached 21 years of age and providing that he entered the business). Toby's Field cottage, garden and orchard were to be sold to pay the funeral and testamentary expenses, debts and death duties. His son was to have the two properties in Charlton Kings which formed the bakery business, unencumbered. The beneficiaries of his remaining properties were required to pay an annual rental to his wife Lucy Elizabeth Oldacre, during her lifetime and these included: Fieldgate House, garden and orchard to his son; Ferndale House, Bishops Cleeve to his eldest daughter Ada; The Willows, two cottages built on land which had formed part of Fieldgate orchard, and the business properties in Winchcombe Street, Cheltenham, jointly between his daughters Anna and Alice. He made small legacies to each of his six grandchildren who had not received shares in the business. His debenture shares in the business and other capital were to be equally divided between William John, Anna and Alice. Ada's name was crossed out of this section of his will and she received no benefit.

The situation was even more serious for William John. His mother still owned The Pollards, the mill and the surrounding land and he knew that his sister Alice would inherit that property under the terms of her mother's will. His position as managing director of the business was intolerable. Anna and Alice would control the majority of the property from which the business functioned, they would again have risk capital in the business and large sums in debentures. There was no doubt in William John's mind that Alice would be demanding a seat on the board and interfering in the management of the business, or she would be demanding that all the money which she had invested in W J Oldacre Ltd be repaid; and also that she would advise Anna to do likewise. He could not possibly meet any demand for repayment of money, and he could not tolerate the interference which he knew would come if Alice was again to be a member of the company.

William John now sank into a deep depression. He became imprisoned within himself and could not communicate with anyone, not even with his wife. Gladys knew that she must bide her time and hope that after a few days the shutters would lift, so that he could open his heart to her. It was on a Sunday morning not long after the death of his father, that Gladys woke to find that her husband was ready to talk about the difficult situation in which he now found himself.

'How can I possibly carry on? Why has Dad done this to me?' he asked. 'I am totally in the hands of Alice and she will break me.'

'You do have control because Mary has 500 shares and this gives you votes on 2,500 shares against a maximum of 1,000 which Alice can muster' said his wife. 'And John's 500 shares are in the hands of both Alice and yourself as joint executors.'

'No! No! I may have the business but I have no capital to protect myself against an attack by Alice' said William John. 'Apart from Charlton Kings, the property is either rented from mother or from other people in the village, I have not the surety to put to the bank against a large overdraft.'

'But the business owns the machinery, the transport and the stock.'

'All that and more will be needed to buy Alice and Annie out.'

Gladys would not let him get away with this defeatist attitude.

'Surely you cannot think that your mother would stand by and watch while all the work which your father did during the whole of their life together is thrown away, nor for that matter, would she stand by and watch her rents disappearing.'

It was Gladys and Jack Charnock who persuaded William John to talk with his mother for they were certain that she would understand his difficulties and in March 1934, Lucy Elizabeth Oldacre signed the first codicil to her earlier will. In it Ada was to join her two sisters as an executor and legacies were added in favour of both Ada and William John. More importantly the codicil made it clear that if she had sold or contracted to sell The Pollards before her death, then her daughter Alice would receive £1,000 in addition to any other bequests.

The changed will caused further problems and divisions between Alice and William John. By August of the same year a second codicil had been signed. In essence it required the estate to sell The Pollards to W J Oldacre Ltd for £1,000, such sum to be paid to Alice free of all expenses and death duties. The dissention between Alice and William John was sufficiently severe for their mother to direct that any beneficiary who disputed that provision would forfeit all benefits and interests in her estate.

William John's worst fears did materialise. Alice did have to be consulted on business matters for the first 12 months after Walter John's death and she did attend the board meetings as an executor of her father's will.

William John was ready for action. A shareholders meeting was held at Crescent Place, Cheltenham, on 21 March 1934. The minutes of that meeting make it clear that Alice did not attend but appointed a solicitor as proxy. From the chair William John ruled that since the proxy was not stamped it did not comply with the law. He then exercised his right as the first named joint holder of 2,000 shares in the names of himself and Alice Redman to vote on their behalf. In his own right he proposed that 20 shares from his personal portfolio be transferred to his wife, Gladys Mary Oldacre, and seconded the proposal under the 2,000 shares held in his father's right. Gladys was immediately appointed a director of the company.

Later that year a final settlement was reached with Anna and Alice. William John took over the 1,000 ordinary shares held in the business by Anna and Alice for a cash sum. The annual interest on £3,800 debentures in their ownership was reduced from six percent to five percent, and this brought them into line with all other debenture holders. Finally it was agreed that four percent interest would be paid to them on all the remainder of the money due to them under the will of their late father, and that they would be paid that interest at three-monthly intervals. This agreement went some way to reducing the financial liability of W J Oldacre Ltd. In 1935, Mary was made a director and Company Secretary.

The final chapter in the rather protracted affair over the wills of Walter John Oldacre and his wife came on 3 July 1935 when Lucy Elizabeth Oldacre signed a third codicil which read:

'I give devise and bequeath all my real and personal estate not effectively disposed of by my said will or any codicil thereto to my daughter Anna Louise Oldacre absolutely as a token of her loving affection and attention to me.'

Anna devoted the next seven years of her life to looking after her mother.

(ii) William John is firmly at the helm

William John was now ready to expand the company. In September 1935, he took over the tenancy of Lynworth Farm, Woodmancote for the sum of £75 per annum, and the landlord agreed to lay water on to the fields and to carry out any other necessary repairs. The company also extended their warehouse building at The Pollards, in order to make more room for the storage of English grain.

Even before any expansion was contemplated, the company was broad based. Their premises were scattered from Charlton Kings to Bishops Cleeve, and the farm stretched from Price's Piece (near to the railway in Stoke Road) to Woodmancote. The business still dealt in hay, corn, and coal; still manufactured their own pig and poultry meals; still acted as agents for Albion Mills and now took on an agency for Blue Cross Feeds; sold seed potatoes, grass seed and Danish seed grain; dealt in lime and fertilisers; baked bread and confectionery; had a retail trade in all these lines and also in pet and pigeon foods; and they farmed. The enterprise needed careful management.

William John had no formal education in business management, and he relied on the background training which had been given to him by his father and on his own natural flair. The general management of the company was firmly in his hands. The Registered Office may have still been at The Pollards, but the headquarters of the company was now established at Fieldgate Farm. The board of directors had their formal meeting at Fieldgate but these meetings were few and far between. However, the board met daily at every main meal, and the dining table became the seat of general management of the company and the scene of regular skirmishes between the family members. Walter John may have run a family business but William John now ran a business to which the whole family were expected to be totally subservient.

After the death of his father, William John took direct management control of the mill at Bishops Cleeve, the bakery at Charlton Kings and the farm, and in carrying out this task, he had three foremen to help him. The day-to-day management at Winchcombe Street, Cheltenham was placed on Mr Hamblin who was already on the staff, and Mr Howard Counsell was appointed to look after all the sales staff working for the company.

It was the job of the foreman at Bishops Cleeve to see that the mill was producing the feeds necessary to meet the orders and to ensure that the orders were ready and despatched on time. In carrying out these duties, he was assisted by Fred Cresswell who operated the mill. This arrangement had worked well enough when Walter John was alive, since he lived on the premises and was always about. The Governor was up early like his father, and cycled down to The Pollards most mornings to see that the men were on time and that the engine and the mill were running properly, before returning home for his breakfast. Within 12 months of his father's death, it was clear to William John that although he had good men at the mill, a greater degree of supervision was needed if everything was to work efficiently and harmoniously.

The foreman announced that he was leaving the district and this gave William John the opportunity to bring in a new manager without causing any ill feeling among the men. The company advertised for a man with appropriate experience and capable of taking responsibility for all the activities at Bishops Cleeve. A number of applicants were interviewed and Mr R A Bick, a man in his mid-thirties was selected and quickly established himself in the business.

The management team of Hamblin, Counsell, Bick, Johnson (the accountant) and John Oldacre was chaired by the Governor and met monthly. The agenda covered the trading figures for the month, advertising, office procedures, sales policy, and staff welfare. From time to time, the second line managers like the bakehouse foreman and the shop managers were invited to join the meeting for specific items, and of course, to account for their stewardship.

The advertising policy was certainly quite well advanced for a small firm like Oldacres in the mid-Thirties. There is no doubt that this was one of the subjects discussed by the Governor when his friend Jack Charnock was staying at Fieldgate. Jack's business extended over the whole of Great Britain and Ireland, and had been built up on American advertising experience which he had studied. Oldacres used the local press to good advantage, often involving a full-page spread with photographs, and they encouraged the press to send reporters to such events as the opening of their new pig house and to their site at the Albion Mills stand at the Three Counties Show. They also sent circulars to their farm, shop and bakery customers, and were early in the field with the production of monthly circulars and a news sheet. A logo was designed and a trade mark registered, this included the picture of a key and the caption 'The key to good feeding'. The logo was used on sacks, paper bags, and on the motor transport. They were also early into cinema advertising.

The management group also developed a fairly sophisticated staff policy. The hours of work of the men were reduced slightly so that they started at 7 am rather than 6 am. The lorry and van drivers were issued with overalls, but the facility was not extended to the carters. Bonuses were paid. A staff suggestion scheme was introduced, and while this caused the usual problems from a lack of good entries the company persevered and Jim Payne, who later became a director of the company, was a regular contributor. Holiday and sick payments were introduced, and Christmas parties and summer outings became a feature in the programme of the company each year.

The monthly management meeting was an ideal forum for ideas to be put forward for discussion and many of those ideas were adopted. The Governor was a benevolent dictator who listened to all, but it was he who made the final decision.

It is interesting to note that John Oldacre proposed that the firm should turn their proprietary meals into pellet form as early as March 1936 but his idea was killed immediately by his father because of the cost of the necessary machinery.

It is apparent from the minutes that Mr Bick had a good appreciation of the animal feed business, and in addition that he could make a major contribution to discussions about all aspects of Oldacres business. He recommended that the quality of poultry meal in winter would be improved by the introduction of cod liver oil to the mix. He suggested that the problems associated with persuading farmers to return hessian sacks would be overcome if paper bags, which were much cheaper than hessian sacks, were used. The paper bag idea was tried, but in those early days, the bags were not strong enough for the purpose. Satisfactory paper bags were introduced a few years later, meanwhile women were employed to mend damaged sacks, and the carters and drivers were given an incentive to encourage farmers to return the sacks.

Sales fluctuated and so did the size of the outstanding debts. Customers who were at fault were reminded of their position by letter and Howard Counsell seems, in his quiet way, to have been successful at encouraging many farmers to pay. The really hard line debts were brought to the attention of the Governor, who then took appropriate steps to get his firm's money from the farmers concerned. The months of May, June and July, were rather slack for sales of cake and meal, and so it was during those months that the travellers made a particular effort to reduce the outstanding debts. However, cash flow was always a problem.

A Cheltenham Corn Merchants Association had been formed in the early 1930s, and Mr Ride was elected chairman. Competition was fierce and one member was soon to be reported to the association for unfair trading. The company were accused of offering goods to the customers of their competitors at unreasonably low prices. Apparently the association demanded that a fine of £50 be paid to a local hospital, but that payment was never made and the association collapsed. The Cheltenham traders then joined the Gloucestershire Association.

Oldacres decided that the best way to fight the competition was to maintain their open trading policy and personal contact with all their customers. Their usual price list rates were followed, but they did offer 5/- per ton cash discount for payment within seven days. The travellers were warned that all complaints must be passed to the office immediately so that proper attention could be given to any complaint.

Bloodworths of Albion Street, Cheltenham clearly found trading difficult and they had to place their business on the market. Bloodworths premises were near to the corn market and Oldacres considered the possibility of making an offer for the company. However, the management team realised that access to their own Winchcombe Street premises was much better than the access to the Albion Street premises of Bloodworths, and so the matter was not taken any further. The company now began a search for premises in Tewkesbury.

In 1935 the total sales for the out of season months of June and July were £3,000. This encouraged the team to look for monthly sales of £4,500 in the season, and this was achieved. The balance sheet for 1935/36 showed a marked improvement over that for the previous year and the company were able to allocate a percentage of their profits to the Employees Bonus Scheme, a scheme very much the brainchild of William John. The employees received a bonus at the rate of five percent per annum of their net wages, and the payments were made in June and December. A special scheme for lorry drivers did lead to dissatisfaction among some men, because the bonus was paid on a tonnage basis and this meant that the drivers of the larger lorries gained over the drivers of the smaller ones. It was abandoned and a higher flat rate was paid and the senior driver put in charge of all transport.

The abundance of grass in the autumn of 1936 and throughout 1937, coupled with high commodity prices, made trading extremely difficult and profits were down. However, the management team decided that they would maintain the quality of their products even though this meant higher prices and agreed that they would only reduce quality when an individual customer specifically asked them to do so, in order to keep the price down for him.

In spite of the difficult trading position all seemed to be going quite well for Oldacres, when the manager of Barclays Bank advised William John that he had been promoted and was moving to London. The change of bank manager proved to be a major headache for the company. Almost as soon as the new manager had taken up his post, letters started to arrive at Oldacres complaining about the size of the overdraft. Relationships with Barclays deteriorated rapidly and the company began a dialogue with the National Provincial Bank.

William John talked over his problems with his friend Jack Charnock. He may have found some consolation from the fact that Jack was having problems with the Midland Bank at about the same time, and that Jack had decided to move his business to Barclays in Liverpool, which were offering him favourable terms. Jack did point out that he had one thing in his favour – his company owned all the property from which they did business and so they had good collateral.

'Yes I know you are right Jack, but the bank holds everything that Gladys and I own, and I decided a long time ago that, like you, we would move towards owning the freehold on every piece of property used by the business, but it will take time to reach that goal,' he pointed out.

Undeterred, Oldacres continued to expand and after much searching, they found suitable premises for a shop and warehouse in Tewkesbury, High Street. Completion was to be on a day in the autumn of 1937, and William John went to see the manager at Barclays Bank to tell him that a cheque would be presented to meet the cost of the transaction. He was dumbfounded by what the manager said to him:

'Mr Oldacre, I have told you that you have already exceeded your agreed overdraft figure, and I can only warn you that the bank will not honour the cheque.'

In his memoirs William John makes it clear that he was at a loss to know what action to take. After talking the matter over with his wife, they decided that he should approach one of his father's former good friends for help, so he set off immediately to see John Cook at his home in Gotherington. He spoke frankly about his financial problems and after a few minutes John Cook pulled his cheque book out of his pocket, signed a blank cheque and handed it to William John:

'There's £40,000 in my account at Lloyds Bank,' he said. 'Help yourself to whatever you want and don't be afraid.'

In his memoirs, William John states that the company moved their account after this episode. However, the company records indicate that the Tewkesbury account was indeed held at the National Provincial Bank, but that after an agreement between Barclays and National Provincial, the main account stayed at Barclays. With the continuing expansion of the company, relationships with both banks were strained. Shortly after the outbreak of the Second World War, the company moved all their accounts to a new branch of Martins Bank, which had opened in High Street, Cheltenham.

The gross profit for 1937/38 was down by four percent, but William John was satisfied that the trading prospects were good and seemed to be improving. The trading figures were good and remained so throughout 1938, but the debit balances were described by the Governor as 'abominable and in need of drastic action'. That drastic action was taken and the cash flow situation improved. By March 1939, it was clear that monthly sales were up by 81 tons over the previous year and that the optimism shown by William John a few months earlier had been fully justified.

The sales staff held regular conferences chaired by Mr Counsell, who then reported on those conferences to the management team. Mr Counsell controlled a regular sales staff of four men, but from time to time Mr Bick, Mr Hamblin and John Oldacre, and a number of the young shop assistants helped canvass for orders. New areas were added to the work of the travellers and, of course, some of the older areas were abandoned because the lack of orders made them uneconomical. The company continued to aim for a turn round of only two days between receipt of order and delivery of goods. This required the most careful coordination between the sales, office and despatch staff, and to help relationships and improve understanding the travellers were taken around the mill at regular intervals. Towards the end of 1938 two of the sales staff left the company but were soon replaced.

The tight delivery schedules required by the management were helped by the introduction of motor transport to replace the horse. The first lorry, a three ton Albion, had come to the firm in the late 1920s in payment of a customer's account. In 1933 that vehicle was exchanged for a five ton Albion, and later an even larger vehicle was purchased but was almost immediately commandeered by the army. In 1936 Fred Weaver took over a new Ford lorry for the Cheltenham work and in 1938 a Bedford lorry came into service at Bishops Cleeve.

Everyone on the staff was expected to give of their best and to encourage the sense of belonging, there were plenty of social functions for all the workforce. For example, each year Oldacres organised a Christmas party and the summer outing.

The Christmas parties were held in the Women's Institute Hall in Bishops Cleeve, and all the employees and their families were invited. The food was prepared by Mrs Oldacre and she was helped by Doris Burnett, the wives of other members of the staff and also by her daughters. The preparation of the food at Fieldgate started many days before the event. The furnace fire and the kitchen range would be lighted up at six o'clock in the morning by Gladys Oldacre and Doris, so as to be ready to start boiling the hams and roasting the chickens. Fieldgate kitchen became an even greater hive of industry than usual, and the young children watched as the jellies, trifles, pastries and cakes were made and the salads prepared and on the day of the party, the kitchen table was filled as the hams and chickens were carved by the Governor, and the meat set out on large serving dishes by Mrs Oldacre.

The evening was indeed a joyful occasion. Party hats were worn, games were played, Mary and Hilda played the piano for carols and songs, and party pieces were performed. Some of the singing may have lacked quality, some of the jokes may have been old chestnuts, but there was laughter in abundance, choruses sung heartily by the assembled company, and at the end of each turn the performer received acclaim with loud bursts of applause and cheering. Finally, the wives joined in with the washing up and the cleaning of the hall, before they led their husbands back home many of them were in a very merry condition indeed.

The summer outings, which were arranged between hay making and harvest, were either to Southsea, Porthcawl, Bournemouth or Blackpool. The party went to Southsea by Black and White coach, but the men preferred to travel by train. The company certainly negotiated some very good deals with the LMS Railway. In 1938 a train left Cheltenham Lansdown station at 6 am on Wednesday 22nd June on the five hour journey to Blackpool and the party finally arrived back in Cheltenham at 12.30 am that night. The outings were, of course, free for all the staff and workforce, but they could take their families at 15s each, or their friends at 16s each. This was a rare treat for it is most unlikely that the workers and their families had any other trip away from home during the year.

On arrival at the destination, everyone was free to do whatever he or she wished. Some enjoyed a walk on the pier; some of the older men were seeing the sea for the first time; some were brave enough to paddle – the men with their trousers rolled up to the knee, their boots and socks on their arms, and their caps on their heads; the ladies with dresses tucked into the elastic of their knicker legs; and all screaming with delight. Some had their fortunes told; others put pennies in slot machines to witness 'What the Butler Saw', and others were simply content to sit and to look at the sea.

The journey home was a time for telling tales of the day at the seaside, singing songs and sleeping. They all knew that it was only on one day of the year that the throb of the engine in the mill could safely stop, and the Governor and his 'greater family' could relax and let down their hair. On every other weekday work had to be done and profit made, if the families in the village were to have food and warmth. The realities of life had to be faced by them all.

(iii) The life of a manager is not easy

Life at the Bishops Cleeve office and in the mill was not easy for Mr Bick. He was a quiet and efficient man but unfortunately he found that his authority was occasionally being undermined by the Governor who could not resist giving direct orders to the men. On top of this there was some resentment among the carters and lorry drivers about the level of control which he exercised over their activities. Fred Cresswell was a particularly difficult man to handle. But within two or three years of his arrival Mr Bick had made major changes at the mill yard. He was well aware that most of the problems at the Bishops Cleeve branch stemmed from the attitude of Fred Cresswell, who also had regular arguments with the Governor. Many of the old hands left Oldacres or were sacked for irregularities over the stocks of animal feed around this time but Fred Cresswell remained with the company until he retired.

The engine at the mill was now looked after by Ern Jeynes who soon had his son, Victor, helping him. Fred's son Douglas, joined the firm and was most valuable not only in the mill, but also in the shops and he did some canvassing. Ted Aston's son Leslie became one of the carters.

The maintenance of a two-day turn round between an order being received and an order being delivered, demanded the most careful organisation. Horse-drawn drays were slowly giving way to motor transport and by 1938, the firm was operating three lorries. The horse-drawn drays provided no major maintenance problems as Alan Aldridge, the wheelwright, was more than capable of handling any repairs. The horses were well stabled, well fed, and well looked after, and on the rare occasion when a horse was unfit for work, a spare horse was always available in the stable. The problem of the dray was that it was slow and the distance that it could travel in a day was limited.

Lorries posed entirely different problems. They were fast and efficient provided that they were kept in good working order, but to keep them on the road they had to be maintained and serviced regularly. If a lorry was off the road for more than an hour or so, then delivery schedules were totally disrupted. The management team had agreed with Mr Bick that lorries were better for the job in hand than horses, and the Governor started selling his horses. As the fleet of lorries was built up, it soon became apparent that a most careful check had to be kept on motor transport costs and maintenance arrangements. A system of log sheets was introduced to enable time schedules, mileages, and petrol consumption to be checked, and the drivers were trained to undertake routine maintenance and servicing of their vehicles at the mill yard, where a petrol pump was installed.

Quite a considerable amount of Oldacres business was in contra sales. Under this system, the farmers arranged for Oldacres to collect all, or an agreed proportion of their grain crop, to mill that grain and to mix it into animal feed. The farmer was then paid for the grain, partly in kind and partly in money. This was generally an excellent arrangement, but if the weather was bad over a prolonged period, then the farmers tended to draw on Oldacres for animal feed, but they were not able to provide grain for the mill. This was one reason why Oldacres suffered from cash flow problems in 1936 and 1937.

The retail corn shops at Winchcombe Street, Cheltenham and at Charlton Kings were under the control of Mr Hamblin who was based at Winchcombe Street. It was almost inevitable that the corn shop at Charlton Kings caused some problems. The shop assistant was young and needed to be kept under fairly close supervision, and so Jim Payne who worked at Winchcombe Street and was showing that he could accept a marked degree of responsibility, was transferred to Charlton Kings and the other man was put under the close eye of Mr Hamblin at Winchcombe Street. The sales at both branches were usually in very small quantities of dog food, bird seed, pigeon corn, and hay and bran for rabbits and other domestic pets. The shops did take orders from some farmers, from stables, and from the owners of small holdings, but the takings were fairly low and competition was

CHELTENHAM FIRMS AND THEIR STAFFS. No. 10.

he firm of W. J. Oldacre, Ltd., corn merchants, etc., was founded by the late Mr. W. J. Oldacre, who in the course of is operations as a farmer bought truck loads of maize and offals, etc., for himself and other farmer friends. He was a ery shrewd and practical man, and this side of his business gradually increased and necessitated the opening of a ore at Bishop's Cleeve, and in 1907 a shop was opened in Winchcombe Street. In 1923 the business was formed into private limited company, of which members of his family are the directors. In 1928 another branch was added at ondon Road, Charlton Kings, which includes a bakery and confectionery department. Following a fire in 1931, the rovender mills at Bishop's Cleeve were replaced by an up-to-date building with a modern plant, to which a further extension to accommodate the ever-growing trade proved necessary in 1935.

Mill and Transport Staff. (A) Mr. G. Hunt, Charlton Kings foreman; (B) Mr. E. Jeynes, chief engineer; (C) Mr. F. Cresswell, Bishop's Cleeve foreman; (D) Mr. C. Nex, head driver.

The late Mr. W. J. Oldacre, founder of the firm.

'heltenham Chronicle" Photographs. Copies 6½in. x 4½in. 1/-, 8½in. x 6½in. 1/9.

4.—Bakery staff. Mr. W. Rowley, manager (X).

Mr. W. J. Oldacre, managing director.

5. Mr. W. J. Oldacre, junior, director.

6.—Sales and Office Staff. (A) Mr. R. A. Bick (Bishop's Cleeve manager); (B) Mr. A. C. Knight (representative); (C) Mr. H. R. Hamblin (Cheltenham manager); (D) Mr. H. N. Counsel (sales manager); (E) Mr. F. L. Johnson (chief accountant).

7. Miss H. M. Oldacre (secretary).

Oldacres Staff – 1937

fierce.

When the Tewkesbury shop was opened, it was put under the management of Mr Counsell. A new shop assistant was employed and he proved to be excellent at the job, so much so that he was given a young helper and provided with a van. This shop was a great success and did not give as many problems as the shops in Cheltenham. Trading in Tewkesbury was different and lower prices had to be charged than in Cheltenham. Competition came mainly from the Co-operative Society which was selling bags of poultry food at a fixed price rather than by weight. If Oldacres prices were lower in Tewkesbury than in Cheltenham, then there were complaints from Hamblin, and so the Governor decided to start selling feed at a fixed price per bag rather than by weight and in this way, to take on the Co-op at their own game. With the introduction of this system he could keep Co-op competition at bay and also maintained a sense of rivalry between the Cheltenham and Tewkesbury branches, without giving cause for any feeling that one branch was being given an unfair advantage over another.

The bakery business posed major problems for William John but he enjoyed the challenge. By 1936 it was clear that the financial results from it were not good enough. The general view was that insufficient care was taken by the foreman baker to ensure that there was a proper relationship between production costs and selling price, that the roundsmen who were expected to canvass for business were inadequately supervised, and that the overall staff was too large. It was clear that the foreman baker would have to go, and that a manager was needed who could take control of all the activities at Charlton Kings – the bakery, the roundsmen, the baker's shop, and the corn trade. The next few years saw a procession of managers. Some lasted less than six months and only one survived for a year.

The difficulties which the Governor was having with managers did not stop him trying new methods and developing the business. In 1936 Mr Bick considered that the introduction of time-clocks would help in controlling costs at Charlton Kings and would be useful throughout the firm but William John was not happy about this idea and ruled against it. In 1937 the company installed new bakery ovens which

CHELTENHAM CHRONICLE AND GLOUCESTERSHIRE GRAPHIC, SATURDAY, MARCH 12, 1938

NEW OVENS AT OLDACRES

With every up-to-date Improvement for making Bread and Confectionery of perfect quality and appetising flavour.

NEW VANS

To bring you promptly and in oven-fresh condition the first-class products of a First-class Bakery.

This splendid equipment is now operating to provide You with Bakery Products that will do credit to your table. The quality and flavour always found in our goods appeal to the housewife who relies upon bread as the nourishing basis of most meals.

May we have the pleasure of supplying you for a trial period? Our Telephone number is 2421.

W. J. OLDACRE, Ltd.,   3 & 4 LONDON ROAD, CHARLTON KINGS

Oldacres' Bakery – 1938

improved efficiency and quality in the bakehouse and in the same year they increased the size of their fleet of vans and eventually had as many as eight salesmen on the road. They also started a bakery round in Bishops Cleeve using a horse drawn van, the bread and cakes being brought daily to the mill yard by motor vehicle from Charlton Kings.

The bakery roundsman in Bishops Cleeve built up a good trade in bread and cakes and as Christmas approached, he often received quite lavish hospitality from customers. Leslie Aston tells a delightful tale about arriving back at the mill yard one Christmas Eve after completing his coal round. He was a trifle merry and found the Governor waiting for him:

'The Governor, noticing the state I was in, told me to go and shake up the horse's bed while he unharnessed the horse' he recalled. 'Just at that moment Bill the bread roundsman came into the yard. He had had a drop too much and couldn't get off the van, he just fell off. The Governor just picked him up and sent him straight off home. When I had made my horse comfortable, he put his hand in his pocket and gave me five shillings.

"There you are Leslie" he said, with a smile. "You had better go and get yourself a drink."'

In July 1938 Mr Hamblin was moved to Charlton Kings to take over all responsibilty at the branch, and Jim Payne was promoted to take charge at Winchcombe Street. These proved to be excellent appointments.

Mr Hamblin found that the staff at Charlton Kings were in poor spirits, and that a great deal of hard work was necessary to restore morale and profitability. It says a great deal for the man that he kept at the task, and at the same time he was able to introduce new lines in fancy cakes, Oldacre brand tea, Oldacre brand butter, and a host of other special lines. Gradually, he gained control of the situation, and even though he did tend to be bullied by the Governor, he retained his confidence.

Three days before Christmas 1938 the bakery at Charlton Kings was in full production when, at 12.15 pm, a 32 foot shaft and pulleys collapsed at the Bishops Cleeve mill. The Governor who was at Charlton Kings, rushed back to the mill and examined the damage with Alan Aldridge and Ern Jeynes. They agreed on the spare parts that were needed, and arranged with a firm in Broad Street, Birmingham to collect the equipment later that afternoon. The Governor made the journey to Birmingham with one of the drivers and in his Memoirs he recalled:

'. . . It was a quarter to five before we left Birmingham with 32 feet of shafting in two sections, all new bearings and a coupling. When we arrived back in Bishops Cleeve, I went home and changed. The men had everything cleared away by the time I reached the mill. We set to work and had assembled the shafting and pulleys by midnight, when my wife arrived with food and a hot drink for us all. It took us until 3 am before we had the belts on and I was able to check each bearing to see that it was in order: the bearings were well greased and we started the mill, running it for about half-an-hour. When I was satisfied that it was safe, I sent Aldridge and Jeynes home but stayed on at the mill myself until the morning shift arrived at 6am. I was thankful that every feed order was fulfilled before Christmas.'

Oldacres sales were down by £2,500 in 1938/39, when compared to the previous year but this was against a drop in grain prices of 40 percent. The business was in fact, very healthy. Arrangements were made for a new shop front to be designed and installed at Charlton Kings; the range of confectionery was increased; and the last horse working from Cheltenham was sold. At Tewkesbury the tenant of the building behind the shop was given notice because additional storage space was needed. At the mill in Bishops Cleeve there was plenty of work but the introduction of new factories at Ashchurch, near to Tewkesbury and nearer to the village, was drawing labour away from Oldacres.

(iv) Life on the farm

Farming offered William John a relaxation from his heavy business responsibilities, and he would set off around the farm whenever the opportunity arose.

After the company acquired the tenancy of Lynworth Farm, William John farmed 130 acres of land on its behalf with the help of Syd Burnett, his farm foreman. Two other men were employed full time with Syd, and a number of part-timers were taken on at busy times. The Governor had little time for contractors, because they were never available at the exact time that he wanted them, but he was forced to use contractors on specialist work, and when heavy and expensive equipment was needed. The greater proportion of the farmland was pasture and orchard, but potatoes and oats were grown, and large numbers of pigs were kept.

Syd Burnett could tackle almost any task on the farm. He was good at drainage and an excellent hedge layer; he could plough, sow and reap, and was very much at home looking after animals. He was tall and his stature was similar to that of Mr Oldacre. When he wore his trilby hat, he was often taken for the Governor and this kept people very much on their toes. In company with his wife Doris and his little daughter Olive, he lived in the farm house at Lynworth, where he gardened and kept his own pigs and poultry. The farm house was about 100 yards below the bridge which carried Two Hedges Road over the GWR railway line. Lynworth farm included an orchard, a pasture, and a plough field adjacent to the farm house, and some thirty acres of land on the opposite side of the road to the house, land now occupied by Cleeve School. The total area of land farmed stretched from Stoke Road to Woodmancote.

Syd had to cover quite long distances each day in order to carry out his duties, and so he had the use of a pony and float. Tommy the pony, was kept in the orchard at Lynworth, an orchard which he shared with Syd's fowls and occasionally with the pigs. Syd would set off each morning in the trap with feed for the animals, and with any tools or equipment which he would need during the day.

When Lynworth first came under the control of William John he began rearing beef cattle but the venture was not worthwhile. Farming was depressed in the early 1930s and beef rearing was not profitable on such a small scale; so Oldacres turned to pig breeding. The situation began to change in 1938 and the Governor began buying Hereford steers and for many years he was successful with the production of beef on a three year cycle.

The breeding and fattening of pigs by Oldacres served as a useful sideline to the main animal feed business. In the summer of 1936, a new pig house was built in the paddock behind the mill, at a cost of £385. This new building was used as a demonstration pig unit, where the Governor could show his customers that Oldacres pig meal was correctly balanced to produce good lean pig meat and bacon. The pig house was a wooden structure standing on a concrete floor and shaped so that the pigs always had a dry bed. Water was laid on to each bay in the pig house and the gates were hung to ensure that the maximum flexibility was achieved in the layout of the interior, and to assist with cleaning. There was a central gangway and a feeding trough which ran the full length of the building, but the trough was divided, so that an accurate feed could be given to the batch of pigs in each bay.

The unit was looked after by 'Chappie' Riddle. There could be as many as 600 pigs in his care at any one time, and he had to clean them out, see that they were watered, mix their meal by hand in a large vat, and carry buckets of food in the correct quantities to each bay. The high-pitched squeals of the pigs while they waited for 'Chappie' to reach their bay was deafening and could be heard throughout the area around the mill. Each bay housed between five and twelve pigs, depending upon size, and they were moved from bay to bay down the length of the house as they grew to maturity. 'Chappie', who was also an expert on ferrets, liked to end his day at the Old Elm Tree enjoying a few drinks and a chat about his ferrets.

The Governor was careful in selecting and crossing the various breeds of pig, and this process was greatly helped when the Lundrace pig became available. The cost of taking a sow to the boar in the 1930s, varied between three shillings and sixpence, and five shillings, and large litters of as many as sixteen piglets were quite common. The Governor bred many of his own pigs, but he also bought piglets at the market.

The unit despatched an average of 30 pigs each week to Ward's of Birmingham for slaughter. Ward's produced a grading sheet for each batch of pigs and the grades were published by Oldacres to assist in the marketing of their pig meal. The regular high grades which were achieved played an important role in the growth of their trade in pig feeds.

William John was interested in animal husbandry, but most of his land in Bishops Cleeve was pasture or arable. The surface of most of the farm land in the village was shaped to assist drainage, the soil being lias clay overlying sand and gravel. The surface shape was made up from a series of 'lands', which gave the ground a corrugated appearance similar to rollers on the ocean.

Ploughing was done by a man walking behind a single furrow steel plough, which was drawn by a pair of horses. It was hard work for man and horse. The Governor insisted that the fields were ploughed as near to the hedges as was humanly possible, and that the ploughing was carefully set out before work began. He then required the furrows to be turned into the bottom of each land, the cut of the plough to be of the correct depth for the soil in any particular field, and that when completed the whole field gave the appearance of a job well done. These high standards were demanded not only because he always looked to achieve the best in everything which he did, but also because he believed that the company benefitted when their customers saw a high standard of workmanship on the farm, and good quality stock in the fields.

Syd and Ern Richins, who lived opposite to the mill, did most of the ploughing. The Governor was always anxious to get the job finished before the weather broke, and would take over the reins when one of the men went for their dinner. The ploughman placed the reins over his shoulder and held them with each hand on the plough handles, and he walked in the furrow which he had just cut. The soil was very likely to build up on the ploughman's boots and the strength required to handle the horses and to guide the plough made him move with a rolling gait.

The job of ridging and lifting potatoes was done in a similar manner to ploughing, with the man walking behind a pair of horses and guiding the equipment by hand.

Once the ploughing was done the men had to cultivate the ground in preparation for planting. Horses were also used for this work, and for mowing, seed drilling and reaping. The farm worker had the doubtful benefit of a steel seat on these pieces of equipment, and the seat was carefully moulded to the average backside! The men had a bumpy and uncomfortable ride and it is not surprising that they covered the seat with a sack or thin cushion.

King Edward potatoes were grown each year and the fields

most used for this purpose were the ground at Lynworth alongside the railway, and the field down Stoke Road known as Brickyard Piece. A gang of men and women were employed to hand plant each potato and to pick the crop at harvest time. The potatoes were loaded onto a horse-drawn dray and taken to one of the farm buildings, usually at Fieldgate, where they were sorted both mechanically and by hand. It was dreary and back breaking work, but the men and women returned to the task each year. Mrs Hamblin (no relation to the Charlton Kings manager), and her two daughters were regular members of the gang, and Mrs Hamblin continued at the work until she was more than one hundred years old.

Winter oats were grown on a three year cycle. Grass and clover seed was planted with the oats in the second year, ready for a hay crop in the third year. The oats were dressed and sown with fertilizer, and in those days, crops of 15 to 20 hundredweight per acre were considered to be very good. Sometimes the oats were sown by broadcasting the seed and here again the gang of workers included Mrs Hamblin and her daughters, at other times a horse drawn seed drill was used. A highly skilled gang was required if broadcasting was to be successful. The workers had the seed in a sack or pouch which they carried low on their chests: they spread out uniformly in a line over a width of the field, and then walked forward at an even rate scattering the seed in an arc in front of them. An experienced gang could sow a field of corn as evenly as a mechanical drill.

Harvesting started with Syd scything the stand of corn around the sides of the field to make way for the horse drawn reaper and binder. The hand-cut corn was tied into sheaves using strands of the straw, but the reaper and binder tied the sheaves with binder twine. The men now had the task of lifting pairs of sheaves off the ground and building them into stooks made up from six to eight sheaves, the ears of the corn at the top of the stook. When they were stooking, the men took the sheaves of corn, one under each arm, and placed them in the form of a tent, so that any water would be cast off and the ears had a better chance of drying. If the weather was extremely wet over a long period of time while the corn was in stooks, then the ears did occasionally sprout although they were off the ground.

The stooks remained in the field until the grain in the ears had dried. The 'ladders' which were purpose-made for the job, were now attached to the bed of the drays, and all the available carters moved their horses into the corn field to help pick up the crop. A man standing on the cart built the sheaves into a stable load as they were passed up to him by men using a 'shupick' (a pitch fork) and then the load was taken to the rick site in one of the fields. The rick was built on top of staddle stones, (mushroom shaped stone supports), and timber to keep the corn off the ground, to allow the air to blow through and to keep rats out of the rick itself. The art of building a rick, or for that matter building a load onto a cart, was to keep the corners out and the middle well filled. Once the rick was completed, it was thatched and the grain was stored in this manner until it was needed.

Farmers are a proud race, and in the days when ricks had to be built in the fields, they would hope to build a rick or group of ricks which was the envy of their neighbours. When the Governor took his wife for a drive through the country-side, he was delighted by the sight of a row of well-thatched, uniform and circular ricks. He seldom had sufficient corn, however, to build more than one or two good sized ricks from his own crop.

When Oldacres required the grain for the mill, the labour intensive and extremely dusty threshing operation began. The contractor brought the threshing machine into the field behind a steam traction engine, and when it was correctly positioned, the engine was turned round. A crossed belt was now attached from the flywheel on the engine to the machine and all was now ready for the threshing operation to begin. The hiss of the steam, the chugging of the engine and the rattle of the threshing machine now deafened the large gang of men involved in the task. The sheaves were cut open and thrown down into the machine and the fearful noise was joined by a cloud of chaff and dust which flew out of one end of the machine to choke all in the vicinity. The straw was dropped out onto the ground to be stock piled or mechanic-ally baled, and the grain was bagged and loaded for transporting to the mill. Before the threshing operation began, the bottom of the rick was surrounded by a net. When the threshing was completed, the dogs were let loose on the rats trapped in the netted area.

A large proportion of the land was still pasture, and hay was made from the grass and clover. The grass was cut with a horse-drawn mower and left to dry in the fields. During the drying stage, the hay was turned three times, raked into windrows, and finally built into haycocks, for final drying. The hay was either picked up on 'shupicks' by a gang of men, loaded and then carted to the rick site, or a pair of horses were used to pull a sweep along a windrow of hay, and drag it to the rick site. The hay was lifted up to the men building the rick either with 'shupicks', by using a hay elevator, or using a monkey pole which was formed from a grab attached to a rope which passed over a pulley so that when a horse pulled on the rope, the hay was lifted to rick level, and when the horse was backed the grab returned to the ground for another load. It was important to ensure that the hay was completely dry before it was put into a rick, or there was always the danger of it catching fire. In a good summer it was sometimes possible to make a second crop of hay after the corn harvest had been gathered.

All harvesting and hay-making operations were dusty and throats became very dry. The traditional remedy for this problem was a tot of cider. Cider was taken into the fields in a stone jar and at regular intervals, the men stopped by the 'jar' and a 'horn' of cider was poured for them to drink. The 'horn' was indeed made from a cow's horn, and the cider tasted particularly good when drunk in this manner.

Syd's full time mate was an old chap called Bill Cox, who had retired from working on the railway. His bald head was always covered by a cap, and his face underneath the cap and a shaggy moustache, was lined with the creases of a smiling countenance. He dressed in a flannel shirt without a collar, but with a neckerchief around his neck, his sleeves were rolled up and on top of the shirt he wore a waistcoat. His corduroy trousers were held up with a two inch wide leather belt, and his boots were stoutly made. When they were working in the harvest field, or at hay making, men from the mill and other villagers joined the gang. Bill Witts was one of the casual workers and he dressed like Bill Cox, but he wore a trilby hat and he did not have the same smiling features. He had a small white moustache and his face was sombre. The men stopped for bait in the morning and went home at dinner time, but when they worked late into the evening, tea was brought to them in the field by Mrs Oldacre. The tea was made and carried in large enamel cans and jugs, and a basket full of thick jam sandwiches and large pieces of fruit cake, made up the meal. The tea break was a time for chatter and Bill Cox often had his leg pulled about an alleged relationship with one of the married ladies in the village. A broad grin would come on Bill's face and he would defend himself by assuring his colleagues that he was far too old for such frollicking:

'No! No! That baint right! It's a long time since that feller did anything but hang down and look at me boots!'

Farming has always been dependent upon the weather and particularly so before the advent of combine harvesters and the development of methods of making sileage. In the days before the war, it was labour intensive, very hard work and the industry was in a very poor state. As the Government realised that war was inevitable, they began to take a greater interest in the farming community and they called upon the farmers to prepare themselves to feed the nation.

(v) The family at Fieldgate

At Fieldgate the family were growing up fast, and William John and Gladys were planning to make improvements to the property. It was only shortly after the death of his father that William John arranged for mains water, the sewer, and electricity to be connected to the house. The bathroom now had a hot water cylinder which fed the tap in the kitchen and the tap on the washbasin, but the bath water still had to be heated by a large electric geyser. These changes made a considerable difference to the quality of life of the family. Some of the drudgery was taken out of the housework not only for Gladys but also for the older girls, for Doris, and for the other women helpers. Of course, the changes ended the cold and often wet trips which the family had to make to the privy in the garden, journeys which young John had made on his bicycle for long enough!

During the next few years William John made other

The Family – c. 1933

changes to Fieldgate. He had the dairy and the sitting room knocked together into one sitting room with a Cotswold stone fireplace for a huge log fire. The door from the old dairy into the yard was replaced by a four light window and the old sitting room window was enlarged; both windows having stone sills, heads and mullions. The floor in the enlarged room was in polished oak.A new stone porch was built on to the front of the house; this gave entry through two heavy oak doors from the garden to the sitting room. The front lawn was extended and made large enough for a full sized tennis court. Later still an old lean-to outside the back door was removed and a stone conservatory built. The alterations were designed and organised by William John himself. The stonework was done by Austin Agg, a free lance worker who also undertook stone walling, hedge laying, fencing and drainage. The carpentry work was done by Alan Aldridge who was on the permanent staff of Oldacres as millwright and carpenter.

In spite of her busy life, Gladys did a great deal of knitting and rug making, and also found time to take an active part in village life and in some social activities in Cheltenham. William John had been invited to join the Rotary Club of

Fieldgate – 1940

Cheltenham when it was formed in 1921, and Gladys became a founder member of the Inner Wheel Club. While her husband found some difficulty in keeping the 60 percent attendance rule of Rotary, she thoroughly enjoyed meeting regularly with the wives of the business and professional men of the town. Although she did not drive herself, she had no difficulty in getting to Cheltenham, because even if her husband was otherwise engaged and therefore unable to take her in his car, there was always a second car which was used by Mary and John, and one of them would be only too happy to take her to, and bring her back from the meetings. She was now also free to accept invitations to join the board of governors of the village school; the committees of the Women's Institute, the flower show, the Red Cross and the management committee of the district nurses. She was delighted to be able to undertake the type of voluntary work which she thoroughly enjoyed.

The three older members of the family were now in their late teens or early twenties. Mary, as the eldest daughter had many family responsibilities when the children were younger, but by this time she was a vital cog in the management of the business. She found time to play hockey, a game at which she excelled and, like her mother, she did a great deal of knitting, and played the piano. John, the son and heir, faced a difficult role. He was expected to react to situations in the same manner as his father, but he was a very different person. In many ways, he was like his grandfather Oldacre, but he had also inherited some of the Beckingsale characteristics. When he was at home, he was often in conflict with his father, not because he was argumentative, but because he did not wish to waste his energy putting forward contrary views. Mildred's knowledge of the family business was somewhat different from that of her eldest sister and her brother. She spent much of her time away from home, but on the occasions when she was at home she was interested in the people who were working for her father rather than the business itself. Mildred knew the men by name, she knew their families and she would spend much time talking with them and, if necessry, she would help their families if they were in difficulties.

Although Mary, Mildred and John lived full business lives, they did find time for plenty of social activities. They were members of the church choir, Sunday school teachers, took part in amateur dramatics in the village and went to dances in Cheltenham. It is surprising today, that a village of the size of Bishops Cleeve could find the talent to produce Gilbert and Sullivan operas and musical comedies, but they did just this under the direction of a Cheltenham musician, and the quality of the productions was outstanding. The Oldacre family were all musical and often provided four or five members of the cast.

Harold Hanks, a hill farmer, was John's cousin and his best friend and they enjoyed themselves in simple but lively pursuits. They ski-ed across the fields on an old door towed behind a car; they toured the district on a motorcycle belonging to Harold, when they were not taking the motorcycle apart. They went shooting pigeons and rabbits accompanied by Nigger, John's black Cocker spaniel. Sometimes they would park one of the cars in the barn in the early evening and then after dark steal out of the house, cross the yard and slip quietly into the barn. The lights of the car were then flashed on, and the boys took pot shots at the rats scurrying along the rafters. John had other hobbies beside motorcycling and shooting, and these included breeding chickens in an incubator in the harness room, and keeping and breeding budgerigars.

Mary, Mildred and John had many friends, but they particularly enjoyed the company of their Hanks cousins. They played tennis and gave house parties at Fieldgate, often on these occasions they would put the clocks on by an hour or so, early in the evening, in order to get their young sisters out of the way well before their guests arrived. On some evenings John and Harold would rig up loudspeakers and floodlights, the latter made with old biscuit tins, so that the party could continue outside in the garden until late into the evening.

Meanwhile Catherine was preparing food and afterwards washing up. She suffered from a speech impediment which meant in a busy household that she received little attention. As she grew to womanhood she took over many of the household chores and spent a great deal of time helping Doris and looking after Hilda and June.

In the early thirties Doris Little had married Syd Burnett, a farmer from Brockhampton, who had joined Oldacres as farm foreman at Lynworth. Before this happy event the family had enjoyed teasing Doris, who lived with them, about a tinker who made regular visits to the village with his horse and van, and always called at Fieldgate. The outside of his van was festooned with pots and pans and because of this a jolly rattling sound was heard as it passed along the country lanes. The van was filled with candles, paraffin, turpentine, galvanised baths and buckets, garden tools, brooms, matches, fly-paper, soap, washing powder and a host of other household articles. If anyone had a damaged oil-lamp or a broken utensil, then the tinker was the man to repair them. He gave an excellent service to the villagers but Doris did not fancy him.

Mobility for the members of the Oldacre family who were in the business was essential, and so William John kept a second car at Fieldgate for their use. This second car was the cause of some conflict between Mary and John. More often than not they would both want the car on the same Saturday afternoon for hockey, shooting or some other activity, or on the same evening. It is fortunate that the Governor soon felt that John needed a car of his own if he was to do his job for the firm adequately: the problem of who should have the use of the second car was overcome for the time being by the provision of a third car!

In the mid-1930s the two older Charnock boys spent many weekends at Fieldgate. Ernest was very fond of Mary and took grave exception to the presence of other young men. John Charnock was still young but he liked to be with Mildred. One of the annual excursions for these young people in company with John Oldacre and other friends was to the military tattoo at Tidworth, which started late in the evening and so they were out late into the night. Another evening might be spent at the theatre in Cheltenham. On one such occasion the whole party was ejected from the front row of the circle because they were distributing oranges from a paper bag and then eating them with far too much noise during the performance. The parties, dances and other activities which the young people organised at home often went on long after Mr and Mrs Oldacre had gone to bed. It was fortunate that the Governor was deaf, for he would not have tolerated the noise as readily as his wife. The girls were always likely to make 'apple-pie-beds' for any boys who were staying the night, or to tie tins or bells onto the bedstead. The boys soon became wise to this and on one occasion at least, they waited in their rooms until all was quiet before making an attack on the girls, tipping them out of bed. On another occasion the Governor learned that the girls had put pepper in the boys' beds. He was very angry and made his daughters change the linen before he allowed them to go out. Mrs Oldacre never knew who, or how many, would still be at Fieldgate at breakfast time, but she did not mind because she always encouraged her family to persuade their guests to stay the night rather than to travel home late or in bad weather. On a Sunday she could well find that she was catering for as many as 18 people for lunch but there was always plenty of food.

In 1937 Mr and Mrs Oldacre were deeply involved with organising the festivities for the Coronation of George VI. *The Cheltenham Chronicle and Gloucestershire Graphic* carried this report on 27 March 1937 about the preparations which

L.H.S., R. Bick – 3rd left, William John
7th Left Fred Cresswell
R.H.S. John Oldacre

were being made in Bishops Cleeve:

'A well attended general meeting to discuss the Coronation activities at Bishops Cleeve was held at the Women's Institute Hall. The Rector (the Rev T Jesson) presided.

The Hon Sec Mr W J Oldacre reported the subscription collectors as follows: Miss Rigby £17.19.0.; Mrs Beard £7.12.6.; Mrs Redman £2.17.0.; Mrs Davey £1.5.0.

The collectors reported that many gifts in kind towards the catering arrangements had been offered, and were to follow.

The Rector expressed the gratitude of the Committee to the collectors for such a satisfactory result.

'After discussion it was agreed that the catering committee should undertake the meat tea for adults, and the members of the Womens Institute the childrens tea. Both would be held at Eversfield Hall, and the pleasure grounds would be used later in the day. The rector had offered to supply a souvenir mug to each child.

'A programme tendered by Mr R A Bick and drawn up by the entertainments committee will include a fancy dress procession through the village and a decorated lorry with music. A cycle maypole dance and a pageant of Empire to be given by school children, will also be included.

'Speaking on behalf of the sports committee, Mr F Cresswell said a programme was proposed to include many events for adults as well as the children, prizes to take the form of souvenirs. A variety entertainment is to be given to the adults later in the day.

'During the morning the rector will hold a service in the church, after which it is hoped to relay by radio part of the actual coronation service in London. The day will conclude with a masked dance, for which a nominal sum is to be charged, for residents of Bishops Cleeve.

'The Chairman expressed the hope that the village would be well decorated by individual residents, to make the day as festive as possible. The committee decided unanimously not to ask for a 2d rate, but to defray the Coronation expenses entirely by subscription. A further meeting is to be held during April.'

The next year a committee involving many of the same members was back at work organising the flower show. This was again a great success and the results from the fancy dress competition were also reported in the local press. The children's prizes were won by Pat Bick who went as a princess, and June Oldacre who was dressed as Mr Middleton, radio's first gardening expert. She was dressed in a gardening apron and hat, both covered with Oldacres garden seeds, and with carrots in every pocket.

Reg Beckingsale was a very cheerful man but he had a hard and tragic life. He and his wife, Ethel, were childless. Their only child was born dead and Ethel was unable to have any more children. Reg loved to call at his sister's home, and he would do this fairly regularly, because he delivered groceries around the district for his father. When Gladys and Reg were together Fieldgate rang with laughter. Ethel herself would often baby-sit for Gladys and she was pleased to look after the family when William John and Gladys went on holiday.

Reg made grocery deliveries around the village daily on foot, or on a bicycle, or much later on, in the smallest van imaginable. His journeys often took a great deal of time and it was quite normal for him to finish work as late as eight

L.H.S. Pat Bick
2nd from left June Oldacre

o'clock in the evening. The late finish was not only because he spent time chatting with his sister, but also because he regularly helped elderly and infirm villagers to get their coal in, and he chopped wood for them or performed other errands. If he thought that his customer had little money, he would all too often allow an overdue grocery bill to go unpaid.

Family parties were a regular feature of life at Fieldgate. It was not unusual for Gladys to make as many as fifteen Christmas puddings in readiness for the festive season. At these parties they played games. On one memorable occasion when Reg was suffering from very bad sciatica, he suddenly jumped out of his chair during a balloon game and with a shout cried:

'Gladys, my sciatica has gone. It's cured the pain!'

They all laughed so heartily that Reg had to catch his false teeth before they fell to the ground. After supper quieter games would be played before the party ended with community singing.

Their nearest neighbours were Mr and Mrs Bert Long at

Pecked Piece Farm; a farm where the timber framed buildings had walls of overlapping elm boards and thatched roofs. Bert and his daughter Ellen would often make their way down to Fieldgate at that time. They would join in the singing of carols in front of a roaring fire and then enjoy a jar of cider which Bert had made. Bert's cider and perry were so good that the Oldacres no longer bothered to make their own. On a summer evening William John would take his friend Jack Charnock for a walk around his farm and call on Bert Long for a jar before returning home. Jack often recalled that after a long session at Bert's you could walk but not always talk, particularly if the brew had been perry.

Hilda and June were at school in Cheltenham during the week and at weekends ran errands for their mother or father. They never stayed in bed in the morning unless they were really ill, because if they did it was assumed that they were unwell and they were given a purgative in the form of a dose of castor oil or syrup of figs.

One of the tasks for the younger girls was to feed fowls in the orchard and to collect the eggs. Over the years, in summer and winter, June seemed to undertake this task clad in a blue gaberdine mackintosh tied tightly around her middle and with Wellington boots on her feet. She enjoyed looking after the fowls, but sometimes in the evening they were not very responsive to her demands that they should return to the hen-house to be protected from becoming a meal for one of the local foxes. June was always likely to pick up a stone to encourage the hens on their way, until the day that she chucked a brick with considerable force at a reluctant hen and later had to explain to her father the cause of the early demise of that particular bird.

Hilda and June also liked to watch the pig meal being mixed with water in a large vat in the barn and then being ladled into buckets by Harry Price. Harry was a small man with short cropped steel grey hair and he could have been taken for a jockey. In fact, he owned and rented a few acres of land in the centre of the village and down Stoke Road. He tended this land, kept his own pigs, and worked for Mr Oldacre for a few hours each day looking after the pigs at Fieldgate. The girls marvelled at Harry's rich language as he opened the door to the pig sty, and held back the pigs who were intent on having the little man over so that they could get at the food.

'Get out of the way yer bloody thing! Get over yer bugger!' he shouted time and time again.

Sunday was even more enlightening for the girls. Harry sang hymns.

'Onward Christian soldiers', he sang, 'marching as to – "Get over yer bugger, damn yer" – marching as to war. With the cross – "Get over yer bugger, get over" – of Jesus going on before . . .', and so on.

Harry's sister Marg Price helped with some of the heavy work in the house. Marg was similar in build to her brother, and her grey hair was tied into a bun at the back of her head. She looked after her elderly mother and found her duties at Fieldgate a pleasant change of company for her. Each morning she scrubbed the stone floor in the kitchen and she joined in with the family conversation and could have sat at the table but preferred to be wrapped in a hessian apron and down on her knees. Everyone had to lift their feet so that she could scrub under them.

A shopping trip to grandfather Beckingsale's shop was a treat for Hilda and June. Grandfather kept huge jars of black and white sweets on the shelves of his grocer's shop; aniseed balls, bulls eyes and sherbert lemon which got up your nose if you sucked too violently on the liquorice straw. After their mother's list of groceries had been purchased, the girls were allowed to dip a hand into one of the sweet jars.

Life for the Oldacre family was enjoyable but certainly not easy. But those of us who had the pleasure of staying at Fieldgate or going on holiday with the Oldacre family, found the experience quite idyllic.

The families of William John Oldacre and Jack Charnock took seaside holidays together on a number of occasions during the 1930s. Both men were fairly serious minded when they were at home and carrying heavy business responsibilities but when on holiday together they relaxed and were always in high spirits. Mrs Oldacre and Mrs Charnock travelled in my father's car and the children went with Mr Oldacre. My father's car usually left Fieldgate first because Mr Oldacre travelled at a much greater speed. Much to the delight of the children Mr Oldacre would blow his horn loudly and wave furiously whenever the car went by a pretty young girl. After he had caught up and passed my father's car he would pull up at the first 'Stop-me-and-buy-one' icecream seller whom he saw. Mr Oldacre and his passangers would be licking ices and waiting for the other car to come into view before setting off again at a cracking pace. The Governor had never learnt to swim but he always joined his friend Jack and the children in the sea. In the evenings the family were allowed to stay up late and join their parents at the theatre or at a restaurant local to the hotel.

As early as 1935, I started visiting Fieldgate and joining the Oldacre family at their home for at least part of my summer holidays. The first time my father took my mother and me to Bishops Cleeve, as we entered the northern outskirts of the village he said to my mother:

'I will take you up the back of the village. John drives far too fast down the middle of the road, and the double bends in the centre of the village are dangerous if he is about.'

And so we travelled up what is now called Station Road, turned right at the green, then along the eastern boundary of the church yard, and finally into Pecked Lane and on to Fieldgate. The village in 1935 had changed little from the village which William Oldacre had reached seventy years before. Only the steady beat of the mill engine at The Pollards and the occasional car on the now tarred lanes indicated the passage of time.

My father's caution about meeting William John on the bends in the village was fully justified. Some years later, June Oldacre had to jump off her bicycle and onto the narrow verge as her father roared round the bend from Pecked Lane towards Fieldgate. June was safe but bruised, but her bicycle suffered damage and the key of the Women's Institute hall which she was carrying for her mother, sailed over the wall and into the thick yew hedge. A great deal of time was then spent in retrieving that key.

My first view of Fieldgate was memorable. The yard, the barns, the Cotswold stone buildings, and standing in the doorway a family of girls; inside the house the stone floors, the sight and smell of sides of bacon hanging in the kitchen, the smell of logs burning on the fire, and the size of the house. I was shown around the house, garden and orchard by Hilda and June, and the whole atmosphere was a wonder to me.

We were soon called for supper, but first Catherine picked up June and me, one under each arm, and carried us across the yard to be weighed on the pig scales. I was then to be weighed again before I went home to see how much I had gained during my stay. Meanwhile, Hilda was filling a jug with cider from a large barrel at the back of the barn, which smelled of pigs, sour meal and cider and the tap on the barrel was surrounded with minute flies. I was then shown how to collect a jug of water from the pump outside the back door – water that was ice cold and so full of bubbles that it sparkled.

The fresh food straight from farm or garden and beautifully cooked, was exactly as my father had always told me that it would be. There were, however, one or two dishes which he had not mentioned. Mrs Oldacre made pastry with plenty of eggs included in the mix, and so the pie crust was thick, short, golden brown and delicious. She also made junket which I had never seen before. At breakfast, I was surprised to see the bacon cut from the side hanging in the kitchen and then put straight into the pan, and I had never seen a dough cake and was surprised to see it included on the breakfast table.

Fieldgate – Garden and Orchard

I returned to Fieldgate every year and spent much time in the company of Mr Oldacre as well as with Hilda and June. With Mr Oldacre I visited the mill, looked around the farm and inspected other business premises. We went to market at Tewkesbury and Gloucester, and when the market was at Hereford, Mrs Oldacre and the girls would come with us. Sometimes I would go with John Oldacre on his canvassing journeys and even though I was under age, he allowed me to drive the car on farm tracks. Fieldgate was often very full and then I would sleep in John's room on the top floor of the house. The room had a window in the gable-end looking over the garden and orchard and John would delight me by firing his shotgun out of that window. The night sounds in the countryside were strange to me, I found much comfort from the chimes of the church clock, and the steam trains which regularly came to a halt at the top of the orchard with a squeal of brakes, the engine making a warm breathing sound as the driver waited for the 'all–clear' signal.

Mr and Mrs Oldacre made Fieldgate a wonderful family home and I looked forward in great anticipation to my every visit.

(vi) The final months before the Second World War

The clouds of war were forming quickly over Europe and moving towards the British Isles. William John and Jack discussed business at their regular meetings, and they agreed that trading had improved from the days of deep depression, but they also spent much time talking about the dangers to world peace. Hitler had moved his storm troopers into the Rhineland, into Austria, and later into Czechoslovakia. The two friends despaired at the lack of action by the Prime Minister, Neville Chamberlain, and waited for the inevitable war to come.

The family at Fieldgate, like those throughout the nation, witnessed the cinema newsreels of the Prime Minister returning from his meeting in Munich with Hitler, Mussolini, and Daladier. They saw him standing to be photographed on the top step as he left his aeroplane, and they saw him waving a piece of paper and telling the world that there would be *'Peace in Our time'*. Many of the young men sensed the dangers, and volunteered for the Royal Naval Volunteer Reserve, the Territorial Army, or the Royal Air Force Volunteer Reserve.

John Oldacre joined the RAFVR and learned to fly at Staverton. Mary joined the Red Cross. Catherine, who had returned home one evening in 1938 and announced that she had been accepted by the Radcliff Infirmary, Oxford, for training as a State Registered Nurse, now became a staff nurse with the Civil Defence Auxilliaries and was the first in the family to leave her old life completely behind her as the world began to change. William John, ready to play his part, became an Air Raid Warden and was soon asked to take on the duties of Chief Warden for Bishops Cleeve. The ARP headquarters were in the mill offices at The Pollards and his friend, Jack Charnock, became an Air Raid Warden in Prenton.

I visited Fieldgate again in the summer of 1939. The Governor and John Oldacre were extremely busy, and although I was occasionally invited to join Mr Oldacre he had little time to spare for a young boy. John was already flying and thrilled us all by flying low over Fieldgate. Meanwhile, I was allowed to go out with Leslie Aston on his deliveries rounds. Leslie was then about 16 or 17 years old and highly regarded by the Governor. I learned how to look after his horse, Turpin, and how to harness him, and how to back him into the shafts. We delivered goods around Bishops Cleeve, Gotherington, Woolston, and Oxenton, and I sat proudly on the carter's seat driving the dray.

Leslie was good to me and prepared to let me join with him when he went ferreting in the early morning or at dusk. A ditch alongside an old orchard in Gotherington Lane was a good place for rats, and when they were chased out of their holes in the bank by the ferret, Leslie took a pot shot at them. One one occasion when Leslie and I had loaded potatoes onto a dray at the station, we both went into the station building to sign for the load leaving the horse, Turpin, on the level ground at the top of the ramp which went from the station down to the road. This was a mistake. When we came out of the building Turpin had gone. . . We knew that the brake, such as it was, was on and could only assume that the horse had moved a little so that the load pushed him down the steep slope. Once moving there was no stopping him. We could see where he had made the right angled turn when he reached Station Road, and the marks of the steel wheels down the road in the direction of the village.

If we had lost Turpin, the Governor found him. He was standing at the entrance to the mill when the horse, still pulling a fully-loaded dray of potatoes, clattered into the yard. William John thought that his guest and his carter must be lying injured somewhere on the road between the station and the village. His car left the yard even faster than usual, and he met us running down the road anxiously looking for Turpin. He was relieved to see that we were both unhurt, but he was not amused. Leslie was at the receiving end of the Governor's wrath. I was denied further opportunity of improving my abilities as a carter.

After Turpin had disgraced himself, he was sent to join Punch, the largest horse from the stable, and he spent the next few weeks working off his excess energy by pulling the plough with that horse. Punch himself was lucky to be alive. Some months earlier, he had been put out to pasture in the orchard at The Pollards, but a severe and unexpected storm brought the apples off the trees, and Punch gorged himself on them. He was found lying on his back kicking frantically in the air with the pain. He was suffering from a violent attack of colic. The vet was called, but gave him little hope of survival, but the Governor would not accept that verdict. He managed to get Punch up onto his legs, and he spent the whole night forcing the horse to trot round the orchard. He did not let Punch rest until the horse was well enough to stay on his feet unaided.

I had hardly left Fieldgate after my summer holidays in 1939, before John Oldacre was called to the colours and my brothers had to join their units. At eleven o'clock on the morning of Sunday, 3 September 1939, the family at Fieldgate listened to the Prime Minister announce that a state of war existed between our country and Nazi Germany. That night, like many people in similar country areas, the family were on the look-out for German paratroopers, and William John went to bed with his shotgun by his side.

$$5$$

OLDACRES AT WAR
1939–1945

(i) The family are mobilized

During the first few months of the war nothing really happened. It was the period of the phoney war during which the British Expeditionary Force waited in France for something to happen.

At Fieldgate William John was proud that his son was serving with the Royal Air Force and happy that Mary had become engaged to Ernest Charnock. Following the outbreak of war Mary planned to be married earlier than originally intended, and the arrangements for that wedding were proceeding smoothly when John Oldacre announced that he had obtained a special licence to marry Kay Stephens on 23 September. William John and Gladys were aware of the friendship between John and Kay but they did not expect them to marry. John was only twenty two years old and Kay's lifestyle seemed very different from that of their son. Kay, brought up in a large family by her widowed mother, had been educated at Malvern Girls College, and was now working as a children's nurse. John's parents were concerned about the hurried wedding but they remembered the hostility and the difficulties which they had experienced in 1913, and they were determined not to interfere in their son's life. Both of the family weddings took place at St Michael and All Angels Church, Bishops Cleeve, and the rector, the Rev Thomas Jesson officiated.

Flight Sergeant John Oldacre was one of the first local boys to be married at the church in uniform. His bride wore a short azure dress under a fitted coat of matching colour with a fur-trimmed collar. Kay's brother, Joe, gave her away and Harold Hanks was John's best man. It was a quiet wedding and the reception was held at the bride's home in Woodmancote.

Mary's wedding took place on the morning of Saturday, 28 October 1939. The Charnock family arrived in the village on the previous evening, Ernest driving mother and me down from Cheshire. Father came by car from South Wales and my brother, John, travelled by train from Cannock where he was stationed with the Royal Horse Artillery. Only Catherine Oldacre was unable to get leave.

Shortly before William John was due to leave for the church he complained about feeling unwell. Gladys was used to being let down by her husband when she was expecting him to escort her on a social engagement so she was not particuarly worried. He had a variety of excuses – a pig had suddenly developed a fatal illness and must be killed before it died and the value of the carcase was lost, or sometimes a crisis had occurred at the mill which demanded his immediate attention. She asked June to cycle up to her brother John's house and to warn him that he would be required to stand in on his father's behalf at the ceremony.

The church was full when the organist played the first chord of the Wedding March and Ernest, in the uniform of a lieutenant in the Royal Tank Regiment, stood up at the chancel steps to receive his bride. Mary walked down the aisle on her brother's arm. She wore a long ecru coloured lace dress with a velvet hat which matched the long dress of her bridesmaid, Mildred. John Charnock, in an ill-fitting battledress, was best man. The marriage service was lengthened by the inclusion of a nuptial mass.

William John was waiting at home to receive his guests. He had made a miraculous recovery and Gladys was quite certain that his problems had stemmed from nervous anxiety coupled with resentment that Mary was leaving home and her duties in the business. The luncheon which Gladys Oldacre provided was up to the very high standards of her pre-war catering. Speeches were made, wedding cake was eaten and champagne was consumed. When the bride and groom set off on their honeymoon they were closely followed by John Oldacre and the younger guests. After travelling

behind the newly-weds for a few miles, the noisy cavalcade
gave up the chase and returned to Fieldgate to finish the food
that was left from the wedding breakfast.

After the guests had paid their respects to William John
and his wife, he decided to take his family and the Charnocks
to see 'Gunga Din' at a cinema in Cheltenham. Three cars
pulled away from Fieldgate and Doris Burnett and the ladies
employed to tidy up the house and garden began their work.
Shortly after the family had driven out of the gate, Doris was
surprised to see June calmly walking down the path from the
orchard with a basket of eggs on her arm. She had been left
behind and her parents did not realise the mistake until Mr
Oldacre went up to the box office to buy the tickets. He was
most disturbed to find that she was missing but the mistake
had been made and all that they could do was to continue
with their planned visit to the cinema. When the party
returned to Fieldgate, June did not appear to be in any way
upset that she had missed the outing. Later that evening the
older members of the two families went dancing at
Cheltenham Town Hall.

Mary now left Bishops Cleeve and over the next 18
months she and her husband lived in rented accommodation
near to the camp in which he was stationed. John and Kay
had a home on Cleeve Hill but soon moved to The Spinney
on Bushcombe Lane, Woodmancote, and they also spent a
good deal of time in accommodation near to John's RAF
base. Mary and John remained as directors of the company
and Mary returned to Fieldgate regularly to continue her job
as company secretary. Mildred was still working in the
fashion trade in Harrogate but her father began to put
pressure upon her to return home so that she could undertake
the routine work which Mary was no longer available to do in
the office. Catherine was nursing and only Hilda and June
remained at home.

John had been taught to fly a Tiger Moth at Staverton near
Gloucester before the war, and had then graduated to the
Hawker Hart and the Hawker Fury, both biplanes with Rolls
Royce engines and the forerunners of the famous Hawker
Hurricane fighter. After just over six hours pre-war instruc-
tion on the Tiger Moth, his instructor had asked,

'Do you ride a horse, Oldacre?'

'Yes sir,' John replied.

'Oh, I thought so' said the instructor. 'You have shown the same delicate touch on the aircraft control that is needed when handling a horse.'

Immediately this exchange was over, John had been sent on his first solo flight.

He had completed more than one hundred hours solo flying before the war started and the closing months of 1939 were very frustrating for him because there were no aeroplanes for him to fly. He was posted to Downing College and later to Emmanuel College, Cambridge for pre–flying training. The colleges were filled with experienced RAFVR sergeant pilots and new recruits who were to be trained as pilots. Each morning after breakfast the recruits marched away from the colleges to attend lectures in Trumpington, followed closely by the sergeants in another squad. When the two groups arrived in Trumpington the recruits made a smart right wheel towards the lecture theatre but the sergeants marched straight down the road to the local pub. The sergeants stayed at the pub until it was time for them to rejoin the recruits and to march back to the colleges for lunch.

In the spring of 1940 the RAFVR pilots were posted to a grass aerodrome at Fairoaks in Wiltshire. Their frustrations continued. They were taught to fly the Tiger Moth again. When this preliminary course was over John was sent to Ternhill in Shropshire where he was flying the twin–engined Avro Anson the body of which was long enough to carry a complete football team behind the pilot.

John was now commissioned as a flying officer and posted to the Central Flying School at Upavon where he was trained to be a flying instructor. Later, in Training Command, he served at Kidlington and Little Rissington where he taught night flying. During the many years that he spent training pilots he made repeated requests to be transferred to operations.

When John and Mary left home, many of the men from W J Oldacre Ltd also joined the forces or went to work in the new factories which had been evacuated to the comparative safety of the Cotswolds. Douglas Cresswell joined the Navy and was killed in action. Leslie Aston failed his Army medical and moved to factory work at Ashchurch. Bill

Washbourne, the gardener, had been badly wounded in the 1914–18 war and now became a gatekeeper at an Army depot at Ashchurch. The village was now to see the start of development which would ultimately lead to its population equalling that of a small town. The first 'shadow' factory was built for Smiths Sectric Clocks on a site at the Newlands on the Cheltenham Road. Smiths came from London and brought many of their workers and their families with them. They were billeted with families in Bishops Cleeve and some of them lived in purpose-built accommodation on land taken from Withy Farm and Gilder's farm in Stoke Road. The Government also requisitioned land for an aerodrome in Stoke Orchard and later for the American Army in Bishops Cleeve.

Fieldgate was a large house and when the size of the family living at home reduced, the spare rooms were occupied by a factory worker and his wife and newly born baby. The young couple had little to cater for the baby's needs, but Gladys Oldacre was there to help them. She had clothes, nappies, and other nursery necessities available and converted a clothes basket for the parents to use as a cot for the child. This family lived at Fieldgate for a few months but soon became homesick and returned to London. Their place was taken by a conscientious objector who had been drafted to work on Oldacres farm. The man knew nothing about farming and was not interested in learning. He only worked the statutory number of hours on the farm and would return to Fieldgate while the other men were still active in the fields. William John could not tolerate a man who would not fight for his country, he could not tolerate laziness and he could not tolerate a smoker on the farm. This man was all of these things and relationships in the home and on the farm were tense. Within one year the man was directed to another farm and the Governor was very relieved to see him go. But the rooms at Fieldgate did not remain empty for long.

The spare beds in the other homes in the village were filled with children evacuated from faraway urban centres, or the space was taken up by workers from the 'shadow' factories. Many of these people had never before been away from their home town. They found the journey to Gloucestershire long and the environment alien. The young evacuees arrived at the local railway station frightened and confused. They carried all their belongings and the children were labelled with their name and address. Mrs Oldacre and the other women from the Red Cross and the Women's Institute did their best to make the children feel that they were wanted and transferred them to their new homes with a minimum of delay. It was not easy for the children to settle down in the quiet countryside and they found the cottages strange indeed. Cows, pigs and other domestic and farm animals were new to them and they had to learn that milk came from a cow's udder before it was put into the familiar bottle. The lack of enemy action led their parents into a false sense of security and some of the homesick children returned to the cities quite soon after their arrival in Bishops Cleeve. When the blitz started many were evacuated again to other areas. Those children who did stay on in the village learned about nature and wondered at its beauty. They also tasted fresh eggs, milk, butter and vegetables for the first time in their lives and many were at last being properly nourished. These new residents settled into village life and enjoyed the experience.

William John was not very successful in selecting schools for his children. A number of the schools closed before his daughters had completed their education and this happened to Hilda and June shortly before the outbreak of war. He moved Hilda to Cheltenham Technical College but June was only nine years old and so she was sent to the junior department of Pate's Grammar School. At the start of the war Pate's had a new building under construction in Pittville, Cheltenham. The headmistress, Miss Jennings, persuaded the authorities that the part completed building should be occupied without delay, to avoid any possibility of the new building being requisitioned. The authorities agreed to her recommendation and the staff, prefects and the girls did all that they could to ensure that the school functioned properly, but they did have to shiver in unglazed corridors and dodge around the building operations. Almost before the work was completed, they were required to share the premises with King Edward School for Girls which had been evacuated from Birmingham. The Pate's girls attended classes between 8.45 am and 1 pm and played sports in the afternoon. The girls from Birmingham had the use of the classrooms from

1.30 pm until 6 pm. It was not a very satisfactory arrangement.

June and many of her fellow pupils travelled to school on their bicycles. It was a cold journey during the severe winters of 1940–41 and 1941–42, and the shortage of long stockings made the cycle ride even more uncomfortable for them. The girls' legs became chilled and many suffered from severe chilblains. William John was determined to protect his youngest daughter from the discomfort of chilblains and he rubbed her legs with 'Polential Oils' which he had found to be a fine embrocation for horses. This preventative treatment was successful.

The rather strict regime which William John had adopted with his older children was more relaxed with June. She was never made to eat everything that was put on her plate but then the food at Fieldgate was so good that she seldom wished to leave anything. The food at school was frightful to June's palate but the girls were not allowed to waste any. June was resourceful and attended school dinners with a large paper bag into which she dropped anything which she did not like and after the meal she flushed the contents down the lavatory. Only on rare occasions did she consider that the contents of the bag were fit to take home for the pigs. A gill of milk was provided for all children to drink at school and June was happy to pass this on to any friend who enjoyed it.

In April 1940 the war news eclipsed any problems which the evacuees or the school children had been experiencing. The Germans attacked Denmark and Norway and the pace of the war quickened. One month later Germany invaded the Low Countries and the Maginot Line, which did not extend along the Belgian border with France, became useless for the defence of French soil. The Chamberlain government in England fell and on 10 May 1940 Winston Churchill became Prime Minister in a Coalition Government. He offered the country nothing but *'Blood, toil, tears and sweat',* but the change of Government was welcomed by William John and the majority of people in the country. In early June the British Expeditionary Force was evacuated from Dunkirk, the Continental powers were occupied by the Germans and Britain stood alone.

(ii) The family prepare for a long struggle

The thought of defeat never entered the Governor's head. He prepared for a long struggle and worked even harder in the business. The defeat of the armies on the Continent came as Hilda was finishing her schooling and the Governor was happy to put her to work in the office at Winchcombe Street. She was soon joined by Mildred who was finding little satisfaction in the fashion trade under wartime conditions. Added to this Mildred was being troubled by swollen glands in her neck and wished to see her Cheltenham doctor. The doctor was most concerned about Mildred's enlarged lymph glands and her anaemic condition and told Gladys Oldacre that she must keep a careful watch on her daughter's health.

William John and Gladys were glad that Jack Charnock was still making regular business trips to Gloucestershire and that they could still talk with their old friend about their family and business problems. In August 1940 Hilda was due to accompany my father back to Prenton for a few days' holiday. At 7 am on the morning of Friday 9 August the telephone rang at Fieldgate. The call came from my mother who was in a very distressed state.

'Jack! Jack! she said, 'We have had a terrible night, there have been bombs dropping everywhere.'

Six of the first bombs to fall on England had fallen on Prenton at about midnight. One bomb had exploded within twenty five yards of our home, one person had been killed, and it was only the chicken wire on the windows of my mother's bedroom which had saved her from injury.

The next few days were exciting but frightening for Hilda, my mother and me. The sirens sounded each night that she was in Prenton but no further bombs landed locally. Later on during the visit she stayed at Mary's home on the other side of the River Mersey in Great Crosby. I was there at the time and when walking along the shoreline together we found it littered with Jaffa oranges which had been washed ashore from a bombed vessel. Oranges were rare during the war and we rushed forward to collect the fruit but they were waterlogged and made a frightful squelch when we touched them.

The country now came under constant attack by German bombers. Bishops Cleeve was relatively free from air raids, but the villagers heard the German planes passing overhead on their way to the Midland or North Western cities. When the target was Bristol they could hear the guns, hear the blast of the bombs and see a red glow in the southern sky. The main dangers for the village came from those planes which did not complete their mission but jettisoned their bombs anywhere along their flightpath. This happened on a number of occasions and it was extremely difficult for William John and his fellow Air Raid Wardens to pin–point the position of any bomb which did not explode. One bomb landed in the back garden of The Spinney where Kay Oldacre was living with her baby daughter Jill, but fortunately it did not explode.

Hilda was 18 years old on 8 January 1941 and at the end of 1940 both she and Mildred volunteered for the Women's Auxiliary Air Force. When the time came for the girls to attend for medical examinations, Mildred had to take a letter from her doctor to the medical board. Hilda was soon serving as a pay clerk in the WAAF, but Mildred failed the medical and was advised to see a specialist in Harley Street. Mary accompanied her to London and the whole family were shocked to learn that Mildred was suffering from Hodgkins Disease, a disease of the lymphatic glands and the spleen and one that was always fatal. Mrs Oldacre was told that her daughter had only five years to live. Mildred now underwent a number of operations for the removal of swollen glands. Coming out of the anaesthetic after one of those operations, she heard the doctors discussing her likely life span. Mildred was a staunch Christian and she had a deep faith. She was dismayed to learn of her fate, but she set about helping the war effort in any way that her strength would allow. She continued to work at Winchcombe Street but gradually was forced to reduce her working hours as she became weaker. She organised the National Savings Campaign in Bishops Cleeve and ran the Penny a Week Hospital Plan. She became a close friend of her sister-in-law, Kay, who was finding it difficult to relax in the company of her husband's mother and father. Wherever she went Mildred was liked and admired for her courage.

Mildred did become very tetchy at home in the constant company of her parents. Her moods were generally at the expense of her mother whom she so much admired, a normal reaction in such cases. She was also irritated by her father if he sat down at the table in his farming clothes and with hands which still looked rather soiled. After being attacked in this manner the Governor could sulk and stop speaking to his daughter for a few days. It was during one such spell that he unexpectedly made a comment to Mildred as he passed her a plate of meat at the dinner table.

Mildred was surprised to be addressed by her father and she made a facetious remark.

'I am in favour!'

'What did you say?' demanded her father only half hearing the remark.

'She says that the meat has a beautiful FLAVOUR' was June's quick reply.

June had saved a major argument by the speed of her reaction, but such exchanges were regular and to be expected in the strained circumstances under which the family were living.

Mildred did get some relief from her enforced confinement with her family at home. She had holidays in Weston–Super–Mare with Mary, Catherine or June, and regularly visited Prenton where she received much love and attention from my mother. On a number of occasions I had the responsibility of travelling with her from Birkenhead to Cheltenham. We would catch the 9am train from the GWR station in Birkenhead bound for Birmingham Snowhill. The train was always full and we had to arrive at the station early if we were to get two seats together for the three hour journey. My mother gave me clear instructions for the journey. I must find a corner seat for Mildred, carry both bags on our walk across Birmingham from Snowhill to New Street, Mildred must rest at the Kahdoma Cafe near to Birmingham Cathedral, and I must find a corner seat for Mildred on the final stage of the journey from New Street to Cheltenham. As the months and years went by it was sad to see the decline in her strength.

Mildred's illness placed a great strain on her mother. During the early years of the war Gladys had to face the death of her father which brought problems over the future of the shop. She was relieved when her sister Enid returned to Bishops Cleeve to look after the shop, thus safeguarding the livelihood of Reg Beckingsale who felt that he could not take on the job himself. Enid's twin sister Alice who had recently married a farmer also came back to the village and lived at Cleevelands Farm where her husband worked for William John.

At about the same time Mary's husband was posted overseas and she returned to Fieldgate. William John was delighted to have his eldest daughter back in the business and knew that her presence in the home would be a great help to her mother. Edith Saxby the wife of a fellow officer, accompanied Mary to Fieldgate where she helped Gladys Oldacre with the housekeeping. Edith and her small daughter stayed with the family until the war ended.

Gladys Oldacre continued with voluntary work in the village. The Government were encouraging housewives and women's voluntary groups to preserve home grown fruit and vegetable crops which were surplus to the immediate needs of the household, for use in the winter. They published information on new methods and recipes requiring less sugar in bottling, canning, jam making and pulping, and also gave advice on salting, drying and making pickles. Gladys was experienced in all these household crafts and her larder was filled with salted beans, eggs in waterglass, bottled tomatoes, gooseberries and many varieties of plum. In addition her husband kept racks of apples in the harness room, stored potatoes, carrots and beetroots in sand and harvested large quantities of honey. Gladys now joined her friends at the Women's Institute Hall where they collected and then bottled and canned all varieties of fruit and vegetables from the gardens and orchards of the villagers. In their homes these ladies helped to keep up the morale of their families and in any spare time knitted socks, scarves and balaclava helmets for the allied troops. These activities coupled with her busy home life helped to keep Gladys from fretting too much about the tragedy of Mildred's illness.

Throughout the war years William John and Gladys opened their home to servicemen from the Commonwealth. The Beckingsales had relations in New Zealand and a number of the neighbours and friends of those families served in England. Bart Hart was in the New Zealand army and during the early years of the war found a second home at

Fieldgate. Sub–Lieutenant Bruce Coleman of the New Zealand Navy stayed at the shop with Mrs Beckingsale and enjoyed reading poetry with her but most of his time was spent with the Oldacre family. He was the son of a farmer and was interested in looking around the farm with Mr Oldacre and talking about farming methods. He was very friendly with June and enjoyed her company at dances, at the cinema and on walks over Cleeve Hill. The Coleman family offered reciprocal hospitality to William John and Gladys when they were in New Zealand. Hilda and her family became life long friends of Bruce and his wife Alice. Catherine and June also stayed on the Coleman farm.

Hilda was stationed in the WAAF at Innsworth, near Gloucester, and was able to live at home. At weekends she invited airmen to Fieldgate and two in particular found friendship and enjoyment in the company of the family. Jack Pike of the Royal Canadian Air Force was a regular visitor and later he entertained William John and Gladys, and Hilda and her family at his home in Edmonton, Alberta. Flight Sergeant Mervyn Cliffe, RNZAF, married Hilda after the war and took her back to New Zealand.

It was not only servicemen who enjoyed the relaxed atmosphere, the country air and the remarkable wartime food at Fieldgate. I was welcome at any time. I made my first winter visit at New Year 1940 and experienced the warm smell of a log fire and the sharp cold of the upper rooms of the house. I had travelled down with Mary who asked me if I would like a hotwater bottle in my bed.

'Denys does not need a hotwater bottle. He puts his feet right to the bottom of the bed as soon as he gets in,' Mrs Oldacre said quickly. 'I've done that all my life and I'm soon snug and warm.'

I did not have the courage to disagree with her and since then I have followed that advice all my life.

Later that year I spent Christmas at Fieldgate when my father and mother were invited to have a break from the constant air raids on Merseyside. I worked on the farm for a month in the summers of 1942, 1943, 1944 and 1945. During these years the house was invariably full to capacity and I never minded if I was given a bed in the tank room, the box room or even on the top landing.

The Governor was a friend to me and when I was a teenager he treated me like an adult. When he set off around the farm he would pick up his hat and stick and call out,

'Are you coming then, young man?'

The Governor would tell me about his hopes and plans for the future of the business as we walked along. He loved to gaze across the fields between Bishops Cleeve and Gothering-ton from a vantage point on the railway embankment.

'Look across there,' he would say. 'One of these days I shall own and farm all that land. Can you see that square ten acre patch? I shall build my house there and look over the whole farm whilst I sit in my own easy chair.'

He held that dream from the days when he was courting Gladys Beckingsale and the dream became a reality in later years.

It was a joy and privilege for me to be with the Governor. He was a wonderful character and a person from whom you could learn a great deal about life. He allowed me a degree of freedom which was far beyond anything that my father would permit, but he expected me to show a sense of self discipline within that freedom. From the age of fourteen he allowed me to turn his car round in the yard at Fieldgate and also to drive him around his fields. I would jump out of the car to open the gate and he would move across to the passenger seat.

'Keep the car on top of the "lands" and you will be fine,' was his usual advice.

When harvesting was in progress, I might be put into the cab of any lorry that was being loaded with hay or corn in the fields, or behind the wheel of a tractor.

'Let the clutch out gently and don't jerk as you move off or you will have the load off,' he would say. 'Off you go then. Hold tight up there.'

In a lorry with a crash gear box it was necessary to double de-clutch every time you changed gear and this was excellent training for me. Add to this the likelihood that injury could be caused to the man building the load on the bed of the lorry if the lorry was jerked as it was moved forwards and the scale of responsibility which the Governor gave to a schoolboy can be judged. The only man I ever saw come off the top of such a load was Ern Jeynes and I was not the driver on that occasion. Ern descended to the ground in slow motion and was covered by sheaves of wheat but he was unhurt.

'You stupid bugger' was the level of concern shown by the Governor, 'I've told you time and time again to keep the corners out and the middle filled when you are loading. Why the blazes don't you do what you have been told?'

I obtained a driving licence as soon as I was old enough and I was then expected to drive the Governor whenever I was available. But even when I was only sixteen the Governor was willing to employ me as a tractor driver during my summer holidays.

The wartime hospitality at Fieldgate did not end there. The Governor was still a Rotarian and one form of Community Services which they encouraged involved entertaining overseas men when they were on leave. William John willingly took part but most of the entertaining was left in the hands of his wife and family. In addition he was likely to pick up men from the Forces as he was driving about on business and to take them home for a good feed. His wife never complained and always managed to find something for them to eat.

The many visitors to Fieldgate during the six years of war found a wonderful welcome. None of the casual guests were aware of the strains under which the family were living. Those who knew the family intimately realised that the friendship was completely genuine but that the relaxed atmosphere could become tense around the dinner table, because of a minor matter of business or a chance comment by one of the family. Gladys Oldacre was the one member of the family who was never angry and never ruffled.

(iii) Wartime activities on the farm and in the business

The Governor was a man of action and not of words. He was fifty years of age but he worked from early morning until late at night in the business, on the farm, in his garden and on his duties as Chief Air Raid Warden. He maintained the output from the mill with a much reduced workforce and increased productivity on the farm. One local farmer was prompted to remark

'John Oldacre be ploughing up the hedges to get more "taters" from his land.'

It was the variety in William John's daily workload that prevented him from becoming stale and overtired during the war.

The Governor handled unaided the general management of the business. He did talk matters over with his wife as they sat at the kitchen table and she was given the task of reading and interpreting the Government circulars and regulations which came through the post regularly. When Mary returned to Fieldgate she was able to relieve her father of office worries and he relied on her for sound financial advice.

The directors met occasionally to ratify decisions which the Governor had already made and for the annual meetings, but the minutes of those meetings are brief. The accounts from all branches of the company were put into the hands of Martins Bank in Cheltenham and the long association with Barclays was terminated. The Governor became anxious that some of his customers might not be able to pay their way and so a reserve fund of £510 was formed against any doubtful debts. The transport fleet was under constant threat of being requisitioned and petrol supplies were a problem. In Autumn 1941, the Governor was able to advise the board that he had managed to purchase a new Bedford lorry to replace the Albion which the Army had taken, and that the vehicle fleet numbered three lorries, six cars, six vans and a Fordson tractor.

After the death of Lucy Oldacre in 1942, The Pollards and other properties in the village were inherited by Alice Redman and Anna Oldacre and, in accordance with the agreement which had been made ten years earlier, Alice sold The Pollards to the company for the sum of £1,000. Two months later the board agreed that all outstanding loans from Alice Redman and Anna Oldacre should be paid off in full. The business was now totally in the hands of William John, Gladys, Mary and John.

The board made far reaching decisions about the farm. In September 1939 the company took the tenancy of Millham Farm from Mrs Ballinger at a rent of £55 per annum and provision was made for any contra account to be deducted from that rent. Two years later the minutes of the company recorded:

'Mr F J Minett of Cleevelands Farm, Bishops Cleeve approached Mr Oldacre to inquire if he would make a bid for his farm as the Gloucestershire Agricultural Committee were compelling him to quit. As the Air Ministry had previously taken over some of the fields included in Withy Farm it was agreed an offer be made to Mr Minett of £5,000. This offer was eventually accepted and the farm taken over by the firm on 3 October with vacant possession on 31 January 1942.'

Following these decisions the area of land farmed by Oldacres was increased to about 250 acres. The newly acquired acreage was situated on both sides of Gotherington Lane and included all the land nearest to Bishops Cleeve, with the exception of one field. William John Oldacre had made a start towards his goal of farming all the land between the two villages.

William John was familiar with the fields which made up Cleevelands Farm and fully aware that the hedges had spread and become wild. Men were set to work on cleaning out the deadwood, cutting back the weeds and brambles, and pollarding the withy trees which stood in the hedgerows. They were told to leave the sturdiest and best stems standing ready for Syd Burnett to lay the hedge. The laying was done by making one clean cut with a bill hook or slasher halfway through the stems and then forcing them down to a nearly horizontal position. Syd then selected the best withy poles and made stakes which he drove into the ground at eighteen inch centres along the hedge line. When the stakes were in position he tied them firmly together by weaving trimmings from the hedge cutting around them. The hedge was now stockproof and tidy.

The gates and fences on the farm were in poor condition and the skills of Alan Aldridge were needed to put them right. He searched for good hardwood in his store and at the local timber yards, looking for stout sections for the gateposts, which had to be squared over the length above ground level and the tops had to be weathered. The five-bar gates which he made in his workshop were ten feet long, four feet high and braced. It was heavy work. The Governor insisted that each gatepost fitted snugly against the hedge, the gates swung freely and catches secured the gate against persistent rubbing by cattle.

Maintenance neglect had led to the drainage becoming faulty over the whole farm. The Governor walked the fields many times searching for signs of water seeping through the sides of ditches, or bubbling up in the fields and through silt laden ditches. He kept a close watch for wet areas and soft spots. He marked all the trouble spots by placing a stake in the ground. He had an excellent eye and could judge drainage lines and levels quickly and accurately. Once he had established the drainage pattern and prepared a mental plan of action, he put his proposals to the Drainage Authority with a request for grant. The drainage was done by contract and the condition in the fields gradually improved.

The farm buildings were as dilapidated as the fences, gates and drainage and the repairs kept Alan Aldridge busy throughout the summer of 1942. The Governor decided to improve the facilities in the farm yard and Aldridge fenced a large stockyard to keep the increased number of cattle safe and warm in winter, and he built covered byres for feeding. The floor of the yard was concreted by one man who mixed and placed all the concrete by hand. A new Dutch barn was erected and was filled with sheaves of corn from the first harvest which was taken from the land.

William John managed the farm himself with the help of his two foremen. Syd was still centred at Lynworth and Harold Keen lived at Cleevelands Farm. The Governor had two very different men to handle. Syd was a farm craftsman and preferred to work alone or with a single mate. For much of the war his assistant was a land girl called Lena and she lived at Lynworth. Syd knew the Governor's ways and when he did not agree on any matter he was quick to make his view known. Arguments were inevitable but in the end agreement was reached. Harold was a tractor driver and when he was criticised he found difficulty in making his views known to the Governor. More often than not he would continue with his own way of working and this approach was bound to lead to serious conflict. He remained foreman at Cleevelands for a number of years, but relationships were fragile. He stayed with Oldacres only because Alice his wife wished to be near her sister Gladys.

The Governor increased the number of Hereford beef steers which he reared. He kept sheep and bred lambs for the first time and maintained his considerable pig unit. In summer the majority of the stock were kept in the fields at Lynworth and Withy Farms and were looked after by Syd, who also had one or two cows and calves at Lynworth. In winter the cattle were split between the stockyards at Withy Farm and at Cleevelands Farm, and Harold had to do his share of the feeding and cleaning out. The men were jealous of each other, each thinking that he was doing the bulk of the work on the farm.

The arable land was farmed by Harold and two permanent farm workers. They had two large rubber-tyred Chase tractors at Cleevelands and all the farm machinery was new or had been converted to being tractor drawn. The ploughing of the vastly increased acreage of land under cultivation was now done using a three furrow plough. Harold found that both he and his colleagues had to set out the ploughing to suit the Governor's requirements and that the depth of cut and the manner in which the soil was turned over had to meet a rigid specification. The soil was hungry when they took the land over and they used lime, basic slag, super phosphate and ammonium nitrate to improve conditions. The manure dug out of the stockyards was also used. Yields of 15 to 18 cwt per acre were achieved and every man, lorry and tractor available in the company was employed to harvest the crops.

The Governor allowed me to help with the harvesting. During the war the Government decided to institute daylight saving and the clocks were kept one hour ahead of Greenwich Mean Time in winter and two hours ahead in summer, which meant that work could go on in the fields until as late as eleven o'clock in the evening. We laboured six long days each week but the Governor insisted that Sunday was a rest day. The farm workers went home for a hot dinner at midday and then stayed out in the fields from 2 pm until nightfall. They were sustained by the cider jar and food provided by Mrs Oldacre. The hours worked on the Governor's farm were repeated by all good farmers and special rations were allowed at harvest so that the men could be fed in the fields. The thickly cut fresh sandwiches, fruit cake and hot tea were always most welcome and each day we

were more than pleased when the Governor or June arrived
with the food.

My tasks varied between tractor driving, stooking corn,
loading and driving waggons and building ricks. It was a
wonderful break from examinations and I had a great deal of
fun mixed with hard work. A hedgehog was put in the sleeve
of my jacket and I only found the animal when my hand
struck the prickles. I filled the cider jar with water when we
arrived back at Cleevelands Farm late one evening and
offered it to one of the men. I made a hasty retreat by ducking
under an overhanging load on one of the lorries and foolishly
lifted my head too soon. Blood poured from a cut on the top
of my head which was caused by a rope-hook under the bed
of the lorry and I was rushed up to the district nurse for first
aid. The Governor was never told the cause of the bald patch
in my hair but I suffered from a very itchy scar for some days.
On another occasion I was working with the Governor
offloading straw bales onto a rick when I slipped between the
load and the rick. The Governor dropped the bale and it
landed on my head driving me down like a tent peg. He was
extremely concerned but I was unhurt because I was only
loosely held by the straw when the bale landed.

The schoolboy son of an Army colleague of John Charnock
also stayed at Fieldgate and worked on the farm, and the
guests from the Services might occasionally be encouraged to
help. In 1944 Bruce Coleman spent two or three weeks leave
in Bishops Cleeve and volunteered for harvesting. We
became good friends in spite of the fact that he seemed to be
a serious rival for June's attention.

Not all the part-time workers were volunteers. Prisoners of
war from Ashchurch near Tewkesbury and from other local
camps were allowed out to help on the farms. They left the
camps under guard in a lorry and were released at the farms
under the custody of the farmer. They remained unguarded
until it was time for them to be picked up and returned to
camp. The Governor planted 30 acres of potatoes each year.
The fields made a fine picture when the crop was in flower
but lifting the crop was labour intensive and hard work. Two
horses were used on the bouting plough and the potatoes
were picked up by prisoners of war. The Governor employed
as many as 25 Italians or 25 Germans, who he preferred

Wartime potato harvest
Syd Burnett, William John, Ern Richins

because they worked harder, on the potato harvest and the crop was sorted and graded by village women. The prisoners enjoyed the work and were fed on sandwiches and home-made jam tart by Mrs Oldacre. Potato picking was also done by school children taken out of lessons. Pate's girls worked on hill farms and it caused the Governor considerable annoyance if June was sent to a hill farm by the school.

The farm was an important part of Oldacres business but the corn trade still formed the backbone. The shortage of petrol meant that farm customers could not be canvassed regularly and so the farmers began to use the telephone to give their orders. One telephone line served the mill office and Fieldgate and during working hours all calls to and from the house had to be routed through Mr Bick who was in overall charge at Bishops Cleeve. At the end of each working day Mr Bick switched the line through to Fieldgate and customers were able to contact the firm at any time. It was quite normal for the family to be awakened by the telephone at six o'clock in the morning if a farmer discovered that he had run out of feeding stuff. William John took these orders and although he never made a note of the name and address or of the goods required, he was able to transmit the information to Mr Bick without any error later in the morning.

When Mr Bick arrived at his small office at the mill, his first task was to transfer the telephone line from Fieldgate back to the office. This simple action might result in the Governor issuing him with detailed instructions; or a list of orders from customers at such a speed that it was difficult for Mr Bick to make a note; or he might get no reaction whatsoever. Mr Bick never knew when the Governor would be coming to the yard and often saw the Governor get out of his car even before it had stopped. This was done by careful judgement of the speed and switching the engine off as he entered the yard; he never seems to have put the hand brake on, nor to have put the gearbox in neutral.

Mr Bick was fully extended through his long working day and this put him under considerable strain. He watched over the output from the mill where Ern Jeynes still tended the engine and Fred Cresswell was still responsible for the milling operations and the warehouse. He took orders by telephone and across the counter of the shop. He assembled orders in a logical sequence for loading and delivery, and ensured that the lorries were routed to minimise the use of petrol. Coal was rationed and he located supplies, looked after the customers fairly, and encouraged a rather reluctant Ern Richins to undertake the coaling task. His office was small and his clerical work was interrupted regularly. If Mr Bick was not at his desk the Governor wanted to know where he was and what he was doing.

Much of Oldacres trade was still with people owning a small acreage of land. The Government was encouraging people to dig or plough up land for corn and vegetable crops and to keep a greater number of pigs and poultry. The houses and cottages in Bishops Cleeve and the surrounding district once more became smallholdings and good farmers increased their output. Oldacres set about the difficult task of providing supplies for this increased market in a period of shortage. The quality of the meal produced in the mill could not be maintained but it was satisfactory and the animals put on weight, hens laid eggs and cockerels were fattened for the table. The Government expected the small pig keepers to join pig clubs rather than to work independently and meal was rationed on that basis. William John organised the clubs and each member was entitled to 70 pounds of meal each month for pigs, which were killed in rotation and the meat and offal shared among the members. William John also helped poultry keepers to obtain permits for feeding stuff. In 1940 ham, bacon, butter and sugar were rationed and the pig keepers had to forfeit their ham and bacon rations. Due to the intensity of U-boat action in the Atlantic, food became more and more scarce and almost all basic foods were rationed. Oldacres sold lentils, oat meal, marrowfat peas, haricot beans, butter beans and other unrationed pulses in their shops for human consumption. Added to their other trade these new outlets kept the shops in a healthy state.

The Governor put considerable pressure on Mr Hamblin. He was good and trustworthy at his job but he suffered from diabetes and lacked the drive which was needed under difficult conditions. The allocations of sugar and fats for Charlton Kings were small when compared with the needs of the bakery. The national wholewheat loaf was baked and to conserve fuel buns, dough cake, doughnuts and slab cakes were cooked in the cooling ovens. Mr Hamblin's transport problems matched those of Mr Bick. The shop sales were substantial but many Oldacre customers lived outside the town and required a delivery service. A number of the van drivers had been called up and some of the bread rounds were taken over by women. Mr Hamblin found some difficulty in handling these women but was helped here by Miss Wise. Mr Hamblin agreed the quantity of bread and cakes for each round, helped the drivers to load up, and when they returned at the end of the day the quantities were cross–checked against the sales. A close check also had to be kept on the relationship between mileage and petrol con-sumption as it was all too easy to find a ready market for syphoned petrol.

Sales of bread and cakes at Charlton Kings increased when the Governor entered into an agreement with Mr Bondolfi, a Swiss confectioner and baker who in 1940 was forced to abandon his shop in Eastbourne because it was near to the Channel coast. At first Mr Bondolfi and his father had an arrangement with a Cheltenham baker to use his ovens but the relationship broke down. Mr Bondolfi then approached Oldacres and negotiated a satisfactory agreement with the Governor. He had the use of the Charlton Kings premises, the ovens and gas and in return Oldacres received a percentage margin on the sales; some sales were made directly by Bondolfi and others through Oldacres establishments. Mr Bondolfi was highly skilled at making homemade Swiss chocolates and in pre-war days his Eastbourne shop had displayed large chocolate animals and eggs, boxes of fine chocolates, decorated wedding cakes and all manner of fancy confectionery. His output during the war was restricted but he had no rival in Cheltenham capable of producing such a high class output.

Oldacres bakery trade did not extend to the Tewkesbury shop where fortunately Purser was still the shopman. This meant that Mr Counsell was able to concentrate on attending markets, purchasing good quality locally grown grain, making occasional visits to customers for orders and keeping payments up to date. He had little assistance throughout the war but he was in regular contact with the Governor who was also doing some of the buying. Mr Counsell kept in close liaison with the clerks at Winchcombe Street to check that the contra sales and payments were in order. And he was a regular visitor to the yard at Bishops Cleeve where he could talk with Mr Bick and rectify any complaints that were coming from farmers, and ensure that supplies of grain from the farms were meeting the needs of the mill, or such of those needs as it was possible to meet in the circumstances of war. Mr Counsell had one advantage over his fellow managers, a close and calm relationship with the Governor and his total confidence.

During the war years the business and the farm prospered. The hard work and dedication of all those involved were rewarded by higher profits and these profits were divided between the directors and the staff and workforce who were paid good bonuses. William John was proud of the achievement and felt that he would be able to show his son that the business was thriving when he returned to civilian life. Like his father before him, William John's labours were channelled towards the creation of a successful family business which could be passed on from father to son generation after generation.

(iv) John Oldacre reported missing

In 1944 the war news was much more encouraging for Britain. Italy had capitulated in the previous autumn and the Allies were preparing for the invasion of the Continent. Bishops Cleeve was host to troops from the United States of America and part of Cleevelands Farm was occupied by GIs.

Flight Lieutenant John Oldacre's transfer to Bomber Command came through at the end of 1943 and by the beginning of 1944 Kay had returned to The Spinney. On 4 April 1944 she gave birth to Susan, their second daughter.

During May there were considerable troop movements reducing the number of soldiers in Bishops Cleeve. Rumours of an impending invasion were rife. John Oldacre spent the early months of 1944 piloting Wellingtons and collecting a crew together ready for operations. The crew made a number of missions dropping leaflets over occupied France and later underwent a conversion course onto four-engined Lancasters.

Before dawn had broken on 6 June the villagers were awakened by the roar of aircraft engines. When they looked up they saw the sky filled with a vast armada of planes flying in strict formation. The roar continued throughout the whole morning and the people sensed that something momentous was afoot. William John went about his normal duties but waited anxiously to learn whether or not the invasion had started. The news of the Normandy landings was broadcast at dinner time.

John and his crew were not part of the invasion armada. It was not until the night of 7/8 July that John made his first bombing raid over enemy territory. He travelled as second pilot with an experienced skipper and crew.

At nine o'clock on the morning of 8 July the telephone rang at Fieldgate and was answered by William John. The caller was Charlie Bayliss, the village postmaster and he asked to speak to Gladys Oldacre.

'I've just taken a telegram down for young Mrs Oldacre at The Spinney,' he said. 'I'm afraid that the news is not good. Your son is missing over enemy territory.'

William John called Mary, Mildred and June into the kitchen where their mother was standing motionless.

'A telegram is on the way to Kay,' Gladys said very quietly, brushing her hand quickly over her eyes. 'John's plane has been shot down and he is missing.'

The family were stunned and William John became ashen as he choked back his feelings. In the heart-breaking circumstances there was no alternative. Gladys had to take command.

'One of you girls fetch Kay and the children here immediately, she must not be alone,' she ordered. 'Come on all of you, we must get back to work. Daddy, you have a business to run, get on with it.'

William John obediently picked up his hat and went out. Gladys busied herself with household chores. Mary went to collect Kay. June set off up the orchard to feed the fowls. Mildred was ill and weak, she could find no occupation to fill her mind, and she wept. Gladys Oldacre never seemed to doubt that her son was alive and in hiding and she was proved to be correct in this belief. His Lancaster had been hit and had caught fire. John attached his parachute to the harness which he was wearing. On the skipper's instruction he sat on the edge of the open forward hatch, put his head on his knees, prayed and rolled out of the burning plane. His parachute jerked open and he floated gently towards the ground. The sky around him was illuminated by flashes from anti-aircraft guns and he watched burning planes crashing to the ground. His first parachute landing was a success and he found himself near the edge of a field. He released his parachute, rolled it up and carefully hid it in a bed of nettles under the hedgerow. His heart was pounding but his brain was clear. Behind him he heard English voices. His first instinct was to join up with the other airmen who were chattering like monkeys on the other side of the hedge. But he was a loner by nature and he also had a strong sense of self-preservation. He moved carefully towards a wooded area and his training for just such a situation took control. Once he was out of sight he checked his pockets. Yes, his water bottle and supply of condensed milk were not lost. He put his hand into his trouser pocket and took out two silk handkerchiefs, opening them to reveal two maps of an area near Beauvais in

France over which the· ʰad been flying. Next he removed two of his trouser buttons and placed one on top of the other. The primitive equipment worked and the small needle swung towards the north point. He set the maps to the correct compass bearing and gained a rough idea of his position.

He found a hollow, removed the RAF insignia, wings and officer's rings from his jacket and covered himself with bracken. It was fine and the weather was mild. He did his best to sleep and waited for darkness.

Over the next few nights he walked in the general direction of Paris. He avoided all towns, villages and main roads. His iron rations were soon finished and he had to search for water and food. He ate raw carrots, suedes and fruit, and filled his water bottle whenever he was near water that appeared to be clean. He rested under cover by day but after a few days he became weak and exhausted. He took cover in a haycock and slept. He was awakened by the sound of voices very near to him. John hailed the couple who he presumed to be the farmer and his wife. They did not understand English and so in schoolboy French he asked them for help. They indicated that he should stay hidden and that they would bring help. Later the local schoolmaster arrived with food and drink and he told John that he would be contacted on the following day.

John returned to his cover in the hay feeling more comfortable after a spartan meal. As darkness fell it began to rain heavily and he anticipated spending a wet and uncomfortable night, but the farmer sensing the airman's plight, invited him into the house. John stayed warm and dry but had to return to his hiding place before dawn.

Late in the morning John's heart sank for a gendarme was approaching on a bicycle. The schoolmaster must have reported his position to the authorities and so the hardships which he had endured had been for nothing. He was about to be captured. The gendarme dismounted, leaned his bicycle against the hedge and then removed a package from the bicycle luggage rack. He advanced towards the haycock and John.

'Monsieur,' he said and then in heavily accented English, 'Quickly put these clothes on and follow me. There is a cycle waiting down the road.'

John quickly dressed in the trousers, jacket and cap which had been handed to him, mounted the bicycle leaning against the wall of the farm building and rode after the gendarme. There were Germans all around but it was not long before the gendarme turned into the yard of the police station at Bresles and John was soon being entertained to a welcome hot meal. He spent two days at the police station where he slept in the loft. He was then handed on to another farmer called Monsieur Pelletiers.

On 14 July, Bastille Day, the war memorial was adorned with flowers and Monsieur Pelletiers gave a great party for his family and friends. Thirty people including John Oldacre assmbled in the farm kitchen surrounded by live pigs, ducks, geese and chickens. The party sat down at the table at 3 pm and were still eating and drinking at 7 pm. John stayed with the farmer for one week and had at least two close encounters with German soldiers. On one occasion he was sitting outside the kitchen door of the farm with an American airman, when they were approached by a German patrol. They steeled their nerves as a German NCO came forward and asked for a drink of water for his men. John casually lifted himself off the chair and sauntered into the kitchen to fetch the water. Their thirst assuaged the Germans continued on their way quite oblivious of the nationality and occupation of the men who had helped them. Later a German dispatch rider rushed through the farm at great speed running over one of the geese. The goose was killed. Before the German had time to pull up and return to the scene to collect his booty, the goose had vanished. John had moved quickly to ensure that the goose graced the table of M. Pelletiers and his friends rather than that of the German Army.

After a short while, John was passed on from the farm to the house of Pauline Toussaint. Pauline's husband was a prisoner of war but, with the help of her daughter Isabel she continued to look after his notary business.

By this time the Allies were advancing through France and as the Germans moved back they commandeered properties for the use of their troops. John was living in one of the rooms in Pauline's house and it was clear that before long the Germans would call. He noticed that his room had a cupboard on each side of the firegrate and, on investigation, he found a trap-door at the back of one cupboard leading to a space behind the chimney. One morning a German officer called at the house and John moved quickly through the trap-door and out of sight behind the chimney. The German inspected the property and liked the room which John had been using and requisitioned it for his use. When the officer left to fetch his kit, John escaped from his hiding place to the safety of the woods where he joined up with a Resistance group who gave him shelter in an old shack where he had to share a bed with a heavily bearded Communist bus conductor.

With the Resistance, John was given the job of setting up lights to act as markers for the RAF which made regular supply drops to the group. The lights were powered by 12 volt car batteries and the markers were laid out to form the corners of a triangle the inside of which was the dropping zone. The lights were switched on at the first sound of an approaching plane but it was not always possible to tell whether the plane was British or German. If a mistake was made, the lights had to be put out quickly or the Resistance was at the receiving end of bombs and bullets rather than supplies. On one occasion a Wellington made a supply drop and the canisters landed in a wood where many remained suspended in the trees. The group had the difficult task of retrieving the supplies and soon came under fire from the Germans. John set off for the other side of the wood with haste and made a two hour detour back to the shack. When he opened the door of the shack, he found the men of the Resistance happily sitting round the table tucking into a hearty breakfast.

Life with the Resistance offered more danger from their bullets than from those of the Germans. They were all anxious to kill the enemy but they were woefully ill-trained. John attempted to discipline them to handle their guns properly and more carefully, but he made little effect on the behaviour of these brave men and women. They were still likely to carry a Sten gun fully cocked and pointing at the back of a colleague walking in front. The results were inevitable and many of them were killed in such accidents. Whenever they came across Germans they fought like tigers and did valuable work for the advancing Allies.

While John was acting out the strange role of infantryman

with the French Resistance, his father was busy harvesting. Once the harvest was gathered he began to brood over the fate of his son and Jack Charnock invited him to take a short break in Prenton. Gladys accompanied her husband and she was able to relax with Freda, but Jack found his friend to be very depressed. Jack decided that he must keep William John fully occupied both during the day and in the evenings. Jack was a keen gardener and he had a friendly gardening rival in Jack Green who lived close by; they compared vegetable crops and the quality of their tomatoes. He decided to show William John the excellent quality of the vegetables which Jack Green was growing. The vegetable crop formed the subject of conversation for some minutes but William John could not keep his mind on sprouts and tomatoes.

'What is your business Mr Green?' he asked.

'Oh, I'm a forwarding agent working from our head office in Liverpool,' Jack Green replied.

'I suppose that it is a public company,' continued William John.

'Yes, I am a director of a public company which operates worldwide. I returned here from our Canadian office only a short time before the war.'

'My business is a family affair,' broke in William John. 'But my son is missing in the RAF and there will be no purpose in carrying on if he doesn't return.'

Jack Green knew the Oldacre family and there was anger in his swift reply. 'Good God man, what a wicked thing to say. You have five daughters and you speak as though they didn't exist. I have no son but I do have two daughters and I'm proud of them. You should damned well be proud of your fine daughters. They could very well carry on your business if you gave them a chance. Pull yourself together man.'

William John was taken aback by this fierce attack and Jack Charnock, aware of the charged atmosphere, touched his friend's arm and said very calmly,

'You know, there is a good deal of truth in what has been said. We are all deeply sad that John is missing. We all pray that Gladys' optimism turns out to be justified. Meanwhile life must go on and you are fortunate to have such wonderful daughters.'

The men began to talk about the progress of the war as they walked back to the house where Mrs Green had prepared coffee and sandwiches. William John had not been spoken to in that manner since his father had died and he was somewhat chastened.

William John did not have to meditate on the words of Jack Green for long. By mid-August the 2nd United States Army had overrun the area where John Oldacre was in hiding. The Americans thought that the tall blond man in civilian clothes with the French Resistance was a German spy. He was taken to the American headquarters which were just being established near to Bresles and interrogated in depth. Finally he was confronted by an intelligence officer who knew Cheltenham well and John was able to satisfy him that he really had been born and bred in Bishops Cleeve.

John was sent by the Americans to Paris en route for England and he entered the city a few hours in advance of General de Gaulle. On the surface Paris seemed little affected by four years of German occupation. The night-clubs were doing a brisk trade and the famous Bluebell Girls were still doing their lavish routines. It was only when John had the opportunity of going backstage at the Lido in the Champs-Elysees, that he saw the guns and ammunition stored under the stage and realised that even in Paris itself men and women had bravely risked their lives to undermine the German hold on the city. In Paris he eventually met a group of the Dutch SAS. The officer in command had been dropped behind the German lines on five occasions and yet he gave the appearance of being meek and timid. John persuaded the Dutchman to allow him to travel with them to Calais, where he found a ship for England.

At eleven o'clock one evening in mid-September 1944 the telephone rang at Fieldgate. Gladys picked up the receiver and heard a familiar voice on the line.

'Hello mother. I'm back!'

'John! John! Where are you? Where are you?'

'I'm in London. Can you let Kay know that I shall be home as early as possible tomorrow.'

Gladys Oldacre never displayed her emotions. She put the receiver down and with a slight flush on her face she climbed the stairs to the bedroom where William John was already in bed.

'John is back' she said as she entered the bedroom.

(v) June's life in danger

The family had hardly settled down after John's return before further trouble was in store for them. June had decided that she wanted to become a children's nurse, but when she left school at the age of 16, she knew that she would have to wait for two years before she would be accepted at any training college so she obtained a job in a war nursery run by the council.

The Government had encouraged local councils to open nurseries to look after the children of factory workers while their mothers were at work. These nurseries were geared to the working hours in the factories and so the staff were employed on two shifts: 6 am to 3 pm and noon to 9 pm, both shifts covering the dinner period. The daily duties were varied. The children were checked in and welcomed, and the mothers of any children new to the nursery were registered. The children's outdoor clothes were removed and some had to be washed and deloused before they were fed. The registration of new children brought with it many problems. Mothers were often reluctant to give personal particulars to the young assistants who had to establish the name and address of both parents, the age of the child and so on. Accurate records were vital as there was always the danger that the child or the parent might be killed or injured by enemy action while the child was in the care of the local authority. If the girls could not persuade the mother to give the required information they had to call the matron. Soon after starting work June had to register a new arrival, and she was anxious to complete the job herself and was successful in obtaining the age of the baby and the name and address of the mother and child.

'What is the father's name?', continued June in an attempt to complete the form.

'I don't know his name,' the mother replied, 'but I know he was an airman from the feel of his buttons.'

June felt that she had done a good job when she entered, 'Airman, present address unknown.'

June cycled to work each day but when one of the family were going to or from Cheltenham in the car, they would strap her bike on the back and give her a lift. In late September 1944, June left home for the 3 pm shift and was told that she could have a lift home if she called at the Winchcombe Street shop. Father and Mildred were going to the cinema.

The work at the nursery followed the usual routine, nappies needed washing, children had to be put on the pot and at the end of the shift they had to be dressed for home. In the early evening June began to feel unwell. By the time the shift ended she was not fit to ride her bike and one of the girls pushed it to Winchcombe Street for her. The shop door was locked and June rested against the wall in the doorway. When her father arrived with Mildred they found her slumped on the ground in the doorway. William John picked his daughter up and rushed her home where Gladys put her to bed and called the doctor. There was a locum on duty and he was not pleased to be called out in the late evening. He was unable to diagnose the trouble, but fortunately Catherine, now working as night sister at Winchcombe Hospital, turned up next morning on her way to Weston for a few days' holiday.

Immediately she entered June's room she knew by the stench that there was no time to waste. She acted swiftly and June was admitted to Winchcombe Hospital without delay. At 11 am the surgeon, Mr. Robinson, removed the gangrenous little finger from June's right hand. The doctors hoped that the action which they had taken would arrest the flow of poison around the body and protect the brain. They told the anxious parents what they had done and of the critical condition of their daughter.

The feeling of helplessness and depression at Fieldgate was much deeper than during the period when John was missing. Gladys never believed that John had been killed, after a time Mildred held the same view and there had been some optimism in the household. June's illness found no one at Fieldgate with any certainty about the eventual outcome. Mildred was convinced that she would never see her little sister again in life. The others in the family tried hard not to think what might happen. The sadness in William John's heart was greater than at any time since his sister Lucy had been severely injured in the accident so long ago. It was often suggested that he favoured June over his other children, and perhaps it was true.

June's condition remained critical. On the third day the surgeon and the doctor agreed that further action was needed if the girl's life was to be saved, and she was prepared for a second operation.

'We must remove the whole arm,' Mr Robinson advised.

'She is only a child,' pleaded Dr Spiridian. 'Give her a chance. Try draining the poison from the hand. Only take the arm as a last resort.'

The doctor's pleading was successful and the surgeon inserted tubes into June's hand.

Slowly the girl began to show signs of improvement. When the hand was dressed each day June suffered excruciating pain and brave as she was, she could not prevent herself screaming at every touch. Her arm was firmly held in the upright position and she could not move. Had she not been physically strong and been born with a fighting spirit she could not have survived the frightful disease and the dreadful daily ordeal.

Gradually the periods of delirium reduced and pain levels began to subside. June was able to have a few visitors in addition to her mother and father. The doctor saw her daily and after checking her condition would sit down for long periods and ask her to go through her routine on the day she was taken ill. He repeated the inquisition with the same intensity each day, looking for any clue to the cause of the gangrene.

'Tell me once again,' the doctor asked, 'What had you done before you began to feel unwell?'

'I cycled to the nursery and after hanging my coat up I put on my overall,' said June, going yet again through the duties of the day. 'There were some dirty nappies and I washed them through. Oh yes, I pricked my finger on a nappy pin. . .'

'You pricked your finger? Which one?' the doctor asked.

'I pricked the little finger on my right hand. I know that I did it and that I complained to the matron that someone had left the pin in a nappy.'

'That's it!' The doctor sat up quickly and made a note on his pad.

As time went on the number of people who were allowed to visit increased. June was delighted and surprised by the anxiety that had been shown not only by the family and close friends, but also by people whom she had hardly known. The treatment which she received at the hospital was excellent. The doctors, sisters and nurses visited her bedside regularly and spent much time talking with her. Mr Shipway the dentist, never visited one of his patients in the hospital without looking into her room.

The doctor told William John and Gladys that it was most unlikely that June would work again. He also explained his theory about the cause of the gangrene. William John did not need to be told that he could sue the council for negligence on June's behalf and with the full support of the doctor he instituted legal action. The case was settled out of court and June was awarded £250 damages. The award was small because it was considered that her father had the means to keep her for the rest of her life. The money was invested in the business on June's behalf.

The doctor had underestimated June's courage and her resolve to make herself fully fit again even if she did have a badly maimed right hand. I had not been able to visit her in hospital but I did write to her for the first time in my life. I was delighted and surprised to receive a reply written with her left hand. She left hospital one month after the accident.

The Governor, relieved that his youngest daughter was still alive, settled back to his life of business and farming. He made the weekly visits to Rotary and towards Christmas sat at lunch with Ernest Ivamy, the principal of the Cheltenham Technical College.

'How is that young daughter of yours John? Has she completely recovered?' he asked.

'She is very much better but her right hand is useless and she will never work again,' William John replied.

'Why don't you get her to come and see me?' Mr Ivamy suggested. 'I am sure that we could give her something to do.'

After the Christmas holidays June started work in the domestic science department of the technical college and was soon offered the chance of taking a special course towards a

City and Guilds Certificate in Domestic Science. Within one year she had gained the certificate, and by that time she was able to use her right hand even though the little finger was missing, the second finger was bent and rigid, and her hand was badly scarred.

Ernest Ivamy was delighted with June's work and the aptitude which she had shown towards catering. He suggested to William John that he should set her up in a high class confectionery business in the centre of Cheltenham but the idea fell on deaf ears. William John was only interested in the family business and if June wanted to become a confectioner then there was room at Charlton Kings Bakery for her. As the youngest member of a large and powerful family, June had no intention of becoming an employee of Oldacres, so she applied for a job at Winchcombe Hospital, but the work was too heavy for her and she had to abandon the idea of qualifying as a nurse.

(vi) The war ends but Mildred's death brings sadness to the family

After returning to England, John spent six weeks' leave with his wife and two young daughters at The Spinney. He did visit his parents but for the most part he was happy to rest after his ordeal and to enjoy the pleasures of the countryside with walks over the hill with his dog. At the end of his leave he was posted to the Operations Room of the 2nd Tactical Glider Division for a short spell, before returning to Bomber Command in the new year as a Squadron Leader. His final job before returning to operational duties was to select a new crew at the Operational Training Unit. He short circuited this task by picking up a scratch crew.

At 4 am on 1 January 1945 Squadron Leader John Oldacre was back at the controls of a Lancaster waiting for take-off clearance for a raid over Germany, his first operation since he had been shot down. It was a harrowing experience. Twelve heavily loaded planes taxied to the end of the runway. The pilot of the first plane received the signal for take-off and gave the four engines full throttle and set off slowly down the runway. John's plane was third in line and he could see that the first Lancaster was in difficulty. He watched horrorstruck as the heavily loaded plane crashed in an earsplitting explosion and burst into flames. The second plane suffered a similar fate. The third Lancaster followed slowly down the runway and gained speed as John eased the nose of the shaking and reluctant plane off the ground. It gradually gained altitude as John willed it up to operational height. He felt that he had lifted the machine into the air with his own bodily strength and was exhausted. The whole crew looked down to see two more of their number failing to take-off, and crashing just beyond the end of the runway and bursting into flames. There was not an airman in John's crew who did not know the horror of being in a burning plane, they could see that few if any from the crews of the crashed planes would survive.

The 'gaggle' of Lancasters came under attack from fighters when they crossed into enemy territory. The heavily laden bombers had considerable fire-power but they were out–manouvred by the light and speedy German planes. John's crew were too busy looking after themselves to know which planes had been lost but they saw Lancasters burning as they crashed to the ground and watched their crews floating down on their parachutes. Over the target area they encountered heavy ack-ack fire and more planes were lost. John held his course until he heard the shout of 'bombs away' over the intercom and set course for home. Only two of the flight joined him for the return journey. Once out of ack-ack range, the fighters came at them again and only John's plane survived the encounter. The battered and solitary crew landed at their home base in Lincolnshire.

Over the next four months John took part in a further fourteen operations. He was a pathfinder on the Dresden raid and remembers well the horrific sight as the whole town burned under the frightful weight of bombs which had been dropped. The conflagration was so intense that they could still see the burning city as they passed over Switzerland.

The Allies crossed the Rhine in March and after heavy fighting to defend the soil of the fatherland, Germany surrendered on 9 May. Hitler was dead and the war in Europe was over. After a brief celebration the Allies turned their attention towards the completion of the war in the Far East and the unconditional surrender of Japan. John was promoted to Wing Commander and became an administrator. He did not relish the thought of a desk bound job in the RAF, nor indeed anywhere else and so he volunteered for operational duties in the Far East, but it was made clear to him that he was needed in administration and that his days of operational flying were over.

John returned to Bishops Cleeve on a short leave early in the summer and he arranged to see his father. He told him that he had been offered a command in India with the rank of Group Captain and with considerable privileges, but was not really interested in it as he would be behind a desk most of the time.

The Governor was fairly certain that Kay was encouraging John to stay in the RAF.

'I can't compete on the matter of salary,' he said. 'It's been a long and hard war, but I've done well. Now I'm about ready to ease back a bit. If you come in now I shall be able to hand the business over to you quite quickly.'

Eventually John left to rejoin his family at The Spinney, his mind made up. He had no intention of staying in the RAF; he was a corn merchant not a professional soldier, and he intended to succeed his grandfather and his father as head of the business.

It was not difficult to obtain release from the RAF. There were plenty of men ready and willing to sign on. John prepared a case for his release based on the role which Oldacres played in feeding the nation; food was in short supply and farmers were still being encouraged to increase production. He approached Alderman Wilfred Waite the Mayor of Cheltenham, who was happy to sign the necessary papers supporting John's application for release. John was back home as a civilian before the Japanese surrendered on 14 August 1945. William John wanted him to live at The Pollards so that he could keep a close watch on the work at the mill and in the yard. Anna Oldacre had been living in the house since the death of her mother and was only too glad to leave the property which belonged to the business. Under the will of her mother she had inherited Owls End, Station Road, which was now empty and ready for her. Anna was happy but Kay felt that her father-in-law was forcing the issue and she took exception to the proposal. The house was modernised, the pollarded trees removed, and the name was changed to Mill House. John and his family moved in during the spring of 1946.

Fieldgate also saw changes as the war in the Far East ended. The house which had been filled to capacity throughout the war was now half empty. William John set Austin Agg to work building a new porch and conservatory at the back of the house and arranged for tarmac to be laid over the whole of the yard. The stable was put back to its proper use when the Governor purchased a grey named Joe, which both he and John used to ride. A new groom/gardner was employed and Gladys had daily help in the house.

Mary had been living at Fieldgate and working full time in the business since her husband went overseas. William John could not mask his disappointment when she told him that her husband had been demobilised and that she was moving to the Wirral where they had bought a house. Ernest became company secretary to the Aintree Race Course Company in Liverpool. William John wanted Mary at his side to look after the office as much as he needed his son. Without any discussion with John, he attempted to persuade Ernest to join the firm as company secretary. On hearing the news, Jack Charnock made it quite clear to Ernest that if he wanted to change jobs he was needed in Thomson and Charnock Ltd. Jack need not have worried. Ernest had no intention of making the change. Mary now agreed to remain as company secretary and to make regular visits to Fieldgate.

By September 1945 only Mildred and June were at home with their parents at Fieldgate. June was making remarkable progress following her accident and was studying at the Technical College, but Mildred's condition was becoming critical. She was losing weight, suffering from a hacking cough and so weak that she had to spend most of the time in bed. June spent much time talking with her sister and reading to her, and Enid Beckingsale and Edith Saxby who now lived with Alice Keen, were two of many regular visitors to Mildred's bedside.

In spite of this sad state of affairs at Fieldgate there was a brief celebration for the family. Flight Sergeant Mervyn Cliffe RNZAF asked William John for the hand of his daughter Hilda. The wedding took place at Bishops Cleeve parish church in October 1945. Hilda had borrowed a long white high-necked gown from Kay's sister Eve, the dress had a train which stretched for more than a yard behind her as she walked down the aisle. She was attended by Catherine and June. Fifty guests assembled at Fieldgate for the reception and shortly after this Mervyn returned to New Zealand where he was soon to be joined by his wife.

There was little to be joyful about once the excitement of the wedding was over. Mildred was becoming very much weaker, her coughing was almost continuous and she was confined to bed.The doctor arranged for a qualified nurse to live at Fieldgate. Mildred had been under medication for almost five years and the effectiveness of the drugs taken in pill form was lessening. The drugs were now administered by injection and the dosage increased. Earlier in the year Mildred had begun to doubt the effectiveness of the treatment which she was being given and had turned to Faith Healing, without success. Christmas came and the family were together but only one or two of them could see Mildred at any one time and she needed a period of rest after each visit. The festivities were subdued.

On the morning of 27 December 1945, the nurse did her best to give Mildred some light food and sips of liquid. She gave her patient a blanket bath, administered the prescribed drugs and made her as comfortable as possible. The day passed slowly. She was visited by the family. Evening came and it was time for another attempt at taking food, another bath and further drugs. At 9.30 pm the nurse settled Mildred for the night, everything was routine.

At 11pm the nurse knocked lightly on the door of the bedroom used by Mr and Mrs Oldacre. She entered and told them that Mildred had passed away. There was little that could be done that night. Catherine had been helping to nurse her sister over the holiday break, she and June were told of Mildred's death and then the family did their best to sleep.

First thing in the morning the doctor was called. Very tactfully he mentioned that Mildred had left her body to rsearch. William John did not think that she had made a will.

'Mildred may have told you that, but unless I see it in writing I cannot agree.'

However there was a will and June knew where it was kept. Mildred had left one or two legacies but the bulk of her small estate was inherited by June and her body was to be used for medical research. It was difficult for the family to accept this wish, but they hoped that some good would come from it. William John was deeply upset at the fact that he could not give his daughter a decent burial, but twenty four hours after removing Mildred's body the hospital informed William John that he could have the body. He was shocked, but the hospital had removed the glands which they needed. So arrangements were made for the funeral which took place early on the morning of 31 December 1945. Mildred was laid to rest in the churchyard at Bishops Cleeve where she joined three previous generations of the family. The church was packed with relatives, friends, and staff paying their respects to someone they loved and admired.

By Easter 1946, William John and Gladys were living alone for the first time since their marriage in 1913.

6

POST-WAR CHANGES
1946–1957

(i) Walter John hands over to his son

The business activities of W J Oldacre Ltd were recognisably the same in 1945 as they had been at the beginning of the war. The company was involved in farming and milling, with three corn and seed retail shops, a bakery and confectionery business, and it was merchanting coal, seeds, fertilizers and compound feeds from Port Millers. However, the scale of the activities had increased and the strength of the company was much greater.

The importance of the farmer and the growth in domestic pig and poultry keeping had doubled the annual sales of the business and increased the profits. Throughout the war William John had a considerable gross income from his salary and the return on his capital. His standard of living was quite high. The business provided him with a car and telephone. He kept a horse and he could be seen riding around the farm. He did not smoke, drink or gamble, and he reinvested everything which he could back into the business. His thrift and careful husbandry of the finances added to the strength of the enterprise. The company now owned The Pollards, Cleevelands and Millham farms, and other land and property in Bishops Cleeve, Cheltenham and Charlton Kings, and by 1944 the board of directors was paying interest on his loan, and by 1946 the capital sum was so considerable that he was given a legal charge on Cleevelands Farm and The Pollards.

William John was true to his word. John Oldacre was appointed joint managing director with his father when he left the RAF. The minutes of the company record a clear understanding that he was eventually to take over the company. He had the total support of his father. The capital in the company was held mainly in their hands. John came back to a very different situation from that which William John had faced in 1933.

The wartime success of Oldacres was due in large part to the hard work and dedication of the Governor and his three managers Messrs Bick, Counsell and Hamblin. William John was determined that the loyalty of these men should be rewarded. So in recognition of their support, he transferred 160 ordinary shares of £1 each from his personal portfolio free of cost, to each of the men, reducing his holding in the company by almost 17½ percent. They were made directors of W J Oldacre Ltd; R A Bick as transport director; H N Counsell as sales director; and H R Hamblin as bakery director.

Demobilization from the forces reached a peak in 1946. Jim Payne and one or two other men came back to Oldacres and Leslie Aston returned from his wartime factory job. Long service staff including Syd Burnett, Fred Cresswell, Alan Aldridge, Charlie Dartnell and Freda Wise still formed the backbone of the employees but they needed additional support, and many new men and women were recruited. Walter Schwab, a former German prisoner of war, was among them and he served the company well for many years. The growth in the number of factories in the area meant that Oldacres was no longer the largest employer in Bishops Cleeve, and there were more employment opportunities open to the villagers. Oldacres was still a family concern but much of the feeling of interdependence between the management and the village workers had disappeared. Individuals still mattered to management but the close personal relationships were no longer to be seen. This was not unique but the nature of the change at Oldacres can be judged from the alterations to their annual social programme. Summer outings to the seaside and Christmas parties for which Mrs Oldacre prepared the food and during which each individual made a contribution to the entertainment were not revived. Post-war staff parties became dances with the added attraction of novelty games. The first was held at St Gregory's Hall

Oldacres Staff Party – c. 1950

in Cheltenham with catering by Mr Bondolfi and the staff from Charlton Kings. Later parties were held at Holy Apostles Hall, Charlton Kings, the Queens Hotel, Cheltenham, and then at the Tythe Barn in Bishops Cleeve. All this was a far cry from the pre–war antics in the Womens Institute Hall in Bishops Cleeve.

The relationship between man and horse which had been so important in earlier years had also lost ground. The horse had ceased to play a major role in the life of the community, and Oldacres haulage was done by a fleet of lorries and vans. It was almost impossible to buy any new lorries and so Oldacres bought second-hand vehicles from the Army. The large pig house at the rear of the mill was converted into a vehicle maintenance and repair workshop. It was in this workshop that Aldridge and Barnett refurbished the vehicles and built new bodies on the lorries to meet the needs of their trade: Barnett had been a sales representative for Oldacres before the war but had been trained as a mechanic and fitter in the RAF.

Other buildings in the village were undergoing a change of

use and land was being taken out of agricultural production. New housing accommodation was urgently needed for the growing population of Bishops Cleeve and land between Tobysfield and Two Hedges, which was part of Oldacres farm, was some of the first to be taken. William John was far from pleased to let it go, however the land from Cleevelands Farm which had been used by the Army was now returned and to some extent this did compensate for the loss. Unfortunately the Army had used Gotherington Lane land as a heavy vehicle park and workshop. The soil was polluted by acid, and it took more than 20 years of ploughing and treatment before it produced a proper crop.

The relationship between William John and Harold Keen, his foreman at Cleevelands Farm, had not improved with the passage of time. Harold handed in his notice shortly after the war ended and his place was taken by Jack Ballinger. Jack only stayed on the farm for a short period but during that time his young son was badly bitten by their dog. The Governor was at Cleevelands at the time and he bundled the boy into his car and set off without delay for Cheltenham Hospital. There he was angered that the standard of treatment which the boy was given would leave him scarred for life. He made his views known to the hospital staff in no uncertain terms, and without further ado took the boy on to Gloucester Infirmary. At Gloucester the stitches were removed and cosmetic treatment was given to the damaged area of the boy's face. The Ballingers were much indebted to the Governor for his prompt and positive action.

The population growth in Bishops Cleeve meant that more land was soon needed for housing and for a secondary school. It came from Lynworth Farm where Oldacres had been the tenants for about 15 years. The farm house, which had been the home of Syd and Doris throughout their married life, was demolished and they moved to Cleevelands which had just been vacated by the Ballingers. The loss of further productive land was a blow to Oldacres farming interests but none of that land had been in their ownership, and so their capital assets were unaffected.

The authorised capital had not changed since the company had been formed in 1923, when only half the 8,000 ordinary shares had been take up and none of the 22,000 preference shares had been allocated. In 1948 John Oldacre applied to the board for an additional 1,000 ordinary shares of £1 each at par, and this request was granted. This change meant that 62½ percent of the ordinary share capital had been issued and fully paid, of which William John held 50 percent, John 30 percent, Mary 10 percent, and the remaining 10 percent was held by Gladys Oldacre and the three employee directors. The board also allocated 11,800 of the 5 percent preference shares to twenty four applicants and they repaid in full the thirty eight debenture shares which had been held by Anna Oldacre and Alice Redman.

The first two or three years after the war were marked by a gradual improvement in trading conditions and by relative calm at the meetings of the board. The family were not at home and were becoming less involved in the day to day running of the business. Business was not discussed at Mill House and there were none of the arguments at meal times which had been a feature at the Fieldgate dining table. Kay was happy with her two young daughters and did not become involved with Oldacres in any way. She knew that her mother-in-law was still fully committed to the company, but she had no intention of becoming so involved. Kay's lack of interest in Oldacres was accepted by John but her reluctance to act as hostess at business functions meant that he had often to ask his sister, June, to be his partner.

William John was approaching 60 years of age and felt that the time had come for him to hand over to his son. He decided to give up as joint managing director and to remain only as chairman of the company. When John was appointed managing director, he considered that he had full responsibility and authority for managing the company and for carrying out the decisions of the board within the agreed company policy, but William John had very different ideas about the respective roles of managing director and chairman. As chairman and head of the family, he believed that he had full authority to give orders to his son or to instruct any member of the staff to do his bidding. The chairman and the managing director were on a collision course, and the many rows which ensued reverberated across the whole family. Family life was far from peaceful but this was not necessarily bad for the company. The dissension sharpened decision making and kept managers fully alert. The company prospered.

In the autumn of 1948 William John was given leave of absence so that he and his wife could make a long-awaited trip to New Zealand. William John was always out and about talking to his friends and customers, and in this way he picked up a considerable amount of information and learned much about the fortunes of his neighbours. Shortly before he left for New Zealand he learned that the owners of Yew Tree Farm, Gotherington were in financial difficulties. The farm stretched along the east side of Gotherington Lane from the boundary of Cleevelands Farm to Gotherington village. He was never one to miss a good business opportunity. The acquisition of the farm would give him ownership of all the land between the road, the railway and the two villages. He made his interest known to the owners and told his son to keep a close watch on the situation. He left for New Zealand in April 1949, a few days before his 60th birthday.

William John and Gladys sailed from Southampton on the *Dominion Monarch*, travelling via South Africa. On arrival in New Zealand they lived in Auckland with Hilda and her family, but made a number of trips around the country. The holiday came to an abrupt end for William John when he learned that the bank were foreclosing on the owners of Yew Tree Farm. He returned home in haste. His offer for the farm was accepted and he was back in New Zealand by August 1950 to rejoin his wife Gladys who had stayed on with Hilda who was expecting a baby.

William John played no major role in management of the business for almost two years, except for the Yew Tree Farm negotiations. When he did come back to the business in the spring of 1951, John was firmly in the saddle and was developing the future management policies of the company. John was a business man and not a trader. His decisions were based on careful market assessment and sound business practice.

On his return, William John was kept busy with the bakery and the farm. Mr Bondolfi had returned to his own business premises in Eastbourne and the management at Charlton Kings was causing problems.

The Governor found himself deeply involved in day to day matters at the bakery. It was always difficult to find and keep a good foreman baker and control of the large fleet of vans taxed Mr Hamblin to the limit. At Christmas, Easter and at other bank holidays, the Governor was kept busy late into the night supervising the outside sales staff. Mrs Oldacre and any of the family who were staying at Fieldgate, began to dislike the thought of hot cross buns because they brought with them such major problems for the Governor. In the winter and particularly on Christmas Eve the problems stemmed from snow, frost or broken down vans. Customers rang because deliveries had not been made or were late. When a van became stuck in snow or otherwise broken down, the Governor charged off in his car armed with spanners, tow rope and cans of oil and petrol.

At Yew Tree Farm there was a great deal of work required to bring the farm up to the standards which William John demanded. The ditches and drains had to be cleaned, repaired and improved. Many of the fields were not large enough for modern farming equipment and hedges had to be removed and other hedges laid. The 150 acre farm included a good house and farm yard, a group of stone buildings and orchards on the opposite side of the road to the house, and there were barns on the north side of the Gretton road. All the buildings and orchards were in the centre of Gotherington and many needed repair. The Governor wanted another stock yard and he built this within the farmyard. The company farm now covered more than 350 acres and included 50 acres of hill land on the east side of the Cheltenham to Honeybourne railway embankment. Oldacres used the farm as a trial and research ground for their products, and as a shop window. Careful records were kept of the types of seed and fertilizer which were used; the specifications and rates of spread of any dressings which were applied to control weeds, pests and diseases; and the yield and quality of the crops. The feeding of pigs, poultry, cattle and sheep was carefully monitored to check on the conversion factors and the quality of the milk, eggs and meat. Customers were invited to visit the farm and John Oldacre organised farm walks. These walks were attended by as many as 100 guests who could see for themselves and have explained to them, the work which was going on and the results which were being achieved.

John knew that it was important for Oldacres to be seen by the farmers as a forward looking and efficient company and that to this end their presence at local agricultural shows was valuable. Shortly after the war the Bath and West Show was held on Smith's sports field at the Newlands, Cheltenham. Oldacres were awarded the contract for the supply of all forage at the show and they provided the sprays and fertilizers for the trial plots at the show ground. The company had a presence at the Blue Cross stand and was well represented by four family directors and Mr Counsell. Later at the permanent home of the show in Malvern, Oldacres had their own stand but this was discontinued when it was found not to be cost effective. Gloucester market moved to its present site in Estcourt Road and Oldacres opened a shop within the market. Throughout these years they offered information about the results which they were achieving with their own products on their own farm.

On market day, Mr Counsell was available at the Gloucester market shop. His contribution to the success of the firm was always recognised by the Governor, but William John's relationship with Mr Bick was somewhat strained and his promotion to a directorship did little towards improving those relationships. After William John returned to England, Mr Bick found that his position was even more difficult than before. He did his best to implement the policies of the company and to carry out the instructions given by John Oldacre, the managing director but William John criticised him constantly and issued instructions contrary to those given by his son. Towards the end of May 1951 Mr Bick asked for an interview with the Governor and on 30 May tendered his resignation. He expressed his regret about severing his connection with the firm after 16 years of faithful and strenuous service, but explained that he had obtained a post in Poole, Dorset. He handed back the shares which William John had given to him and he left the company on 30 June 1951. Jim Payne was promoted to undertake some of Mr Bick's work but he was not made a director until 1953, when Mr Hamblin resigned on the grounds of ill health. Mr Counsell now trebled his holding of ordinary shares and two new managers were appointed – Ken Talbot as accountant and Joe Stephens as mill manager.

The departure of Mr Bick came at a time when the company was preparing to make major strides forward. William John had taken many commercial risks since he had joined his father in 1904 and in 1951 he showed his total confidence in his own business abilities and those of his son. Although he had a legal charge on Cleevelands Farm and The Pollards, he agreed to deposit those deeds together with the deeds of Yew Tree Farm and 40 Winchcombe Street with Martins Bank against a greatly enhanced overdraft provision. The Governor's money was tied to the business but he was prepared to risk all of his capital in the interest of expansion. It was his readiness to take such risks which gave Oldacres the opportunity to become a major animal feed company.

An opportunity arose in March 1953. At a special meeting the directors were told that W Ride and Company, one of the largest corn merchants in Cheltenham and a major competitor was on the market. Ride's owned a large shop and warehouse at 31 Winchcombe Street, two further shops and other properties in the town and the directors agreed that a firm offer of £23,000 should be made for the property, plant and transport, plus a sum for the stock at an agreed value. Two extraordinary General Meetings of the company and a number of board meetings were held over the next six months. Authority was given for the directors to overdraw the company bank account to a sum exceeding the amount of the issued capital. The bid for Ride's was accepted. Oldacres sold a store in Alstone Road to Cheltenham Agricultural Traders, another competitor; deposited the deeds of all the former Ride's property with the bank; sold 40 Winchcombe Street; and exchanged the 52 acres of hill land at Yew Tree Farm for six acres of land adjoining Cleevelands Farm on the west side of Gotherington Lane and a financial consideration. During this period of intense activity, William John was taken ill and underwent a prostate operation.

The purchase of Ride's had hardly been completed before Oldacres were making an offer for the business of C H Dee.

This offer was not accepted for another three years by which time Oldacres annual sales had doubled again and 5,000 tons of animal feed compounds were being produced in their mill. During these years they increased their transport fleet with the introduction of lorries fitted with telehoists and lorries, equipment and stock were purchased from the old established Kidderminster corn merchant, Clement Dalley, which had ceased to trade. Old buildings behind the original mill at Bishops Cleeve were demolished, a new warehouse was built, a larger cuber installed, alterations were made at Tewkesbury and 31 Winchcombe Street and a wooden office extension was built at Bishops Cleeve. Shortly after the war Oldacres had bought the land and cottage alongside Mill House from Charlie Trapp for the sum of £1,000. Charlie had been given a rent free tenancy of the cottage but the land was used by Cleeve Motors, a separate company formed by John and involved in motor car sales and maintenance. When Charlie Trapp died, Oldacres decided to carry out improvements on the land and to refurbish the cottage.

Changes were also made in office procedure and in the management structure. Mary Charnock resigned as company secretary but remained a director, and her duties as company secretary were taken over by Ken Talbot. John Oldacre was not satisfied with the method of calculating staff bonus, nor with the accounting procedure. Mechanical accounting was introduced and separate trading and profit and loss accounts were in future to be produced for the corn side; the bakery, which now included Boskett's Bakery, Gloucester Road, Cheltenham; and the farm. It had long been of concern to John that resources from the milling side of the business had been diverted to both the bakery and the farm without financial adjustment. These changes meant that the staff bonus could be based on branch performance and branch profit on earning power, and could be paid earlier. These were not changes which the Governor really welcomed. However, the factors leading up to the change were similar to those which the Governor himself had complained about when his father was running the farm as a separate entity from the business; the animal feed company was subsidising other activities. The Governor retaliated by questioning the running of Cleeve Motors as a company independent of Oldacres, but the accounts showed that all was in order.

William John was in hospital briefly in 1956, for a check up on his condition following the prostate operation.

John Oldacre was anxious to expand on feed compounding and this demanded considerable capital investment. In his opinion, the bakery did not fit comfortably with the other activities of the company and the capital employed could be better utilised. In April 1957, British Bakeries Ltd made an offer of £30,000 for the freehold of the Charlton Kings properties and the bakery business, plus stock at valuation. The offer was accepted and agreement was reached whereby Oldacres had the use of the corn shop at Charlton Kings in return for them garaging the ten bakery vans taken over by British Bakeries Ltd. John was appointed as a local non-executive director by British Bakeries and held that position for five years.

(ii) New Zealand holidays

William John and his wife had much enjoyed their first visit to New Zealand. They had had an excellent sea voyage on *SS Dominion Monarch*, at the end of which they had the joy of seeing Hilda after almost four years, and of meeting Bruce their first grandson. Hilda and Mervyn had had a difficult start to their married life in New Zealand, but had at last found a comfortable home on the North Shore at Auckland where they were able to accommodate Hilda's parents. The pace and quality of life in New Zealand had suited William John and Gladys and made them wonder about the changed life they would have led, if they had not given up their passage to that country in 1923. The holiday was cut short for William John by news that Yew Tree Farm was on the market. William John returned home alone. Unfortunately, his wife had broken her ankle and was not fit to travel, but also she wanted to stay in Auckland because Hilda was expecting her second child. William John sailed on the *Rangitiki* and travelled across the Pacific and through the Panama Canal. He was occasionally seasick but he loved the sea and he always felt completely relaxed on board ship. He

William John and Gladys Oldacre – 1949

was friendly with his fellow passengers and liked to talk with them about New Zealand, the places which he had visited around the world, and about his business. He was good company and on the four week voyage he received many invitations to join the Captain for cocktails. He was also in great demand at other social events which were held on board. He was handsome, jovial and looked much younger than his 60 years. He could find plenty of partners and by the time the ship reached Balboa, he had a regular following. He invited four of the ladies to join him on a daring escapade to the night life of the town. The party do not appear to have come to any harm and after Gladys had returned home these ladies visited Fieldgate.

Once he had completed the negotiations for Yew Tree Farm successfully, William John was ready to return to New Zealand. He knew that Hilda had been pressing Catherine and June to visit her new home and so he suggested that they should accompany him. At that time, Catherine was still nursing and June was employed as nanny to Timothy the young son of Hugh Clutton–Brock, the headmaster of Cheltenham College junior school. Before the family left

England they visited the Wirral where William John talked endlessly to my father about the wonders of New Zealand, and the excellent manner in which John was running the business.

William John and his daughters sailed out of Tilbury on the *Rangitata* on 17 June, 1950. Catherine and June had both paid their own fare but their father paid all other expenses which they incurred. The girls travelled together in a first class twin-bedded cabin on the verandah deck quite close to the one occupied by their father. Alice and Arthur Redman were also aboard and William John found their company restricting and rather heavy. He was out to enjoy himself and to give his daughters a real taste of the world. He was extremely generous to them. Alice did not approve of her brother's light hearted mood and was shocked by the freedom which he gave to his daughters.

When the ship arrived at Balboa, the girls found the conditions extremely hot and humid. But William John was determined to entertain them well and persuaded five other passengers to share a taxi into town with him and his daughters. He was looking forward to returning to the night club which he had visited on his way home with his lady admirers. When they arrived at the venue which he had chosen for the evening, the outside of the building was brightly lighted with neon tubes and decorated with coloured pictures of scantily clad girls. Inside the atmosphere was sultry, the lights were dim and the clientele mainly sailors. The sailors were buying beer for themselves and coloured water for the hostesses, who in turn were getting commission on every drink which was purchased. Catherine and June were amused that their father had thought that this atmosphere would be educational. But, William John was paying, they enjoyed the light refreshments and drinks, watched the antics of the couples, and waited for the much acclaimed cabaret. The lights on the small stage came up, there was a roll of drums, and the master of ceremonies entered.

'Ladies and gentlemen, the moment for which you have all been waiting. I give you the star of our show. Straight from Brighton, England. The magnificent Lola.'

Catherine and June could not contain their mirth. Lola made her entrance clad in a G-string and with a tassel attached to each nipple. Lola began to move her hips provocatively to the sound of sensual music. These movements together with outrageous contortions, persuaded the tassel on her right nipple to swing in a clockwise direction and the tassel on her left nipple to swing in an anti-clockwise direction. They watched the great concentration on their father's face with much more interest. Eventually it was time to return to the ship and the girls assured their father that they had found the performance most interesting but a trifle difficult to emulate.

The voyage continued across the Pacific. The crew enacted the Father Neptune ritual as the vessel crossed the equator but it was only men new to the experience who suffered the indignity of a ducking in the pool. Catherine, June and the other ladies were only required to watch the ceremony. At 11 am on 18 August the *Rangitata* sailed into Wellington harbour. The family dis-embarked and after a quick look around the sights of the capital, boarded the overnight train for Auckland.

At Auckland station they were met by Hilda and taken to her home for a welcoming party. During the Governor's absence his second grandson, John Cliffe had been born. Hilda's house was full amd Catherine and June took lodgings with George and Ethyl Oak, her next door neighbours where they felt very much at home. The girls made a number of holiday trips around both the North and South Islands, but they had to find work in order to keep themselves. A maternity home had offered them both jobs immediately they arrived in Auckland but they decided not to take the posts. Catherine wanted a change from nursing and worked at Rainsters, a company which made mackintoshes. June was employed at a home for polio victims.

William John and Gladys continued to live with Hilda on the north shore. The house had a wonderful view of Rangitoto Island and across the harbour. Auckland has now spread over a vast area, but in 1950 there was little development on the north shore and much of the area was swamp land. New cars were almost unobtainable but visitors were allowed to import a car for their own use and then to sell it in New Zealand at the end of their stay. William John took a new car with him on each visit. He and his wife saw places of interest in New Zealand before they became major tourist attractions. At the hot sulphur springs in Rotorua there were no defined routes and no protective railings. The public buildings at Wellington which lies across the Great Pacific fault had not then been designed to resist earthquake shock, and visits to St Joseph glacier on the South Island were very adventurous. On these journeys they called on relations and friends. George Redman, a brother of Alice's husband Arthur, farmed over 2,000 acres of hill land near to Masterton. He had been a boyhood friend of William John and they were able to re-establish their old relationship when they went out riding together. They would mount up as dawn was breaking and spend the day riding the boundary of the farm, repairing fences and keeping an eye on the vast number of sheep which George shepherded. Jack Denley, another old friend and a cousin to Hanks Beckingsale's first wife, a butcher in Ashburton on the South Island, was delighted to see the Oldacres again after so many years. Many friends also welcomed them into their homes. William John and Gladys found a close affinity to Bruce Coleman's parents, Reg and Ethyl. Reg owned a small mixed farm at Ohingaiti near to Levin. The atmosphere in the home and on the farm, and the lifestyle of the Coleman's was similar to that which William John had known when he was a boy. When they arrived at Ohingaiti, Bruce was still at home but was engaged to be married. Gladys did not like to be away from Hilda and her children for too long and so the trips never stretched over too many weeks.

On his second visit to New Zealand, William John was anxious to return to England with his wife without too much delay. He booked a passage on the *Dominion Monarch*, a ship which he very much liked and on which he made three voyages between 1949 and 1958. The captain of the *Dominion Monarch* was a Quaker. On their first voyage the captain had invited Mr and Mrs Oldacre to a number of his cocktail parties and soon realised that Gladys Oldacre did not take alcoholic drink. On subsequent voyages he invited them to sit at his table in the dining saloon. William John was flattered, but he resented the fact that at the Captain's table he could not have wine with his meals. This voyage with his wife was more subdued than his earlier trip home on the *Rangitiki*, but

Fieldgate – 1952

he was happy and contented to have Gladys with him again.
The Governor and Mrs Oldacre arrived back in England
before Christmas 1950.

(iii) June's wedding

After a year in New Zealand, June felt that the time had
come for her to return home. She booked a passage on *SS
Stratheden* from Auckland via Australia, Ceylon and the Suez
Canal. She was due to sail in August 1951, but the New
Zealand dock workers were on strike and so she had to fly to
Sydney, Australia to catch the *Stratheden.* She left Auckland
in a Solent flying boat which carried 47 passengers at a speed
of 255 miles per hour. The aircraft developed engine trouble
two hours out from Sydney and the final stage of the flight
was made a few feet above sea level but they arrived
safely.The *Stratheden* called at Melbourne, Adelaide and
Perth, and at each port June was greeted by Australian
friends whom she had met on holiday in New Zealand. She

was well looked after in Australia and on the ship itself. Kim, her cabin steward turned out to be a relation of the family who lived next door to Beckingsale's shop at Bishops Cleeve. Cabin stewards were not allowed to drink on duty. Much to the delight of Kim, June ordered a pint of beer to be served in her cabin before dinner each evening. The *Stratheden* called at Columbo, Aden, Port Said and Marseilles before docking at Tilbury on 24 September 1951.

The Governor and Mrs Oldacre met June at the dockside. The family then spent a few days in London and saw the musicals *Carousel* and *South Pacific* before returning to Fieldgate. On her first evening in England June telephone me and we arranged that I should spend a holiday at Fieldgate starting on 8 October.

I drove down to Bishops Cleeve in my 1936 Ford 8, and for the first time I was nervous as I entered the yard at Fieldgate. June was in a similar state but as soon as we greeted one another the tension eased. The next evening we told June's mother that we wished to become engaged and that I would be speaking to the Governor on the following day. I suppose we hoped that she would pave the way for me. The next morning, I walked around the farm with the Governor with the intention of raising my urgent question with him, but I was not given the opportunity. He was playing with me. Finally after lunch, while June and her mother were doing the washing up, I rushed into the matter with the Governor before he dozed off.

'Governor. June and I wish to be married.'

His first response was to chortle in a manner to which we were all accustomed. Eventually he said, 'Oh you do! You'll find her expensive to keep.'

I was satisfied with his answer. Meanwhile, June had to prevent her mother from listening at the door by attacking her with a wet dishcloth. I rang my parents who were delighted with the news.

The Governor was a generous man but it never paid to ask him for anything. He seldom gave his children a Christmas or birthday present but on occasions he was willing to dig deep into his pocket. If he thought his daughters looked well in a new set of clothes, he would say,

'You do look nice. What did that cost you?'

On being told the price, he might open his wallet and pass the sum over to them. He took the whole family out to dinner quite regularly, often in company with my mother and father. The two men would take it in turns to pay the bill and both mother and Mrs Oldacre really enjoyed the outings. Mrs Oldacre was not fond of the main course but loved sweets, particularly when there was plenty of cream. One evening at the Worcestershire Hotel in Droitwich the head waiter realised that she had a passion for peach melba. She had consumed two helpings. The waiter came up to the table with another peach melba.

'Excuse me madam. We have just one peach melba left. I am sure you would enjoy it.'

'Thank you very much,' and she proceeded to tuck into her third sweet.

While we were engaged, the Governor took us to the theatre on a number of occasions. In January we dined at the Randolph Hotel in Oxford and then set off for the theatre to see an ice pantomime. On the way we stopped to look into the window of a furniture shop.

'Do you like that suite?' the Governor asked June.

It was a three piece utility suite with a light wooden frame. 'It's very nice and as much as we could afford,' replied June.

'You had better order it then,' the Governor remarked and he moved towards the shop door.

Inside the shop we made a closer inspection and June told the assistant that we would have the suite. While June was telling the assistant the address to which the goods must be sent, the Governor signed a cheque.

The wedding was planned for 23 August 1952 and the Governor decided that he would make the affair a real family celebration. As the wedding day approached he saw a gold lame wedding gown at Cavendish House, Cheltenham. He told June and her mother about it and said that if they liked it they could charge it to his account. They went straight to the shop and tried on the dress which fitted June perfectly. This was fortunate because they knew that he would not meet the cost of any other gown which they chose.

The preparation of the guest list did not pass without incident. The Governor was anxious to invite some friends who were not well known to June. She would not have objected to this if he had not crossed off the list some of her friends because he felt that the numbers were becoming too large. Strong words were exchanged and the Governor walked out of the house in high dudgeon. When he presented himself for the next meal it was clear that he was in no mood to speak to his wife or daughter. His mood was ended abruptly by June.

'Mother and I have a very great deal to do and so it's no use you behaving in that stupid manner,' she told him.

Gladys waited for her husband to explode with anger. There was a pause and then the Governor laughed loudly. The crisis was over and a compromise was reached over the guest list.

Housing was difficult in 1953 but we managed to find a suitable semi-detached property near to Heswall in the Wirral. We had sufficient capital to meet about half the cost of the property and we knew that neither my father nor the Governor would approve of us going to a building society. We did not know the best way to solve the problem, but we need not have worried. The Governor made us a handsome wedding present.

It rained heavily for days before the wedding. The reception was to be held in a marquee on the lawn at Fieldgate and when the men arrived they were doubtful about erecting it on the soft ground, but all went well. Charlton Kings Bakery were commissioned to do the catering and the tiered wedding cake was baked in three square boxes made especially for the task by Alan Aldridge. Mr Hamblin and Miss Wise took charge of the catering and Doris and her helpers were ready to look after the guests.

The sun was shining in a clear blue sky on the morning of 23 August 1952, and the Governor was a proud man when he walked down the aisle of St Michael and All Angels with his youngest daughter. She was dressed in her gold lame gown and was wearing the same Brussels lace veil which had earlier been worn by Hilda and other members of the family. Catherine and her nieces Jill and Susan Oldacre were bridesmaids. Catherine was dressed in a patterned pink brocade and the children were in turquoise satin. The ceremony was conducted by Canon E C Hanson from Emmanuel Church, Cheltenham who had earlier been curate

Wedding of June Oldacre to Denys Charnock

at Bishops Cleeve and was a friend of the family. Canon Barton from St Stephens, Prenton also took part in the service.

When the guests arrived at Fieldgate for the reception they found the lounge overflowing with wedding presents. The austerity of the previous 13 years had eased and we received presents sufficient to complete the furnishing of our new home. The reception was lavish. My best man, Geoffrey Harper, read telegrams from all over the world. My father, as the oldest friend of the bride's family, proposed the toast to the bride and bridegroom. He spoke of the long association of our two families and his delight that with the marriages of Mary and Ernest and now June and me, we had become the 'United Families'.

(iv) The last months at Fieldgate

In January 1954, I was appointed to a post in Gloucester and we stayed at Fieldgate for a short time before buying a house in Churchdown. At the same time Hilda, Mervyn and their two sons came to spend 12 months in England and lived at Fieldgate. The Governor was happy to preside once again at the dining table surrounded by a large family. He was even more delighted when all 16 members were present at dinner on Christmas Day 1954 – he and his wife; Mary, Ernest and their children Helen and Christopher; John and Kay with Jill and Susan; Catherine; Hilda and Mervyn with Bruce and John; and June and me with our daughter Sarah. This great occasion was only marred when a few days later, a number of the party went down with influenza.

The Christmas party was the final chapter in the 30 year history of the Oldacre family at Fieldgate. This very ordinary Cotswold stone farm house had been turned into a wonderful family home by William John and Gladys. A warm welcome had been given to guests from all over the world. We all loved the house but Gladys Oldacre had found it to be hard work to keep clean and to keep warm in the winter. She wanted her husband to build a modern house in the village.

The orchards and fields in the centre of Bishops Cleeve were slowly being eaten up by housing, and during 1954 Bert Long sold his farm for building. William John was deeply disappointed. He had once thought that Pecked Piece Farm could be added to Fieldgate, but he now realised that the changes occuring in the village meant that the land at Fieldgate would also soon go for building. A few months earlier, Yew Tree Farm house in Gotherington had become vacant, and much to Gladys' disappointment, her husband decided to refurbish that house for their own use. Yew Tree was in the centre of Gotherington and only a few feet behind the road line on Gotherington lane. The back of the house opened directly onto the barns and stockyard and there was no lawn and hardly any flower garden. Gladys had always loved her garden and on fine days in summer had always served tea on the lawn. Yew Tree was a solid stone building but only the kitchen and the main bedroom could be compared with the accommodation at Fieldgate. Improvements were made and Yew Tree was their home for three years. The Governor always claimed that he grew better vegetables in the kitchen garden at Yew Tree than anywhere else.

The family did their best to support their mother in her attempts to persuade William John to build a new house. We all thought that the best site on the farm was on the higher ground in Gotherington where one of the orchards abutted the road to Gretton. The Governor did not agree. When he did decide to build a new home he chose a field near to Bishops Cleeve which he had pointed out to me many years before as we walked along the railway embankment. It was part of Millham Farm, adjacent to Gotherington Lane and within easy walking distance of Bishops Cleeve. It was a field from which he could see the whole of his farm while sitting in his own armchair. William John and Gladys decided that they would build a bungalow on the site and that the design would be based on the homes which they had seen on their travels; an L-shape with the angle of the L facing south to form a sun trap. The basic design was spoiled by the local planning committee which refused to allow them to put the front door in the angle of the L and also refused the use of green tiles. Construction of the bungalow began in 1957 while they were away in New Zealand again.

7

WILLIAM JOHN'S THREE SISTERS

William John had many acquaintances but Jack Charnock was his only close friend. His family totally fulfilled his need for personal relationships. His sisters Ada, Anna, and Alice were becoming elderly. Family loyalty dominated their lives and far exceeded any differences which had arisen between brother and sisters over the years. After the death of their father they accepted William John as head of the family and they became proud of his success and the loving care which he showed towards his mother. William John visited his mother daily at The Pollards until she died.

His sister, Ada, had shaken off the ties of the family business early in her life and she was a successful teacher and headmistress. Much of her strength came from an open mind and her deep Christian faith. She knew what she wanted from life, she was sure of the path to take, and she set course resolutely to reach her goals. She had the ability to encourage and stimulate her students to achieve the maximum from the talents with which they had been endowed. She was a farmer's wife and a mother, but her interests were intellectual rather than domestic. During her early married life her mother-in-law kept house for her family and later the task was taken on by her daughter Dorothy. Ada was widowed shortly after the end of the war. She continued living at Corse Lawn where she was still the headmistress of the school and organist at Eldersfield Church. As time went on she felt that her roots in Bishops Cleeve were deep and she returned to the village to live in a pleasant bungalow which she built in the garden of Owls End, a garden which had become much too large for her sister Anna. Ada was interested in people and she was pleased to be near to her family again and to be with some of her childhood friends. She knew the men at Oldacres who came from the old village families, and she was pleased to find that Leslie Aston delivered her coal. Leslie still remembers her with affection.

'Good morning Leslie, how are your family?' was the usual greeting.

'Good morning Mrs Irons. Nicely thank you.'

On one memorable occasion Mrs Irons followed this friendly greeting by adding 'It's always good to see you. My brother has a very high regard for you and all that you do for the firm.'

'I don't know about that,' replied Leslie, 'We've just had a bloody great row, – Beg your pardon mam.'

Mrs Irons smiled. 'Ah well. He speaks well of you and he always did prefer men who could stand up to him.'

In her own way her younger sister, Alice, was equally as capable as Ada. She was cautious and meticulous in the home and in her business life. Alice should have been encouraged to become a professional accountant like her uncle Richard Minett rather than a book–keeper in the family business, but duty kept her in that role and her childless late marriage failed to give her a sense of fulfilment in life. She was frustrated by her position. Her brother took far too many risks, and in those risks she saw danger to both the business and the standing of her father and the family. Early in her business life, Alice had challenged her brother and invariably lost. Later she used more covert methods when she wished to influence her father and her sister Anna against the ideas or actions of William John.

Arthur Redman seemed to be little help to Alice. He was some years younger than she and became a farmer when he retired from the Guards. He farmed land at Twyning near Tewkesbury which had been given to his wife by her father. William John did not consider that his brother-in-law was hard-working nor did he think that Arthur was a good farmer. William John openly criticised Arthur's farming methods and achievements, and this did little to heal the wounds which Alice felt that she had suffered at the hands of her brother in the business. It is surprising that Alice could applaud William John's success and at the same criticise the man and his approach to business. Alice sold the farm in the early 1950s and moved to Owls End where she and her husband lived in a separate part of the house from Anna. Alice died from cancer in 1956. The bulk of her estate went to her husband but she left a small legacy to Catherine, Hilda and June. It was generally accepted that the gifts were given to her three younger nieces because Mary and John had inherited shares in Oldacres from her father.

Anna only remained at Owls End for a short time after the death of her sister. She had reduced the size of the garden by allowing Ada to build a bungalow and had sold the orchard for housing, but the house was far too large for one person on their own. She owned land on the opposite side of the road to Owls End and had a bungalow built for herself. She then sold Owls End and used the money that was left over to supplement her income.

As the second child Anna was sandwiched between two sisters of strong personality, and she found it difficult to compete with them. She was a woman of high ideals and a strong sense of duty towards her parents. Although it was never mentioned in the family the baptismal records at the church indicate that she had a twin sister who died in infancy. When her youngest sister Lucy died, Anna was 36 years old and she had selflessly devoted the previous ten years of her life to nursing her ailing sister. She never married. She seemed to lack the boldness of other members of the family and William John always believed that she would have loved to kick over the traces but lacked the courage to do so.

Anna may have been reserved but she had many good friends and became contented in later life. In her youth she had travelled over much of Europe and throughout her long life she had regular seaside holidays in England. She appreciated simple pleasures, sitting quietly to enjoy the beauty of her garden and the countryside, or at the seaside watching the waves break on the shore. Even at 80 years old she occasionally showed an adventurous spirit. Towards the end of her life she was a regular visitor to our home in Sussex and it was difficult to prevent her from taking a day trip across the Channel from Newhaven to Dieppe, and she was ready for a pleasure boat trip around Beachy Head whatever the condition of the sea.

When William John returned from New Zealand for the

third time, Ada and Anna were both living within a short distance of the place where the family had been born and he visited them regularly. Ada and William John showed great respect for each other and neither attempted to interfere with the other. On the other hand, William John was always ready to offer advice and guidance to Anna although she seldom asked for it.

Ada and Anna both lived until they were 89 years of age in the mid-1970s.

8

CHARTING THE COURSE
1958–1970

(i) Changes in the air

On their return from New Zealand, William John and Gladys lived with John and Kay for a few weeks but in the early summer of 1958, they were able to move into Homelands, the bungalow which long ago they had dreamed of building in that field in Gotherington Lane. The bungalow was designed to suit their needs, to be comfortable when they were on their own, and yet to have sufficient accommodation to house the family when they visited their parents. William John was a big man and hated to be confined and so the rooms were large. The double glazed picture windows in the lounge allowed a clear view across the farm to the north, west and south, and double doors in the south window gave access to a terrace contained in the angle of the L-shaped building. This terrace offered a sun trap and an excellent place for them to sit and take their tea on warm days, a habit they wished to continue in their new home. The kitchen and dining room were separated only by a divider unit which served as both a sideboard and a china cabinet. The arrangement was designed to reduce the distance between the stove and the dining table which could then be used at every meal without adding to the domestic workload. Gladys had insisted upon an Aga Cooker which also provided hot water and had the added advantage of warming the kitchen and the dining area. There was a small office for the Governor and two large bedrooms on the ground floor. The most southerly bedroom, which extended over the full width of that wing of the bungalow, was used by William John and

Gladys and gave them views of Cleeve Hill, Nottingham Hill and the Malverns as they lay in bed savouring a pot of morning tea. The roof area was vast. Some of the space was taken up with two further bedrooms which could be shut off from the rest of the bungalow until members of the family came to stay. Homelands offered an ideal residence for a couple in their seventies and they should have been able to relax and enjoy life to the full.

Gladys was delighted with her new home. She had lived all her life in old stone properties which always seemed to her to be cold and draughty, and to demand constant and fruitless cleaning. There were carpets on all the floors of the new bungalow, it was heated by electric storage heaters, easily cleaned and she had the Aga for cooking. Gladys felt that she needed little help to run the home but she did have Doris in for a few hours each week. Her children and grandchildren, all of whom meant a great deal to her, were widely scattered, but they made regular visits to Homelands whether they lived in Bishops Cleeve or New Zealand. Gladys was thoroughly happy and contented. Unfortunately the same was not always true of her husband.

The Governor managed the half-acre garden himself, looked after the stoking of the Aga, and the cleaning and maintenance of the Baxi fire in the lounge which gave them comfort and cheer on a winter's day even in a centrally heated home. He worked with great vigour in the garden, but the plot was too small to keep him fully occupied and before long he had extended the vegetable patch deep into the field behind the bungalow. The soil was a heavy clay but he found no difficulty in doing all the manual tasks himself. But the Governor was soon bored at home and was once again anxious to play a major part in the management of W J Oldacre Ltd.

The shortage of capital for expansion was a constant problem for Oldacres. The sale of the bakery had been followed by improvements at the Bishops Cleeve mill and at the shop in Cheltenham High Street; the updating and renewal of the transport fleet; and the construction of a new pig fattening house and a deep litter house for poultry in the farm buildings at Yew Tree. Output and productivity increased at the mills and sales were approaching £500,000

Bishops Cleeve Mill, Bishops Cleeve, Cheltenham

per annum. The company was now moving forward at an increasing pace and there was a growing momentum for expansion. William John wanted to be involved and while his son was prepared to talk with him, he would not tolerate interference with management.

They had made a wise decision when they transferred to Martins Bank. Martins was not one of the big five banks and Oldacres became customers almost as soon as the Cheltenham branch was opened. The company account was large when compared with the accounts of most other customers. John and his father had regular meetings with the district general manager and relationships were excellent at both district and local level. Martins were satisfied with the management and organisation at Oldacres, and offered relatively large overdraft facilities but by 1959 they were suggesting the formation of a public limited company. The Governor and John were prepared to consider the possibility of a flotation on the Stock Market but they preferred to maintain the status of a family company. They agreed with the bank that the success of any flotation would be influenced mainly by healthy accounts, but while bearing the matter in mind they looked towards ways and means of raising more capital themselves.

John Oldacre and the other directors paid particular attention to future financial planning. They were satisfied that sufficient reserves would be forthcoming each financial year to finance the anticipated expansion on turnover, but that they would not at the same time be able to reduce borrowing from the bank, or increase investment in fixed assets without releasing more of their freehold property. The farm represented the most readily realisable asset, but it was invaluable as an advertising media for the business and was producing a healthy return on the capital employed. The financial evaluation concluded that if Oldacres was to remain a private company, then there would have to be strict budgetry discipline and that shareholders would have to be content with a fairly small distribution of profit. One problem was highlighted – the early death of either the Governor or his son as the major shareholders would greatly embarrass the company and they agreed that further consideration must be given to that matter.

During the financial appraisal John Oldacre was approached by J Reynolds and Company Ltd of Gloucester. Reynolds were flour millers with whom Oldacres had had friendly trade relations for many years. Both companies were aware that Holton and Son of Ducklington Mill, near Witney was on the market privately. Holtons was a combined flour and provender business with a small turnover. Reynolds were interested in acquiring the flour datum of Holtons and suggested that Oldacres and Reynolds should form a separate joint company to run the provender side of the business. John realised that the total input for any joint company would come from Oldacres and after talking the matter over with his father, advised Reynolds that the proposition would not be acceptable to his company. As an alternative he suggested that Reynolds should take a minority holding in Oldacres which he believed would be advantageous to both companies and would offer the opportunity to strengthen his board. Holtons operated in an area adjoining Oldacres eastern boundary and was situated in a good barley growing district. The fixed assets included an 84½ acre farm, six cottages, two houses and flour milling machinery. If Holtons was acquired all the property with the exception of the mill could be sold leaving a net outlay in the order of £10,000. Further, John knew that Herbert Bull, the manager of Holtons would be a valuable addition to his management team, and that an arrangement with Reynolds would fit in well with Oldacres expansion plans and give a broader base for their board meetings than around the kitchen table.

The purchase of Holton's was completed by June 1959. J Reynolds and Co Ltd invested £20,000 in Oldacres in return for the allocation of 4,710 ordinary shares of £1 each. The agreement included the right for Reynolds to nominate one representative to serve on the board of Oldacres. In addition Mr G Collier of Reynolds became a shareholder in Oldacres in his own right and was elected to the board.

The purchase of Ducklington Mill and the agreement with Reynolds were preceded by a capitalisation of some of the reserves held by Oldacres. The minutes of the 36th annual general meeting held on 28 September 1959 record:

> 'That the outstanding capital of the company be increased to £62,000 by the creation of 32,000 additional ordinary shares of £1 each, such shares to rank parri passu with the existing ordinary shares.'

> That the sum of £22,000 representing undistributed profits of the company and now standing to the credit of the company reserve account be and is hereby capitalised to be distributed in proportion to the ordinary shares held by members of the company whose names appear on the Register of Members on the 28 September 1959.'

William John had transferred a small number of his ordinary shares to Catherine, Hilda and June when the bakery was sold, and in the intervening years ordinary shares had also been allocated to four more of the senior managers. The changed capital structure left William John holding 30 percent of the issued ordinary share capital, John 22½ percent, the remainder of the family 17½ percent, the employees 12 percent, and Reynolds and Mr Collier 18 percent. The board of directors was strengthened by the election of Mr G Collier and Mr W A Roberts both of Reynolds, and Mr Joe Stephens the production manager at Oldacres. John Oldacre had effective control of the company. On most occasions he could rely on support for his management and development proposals from the majority of the board, and he could similarly command the votes of over 50 percent of shareholders at an annual general meeting. The board now made decisions which would have a far reaching effect on the future of the company.

By this time the Governor had again accumulated a considerable sum in his unsecured loan account with the company. In order to formalise the position, the whole farm was transferred to him at an agreed valuation. Oldacres took the tenancy of the farm until 1970 and the agreement included the option for them to renew the tenancy for a further 10 years. Although the farm had been used to demonstrate the results which could be obtained by using Oldacre feeds, fertilizers and seeds, the nature of the farming had remained unchanged. Hereford steers were fed and grazed in the fields during the summer months and taken into stockyards in winter. Lambs were delivered out in the fields in the spring. Pigs were fattened in purpose built houses. Corn was generally cut with a reaper and binder, stored in Dutch barns and later threshed. It was realised that the time was fast approaching when these methods would fail to produce an adequate return on the capital employed and would have to be changed.

The farms took on a new look. Cleevelands farm house, yard and some of the small fields and orchards immediately adjacent to the farm were sold for building. Two farm cottages were built on land halfway between the villages of Bishops Cleeve and Gotherington on the west side of Gotherington Lane. Barns, tractor sheds, calf rearing houses, and covered accommodation for cattle were all built adjacent to the cottages, and warm and dry areas were allocated for rearing lambs. Pigs and poultry were moved to the farm buildings in Gotherington. Modern plant was purchased to cultivate the arable land and the farm was generally made ready for the revolution in methods which was taking place.

Syd and Doris Burnett moved into one of the new cottages. Syd gave up his horse and trap and became the driver of a Land Rover. The second new cottage was the home of a succession of college–trained farm managers. Gentle husbandry methods gave way to deep litter hens, winter lambing, calf rearing and barley beef. The land was put under intensive cultivation and new types of seed which yielded heavier crops were planted. Under the influence of the combine harvester, corn stooks and ricks disappeared from the fields. The countryside lost much of its charm but the customer benefitted from reduced imports and relatively cheap food.

Oldacres' farm still had to serve a useful function in testing improved formulations and feeding techniques and at the same time show an adequate return on the capital employed. A visit by John Oldacre to Dutch veal farms led to the successful introduction of 200 Fresian beef cattle reared on a high nutritional plane. Calves were bought at between seven and ten days old, housed in single pens, weaned at four weeks, and then moved to a follow–on house. These calves gained one pound each day during the four week period, the daily gain in weight gradually increased to two pounds and at the end of ten weeks the cattle weight 200 pounds. The beef was ready for market in 48 weeks when the beasts reached 900 pounds live-weight. The disposal of the grass eating Hereford beef herd allowed the grassland to be used for fat lamb production. The farm carried 420 ewes which were divided into two flocks, one flock lambing before Christmas and the other in April. The two flocks produced 600 fat lambs and the grass land gave a return of £40 per acre per year. In the farm buildings at Yew Tree, 2,000 hens produced 1,250 boxes of eggs each year, and 36-six pedigree Large White sows produced 600 quality bacon pigs. On the land one tractor driver was able to cultivate 120 acres of arable land and yields of 45 hundredweight per acre became quite normal. Beef no longer took three to four years to mature and crop yields increased three fold. The Governor watched the changes with great interest but missed the majestic sight of matched herds of Hereford steers in his fields, and the pleasing comments from his neighbours.

William John had been proud of his cattle and of the neatly cut hedges and well drained fields. Although he looked to achieving maximum profit from his other business ventures, in farming the quality of his stock and the general appearance of his farm had always been enough to satisfy him. John and the other members of the board of Oldacres Ltd did not share that philosophy, leading to many heated skirmishes between father and son.

The output from the refurbished mill at Bishops Cleeve was increasing steadily and all the machinery at Ducklington Mill was newly installed. The steam engine and stone mills of the 19th century had vanished. The diesel power, the impact grinder and fountain mixer of which William John had been so proud in the 1920s had gone. The electrically driven provender press which John Oldacre installed when he first returned to the company after the war was obsolete. Oldacres were early to install electronic equipment to control both their mills. Cereals and proteins were delivered in bulk and conveyed to storage, grinding and blending bins. The one hundred horsepower grinding units were remotely controlled and they automatically reset their own maximum feed rate when changing from one material to another. The blending was done by formulae capsules programmed in the laboratory. A single operator set the mixer time, the requirements for single or repeat batching and then the blender delivered the correct ingredients in the correct amounts. Simon Hyflo presses were used for cubing and the finished feed was either stored in bins for bulk delivery, or bagged ready for despatch.

Simon-Barron pelletizing plant

Ron Chambler was now appointed as technical and scientific officer to keep pace with the developing science of animal feeding. This officer designed the feeds and controlled the preparation of the formulae capsules. A vigorous advertising campaign in the press and on film introduced Oldacres as modern and forward thinking millers. The campaign stressed that separate formulations were designed for feeding cattle, sheep, pigs and poultry, and within those species separate formulations to meet specific needs, such as beef or milk production. Also that in the light of further development and monitoring, the feeds were constantly being improved.

The annual output from the mills at Bishops Cleeve and Witney soon reached 15,000 tons, the staff numbered in excess of one hundred and the sales reached £750,000. John Oldacre now considered that the company should expand northwards and the board opened negotiations with a firm at Evesham. After inspecting the premises and the accounts, John advised that the Evesham business was not one which should be incorporated with Oldacres. While this examination was in progress, Jim Payne suffered a heart attack and

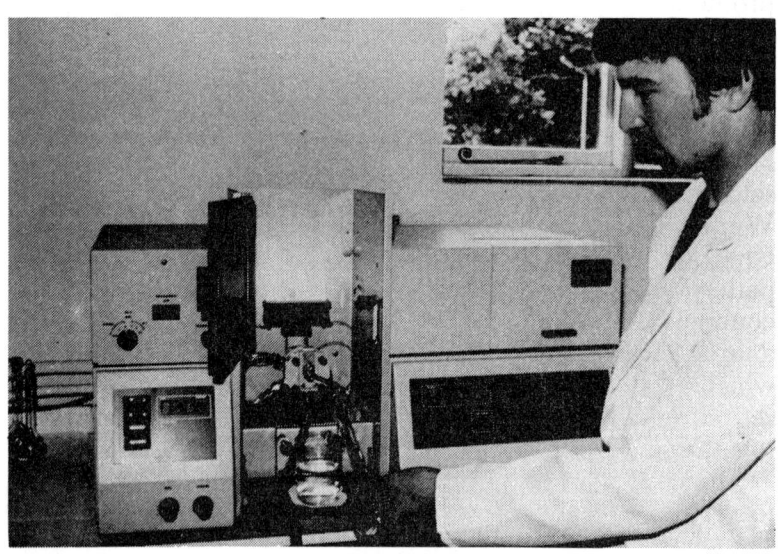

The Laboratory

died. Jim had joined the company when he left school and had always been hard working and popular. Jim's death was closely followed by the resignation of Joe Stephens and Ron Chambler from the company. John now had a chance to make major changes in the senior management of the company.

John believed that the progress which the company were making in the animal feed market demanded the appointment of a manager who could take responsibility for production at both Bishops Cleeve and Witney. The post was advertised but the response was disappointing. John talked the matter over with his father but they were undecided about the action which they should take when a letter arrived from Henry Shouler.

Henry Shouler's home was in Oxfordshire and he had been working for Spillers since leaving school. After a spell in management at Spillers feed plant in Somerset, he was promoted and moved by the company to the former Vernons Mill at Birkenhead docks. He was unhappy on Merseyside and returned home whenever the opportunity arose. It was when he was playing cricket in Oxfordshire that he was told by a friend that Oldacres had been advertising for a production manager. He made contact with John Oldacre and there was an immediate rapport between the two men. Henry joined Oldacres and so began a most successful business relationship.

The new team which John now commanded included Henry Shouler as production manager; Howard Counsell, sales manager, Bishops Cleeve; Herbert Bull, sales manager, Witney; and Bob Phillips, technical manager in place of Ron Chambler. These men came together at a time when the pattern of trade was changing and there was a need for the company to concentrate on the production of compound animal feeds to the exclusion of the peripheral activities in which Oldacres had earlier been engaged. Howard Counsell retired soon afterwards but the remainder of the team stayed together for more than 20 years.

The pattern of retail trade was also changing. The sale of feeding stuff across the counter decreased and Oldacres shops became pet and garden centres supplying the needs of an increasing number of pet lovers and amateur and professional gardeners. Sales counters, scales and tills disappeared. Packaged goods were more easily displayed in an open plan shop and customers were becoming used to picking up goods directly from the shelves and paying for them at a check-out point. A new manager was appointed to reorganise the retail business and the shops were modified to meet the new trading methods. The Bath Road shop had been in poor repair when taken over from Ride's and now needed major repairs but it was clear that it would never show a profit so the shop was closed and the site was sold. A mobile shop had been introduced some years earlier but this was also found to be non-profit making and the mobile service to the rural community was discontinued. By the mid-1960s the board had decided that the capital invested in shop premises could be more profitably employed in the main line milling activity, and all the shops were closed and the buildings sold. The Tewkesbury business was taken over by Mr Counsell's son.

A new showroom and office was opened in Bishops Cleeve in 1961 and the whole of the administrative and sales staff were transferred from 31 Winchcombe Street to that location. The loss of the retail business was a further blow to William John who had opened the first shop at 40 Winchcombe Street more than 50 years earlier. The Governor felt that the nature of the business which he had worked so hard to create was being destroyed and he made his views known to his son in the strongest terms, but he was fully behind the development of compound milling.

In the changing trading conditions, Oldacres had maintained their status as a private company but the same was not the case for William John's friend Jack Charnock. My father had built up an excellent business which extended across the length and breadth of the British Isles. Unlike Oldacres, it was a company which had no shortage of full-time family executives and as the youngest in the family my father had made it clear to me at an early age that there would be no room for me in that business. Over the years Thomson and Charnock Ltd had purchased a number of corn merchant businesses in Liverpool but by 1959, the scale of the operation was still too small to meet the salary demands made by some of the directors. The crisis was resolved when the company was taken over by James Laing and Company Ltd. My brother Ernest, who earlier had gained a Diploma in Theology at London University now achieved a lifelong ambition, and was ordained deacon and then priest by the Bishop of Chester; Mary found herself in the role of a parson's wife. The sale of Thomson and Charnock to a company listed on the Stock Exchange and her husband's change of profession, were sufficient disturbance for Mary without added problems at Oldacres.

My father was 75 years old when he agreed to the sale of his business. He had handed over the management to his two sons and a nephew more than ten years earlier, but he put in an appearance at the office each morning where he looked after the private ledger and the banking work. In his own words, he acted as office boy.

My only involvement was as a shareholder, but it appeared to me that a wise decision had been made when the business was sold and everyone concerned seemed satisfied with the outcome. My father and mother together had more than sufficient capital to maintain their standard of living. My father was an avid reader and a keen gardener and seemed to be contented, provided he had my mother by his side.

William John Oldacre was the person who took exception to the actions which my brothers had taken. He was angry and devastated that they had sold the business which my father had created, and had given away so lightly the years of hard work and sacrifice which his friend had endured in the development and growth of that business. The Governor left me in no doubt of his opinions. In his view, my brothers had broken the heart of his oldest and dearest friend and he considered that my younger brother John had led Ernest astray. Mary stayed with her parents at Homelands when she attended board meetings at Oldacres and also when she took her son Christopher back to school at Dean Close, Cheltenham, or out on exeat. She was seldom accompanied by her husband who was busy on parochial matters. She arrived alone at Homelands and these visits were often fractious; her father complaining about the actions of both her brother and her husband.

The Governor had no financial worries. He had the style of home for which he and his wife had always craved, his business was flourishing and in capable hands, but he was bored, restless and far from contented. He had no troubles save those which he created for himself but he became subject to deep and agonising depressions. He was the patriarch of the family and of the business but it seemed that his generosity had left him unable to exercise his rightful authority. He was tormented by his own frustrations.

(ii) Predators cast their eyes on Oldacres

It was only a short time after the end of the war that John Oldacre realised that his marriage to Kay was foundering because of his dedication to the business and the close proximity of his work to the home. In an attempt to stabilise and hopefully improve relationships with his wife, he purchased with the help of his father, Cockbury Court on Cleeve Hill. Mill House was vacated for use by the mill manager. Cockbury Court was a beautiful Cotswold home, in a wonderful setting and ideal for entertaining friends and business acquaintances but Kay did not settle there. The house was difficult to manage, she was alone for long periods and found the location rather remote from friends and her own closely knit family. In an attempt to save the marriage, John and Kay moved again. They purchased The Round House on Bushcombe Lane, Woodmancote which was somewhat smaller and nearer to Kay's mother and sisters.

William John and Gladys were powerless to help as they watched the marriage breaking up. At times they blamed themselves because they had not expressed reservations about the match when John first announced his intention to marry Kay, but they were aware that any such intervention at that time would have been useless. They hoped and prayed that their grandchildren, Jill and Susan, who were in their teens, would not suffer too much whatever the outcome.

John and Kay were divorced in 1963 and their children suffered the inevitable pain, torn as they were in their love for their parents. Jill had completed a secretarial course and was working in London. Susan was at school studying for her A levels, after which she read for a BA. degree in general arts at Manchester University, before joining Macmillans, the publishing firm.

John lived briefly with his parents and then in a flat in Pittville, Cheltenham before the divorce came through. He then moved to The Lammas in the centre of Minchinhampton with his second wife Virginia Hurt, an American whom he had met whilst ski-ing in Europe. They also owned a lakeside property in Salzburg, Austria. John now had a partner who gave him full support in all his business ventures and was happy to make The Lammas a centre where he could entertain his friends and business associates. Virginia was knowledgeable about literature and music, accomplished at tapestry and book-binding, a good hostess and a conversationalist who expressed her views forcefully. The Lammas was a home of distinction and their beautiful gardens were open to the public on some summer weekends. The happiness and companionship which John found with Virginia was shortlived – she became ill with a virulent form of Parkinson's Disease and tragically died in 1976.

The help and support which Virginia was able to give to John could not have come at a more opportune time. Serious attempts were being made by outside companies to gain control of Oldacres. J Reynolds and Co Ltd., were now a part of Associated British Foods Ltd. In 1963 that company offered to purchase all the shares in Oldacres other than those owned by Reynolds. The offer was made on the basis of £125,000 cash, plus 125,000 6½ percent Preference shares of £1 each in Associated British Foods. They agreed that John Oldacre would remain as managing director, that the company would continue to be run by the existing management and that the rights of the workforce would be safeguarded. Nitrovit Ltd., a company with whom Oldacres had done business for many years, also showed interest in the company. And Oldacres considered forming a group themselves under a holding company. The proposals were discussed with the district general manager at Martins Bank, who pointed out that, with Associated British Foods, Oldacres would be a small cog in a big wheel, and with Nitrovit a big cog in a smaller wheel. The Governor was in no doubt about the proper course for Oldacres to take and it was not long before the board agreed the firm should remain independent. Further freehold property was sold and new overdraft facilities were agreed with the bank but almost immediately Oldacres suffered a series of severe financial blows.

The nature of the feed market had changed. In the interest of reducing imports and their effect on the balance of payments, the Government was continuing the wartime practice of encouraging farmers to produce more and more of the nation's food at home. Milk production was subsidised and the lack of a market economy in milk soon showed healthy returns for farmers. They quickly realised that there was a direct relationship between the amount of food which they fed to their obliging cows and milk production, and that every additional pound spent on concentrates produced a return of two pounds. Dairy herds increased in size and the industry became dominated by men who farmed considerable acreages of land and such customers ordered large quantities of feed and required deliveries to be made in bulk. They expected credit over a three month period and Oldacres could therefore be owed many thousands of pounds by any one farmer. This was a situation which the Governor deplored and in his opinion the inevitable occurred. One farmer who was heavily in debt to the company became bankrupt and others failed to meet their bills. The policy which the Government was following had shown a steady growth in profits for Oldacres since the war, but the failure of these debtors changed the pattern and shareholders received no dividend for two years.

Slowly the financial position stabilised. The bank now suggested that Bartlett and Partners Ltd., a firm of financial consultants and corporate planners might be helpful to the board. John and Mary met Alan Bartlett who said his company could give a service which would be tailored to ensure through regular meetings with the policy makers, that targets were set to gauge achievements and progress. The Governor voiced strong opposition to the whole idea but after slight modification, Alan Bartlett's plan was approved by the board. Later and against further opposition from the Governor, he became a director of Oldacres.

The rate of return on capital invested in the ordinary shares of the company had always been the source of disappointment to some members of the family. The introduction of financial consultants was closely followed by an attempt by the board to ensure that a reasonable rate of return was given to those shareholders requiring income, while those more interested in company growth received a smaller return on their capital. On a majority decision, the board wrote to the shareholders saying:

> That in the event of the company declaring an ordinary dividend each 'A' share shall receive an amount equal to twice that received by a 'B' share.
> That each 'A' share shall entitle its holder to one vote.
> That in all other respects the 'A' share shall rank equally with the 'B' share.
> The rights of the 'B' ordinary shares would be inter alia as hereunder:
> That in the event of the company declaring an ordinary dividend each 'B' share shall receive a proportion of such dividend equal to half that paid to each 'A' share.
> That each 'B' share shall entitle its holder to two votes.
> That in all other respects the 'B' share shall rank equally with the 'A' share.

The Governor was enraged by the whole affair and blamed Alan Bartlett for encouraging his son in the destruction of the family business which he and his father had founded. His earlier generosity meant that his shareholding now represented a small percentage of the voting power of the company, unless he gained the support of his daughters. The lower voting power of 'A' shares seemed to him to be designed to undermine the limited control which the family could exercise and yet the family would still be taking the vast majority of the financial risk. The family were not in favour and the board did not proceed with the proposal.

Although the Governor felt that he had less and less power over policy decisions, he agreed to purchase the shares which were held by J Reynolds and Co Ltd. A sum of £25,000 was paid in his name and he immediately placed the shares into a discretionary trust with John, Catherine and the family solicitor as the trustees. The bulk of the capital was to remain in trust until William John's youngest grandchild reached 21 years of age, but any grandson who entered the family business would be eligible to receive a substantial block of the shares after four years satisfactory service to the company, and a further block after eight years. The residue was to be divided equally between the other grandchildren. The Governor was clearly anxious to make every effort to safeguard succession in the family business. The formation of the trust meant that over the years he had given away to his family more than half the capital which he held in Oldacres. In addition he made regular gifts of cash to former employees through the good offices of the district nurse; the Salvation Army; St Michael and All Angels Church; the Cheshire Home; and a host of other charities.

Mary's position in the family was never easy. June was more fortunate in two respects – she had never been involved in the business, and our home was reasonably close to Homelands where she could call regularly. We now lived in Worcester where I was working on the design and construction of the M5 and M50 motorways. June had acquired a second hand Morris Minor and it was easy for her to make the 23 mile journey to Bishops Cleeve. Sarah was attending the Alice Ottley School in Worcester and Stephen was shortly to join his cousin Christopher at Dean Close, Cheltenham. Each Sunday morning during the term we attended chapel at Dean Close and then went back to Homelands for lunch. A week seldom went by without us seeing June's parents at least once. If we failed to visit Homelands then they would drive up to Worcester, more often than not arriving for a tea appointment as early as 2 pm. The children were allowed considerable freedom at Homelands and they were happy to be there.

Jill and Susan Oldacre, and Helen Charnock also made regular visits to their grandparents, but their time was more limited. All three of the girls lived outside the county, Helen boarding at Huyton College in Lancashire and later nursing in Liverpool. William John and Gladys were always delighted to welcome any of their grandchildren. Granny was ready at all times to play cards, scrabble or other board games and on fine days she would have croquet set up on the lawn before any of the children arrived. Granny only needed the slightest excuse to suggest a drive through the Cotswolds or a visit to a motor cross rally, a motor-cycle scramble or a game of polo, and on these occasions she packed one of her famous picnics. Grandpa indulged his grandsons and adored his grand-daughters. The boys were allowed to drive his cars around the farm before they could really reach the pedals, and he made no complaint if they landed in the hedge.

'Come on boy you can do better than that', was about the level of concern which he showed. While these mechanical adventures were in progress any girl who was present was content to enjoy her grandmother's company; this was sensible of them because they would not have been given the same opportunities by their grandfather.

The Governor liked to get away on short holidays and he and his wife were regular visitors to Buglawton, near Congleton where Ernest was vicar, and where they had the opportunity of meeting my father and mother again. They also enjoyed short breaks in the Lake District when we would join them, staying at the Belsfield Hotel in Bowness. On the journey north we would pick up Christopher at the Sandbach junction on the M6, and arrive at the hotel in time for an early dinner. At meal times, Christopher and Stephen sat one on each side of their grandfather. The Governor staged competitions between the boys to see which of them could eat the greatest number of prunes, the greatest number of kippers or whatever. For his part, he would order the ripest cheese and then chortle at the complaints which the boys made about the frightful smell. He would keep the cheese covered and only flick the cover aside when he wished to cut a morsel, but this did not prevent the rich aroma pervading the table or the complaints from the boys. Granny and Sarah sat at the other end of the table and behaved with greater propriety. We enjoyed the beautiful scenery of the Lake District, we ate picnics excellently prepared by the hotel staff, we played pitch and putt, walked the hills and rowed on Lake Windermere. The Governor was in his mid–seventies but on these holidays, the years fell away from him and he walked and played like a young man.

The Governor placed his own son on a pedestal from which John was likely to come crashing to the ground at regular intervals. He was fully aware of the excellent manner in which Oldacres was being managed and the progress which they were making, but clashes between father and son were regular and violent when the Governor did not agree with company policy, or when he did not get his own way.

These clashes could send the Governor into a state of deep depression. On occasions his frustrations became so overwhelming that he had to get away from Homelands and close proximity to the business. He needed to spend time on his own. These moods made great difficulties for his wife who might not know of his whereabouts for days on end. We all did our best to ease her burden and to ensure that someone was on hand when the Governor's deep love for his wife led him to make a telephone call to inquire about her health. When the call came, we tried to persuade him that mother was quite well, but was anxious to meet him for lunch as soon as possible. If we could encourage him to make such an appointment then it was probable that he would return home. Sometimes he would try to persuade her that life would be easier if they moved their home right away from Bishops Cleeve, but Gladys had no intention of moving.

(iii) William John's eldest grandson enters the business but he loses his best friend

In the autumn of 1964, William John and Gladys took another trip to New Zealand. They were accompanied by Jill who remained there and in Australia for some years before returning home with her husband, Alec Bristoe and their small son Andrew, the Governor's first great-grandchild. In Auckland, William John and Gladys stayed with Hilda whose family had increased by two, Delwyn and Ian both having been born since the grandparents' last visit. Bruce and John were now in their teens and their grandfather spent many hours giving them the background to the family business in England. He pointed out the success which had been achieved over more than eighty years, and he made every effort to persuade them that their future lay in W J Oldacre Ltd. He was determined that the dynasty which his father had founded should continue and was looking for a male member of the family to succeed his son. He was still unable to consider the girls in the family as possible business managers.

At the end of their holiday William John and Gladys returned to England by air for the first time. They visited Jack Pike at Edmonton, Alberta, after a rather fruitless trip to

Vancouver Island, British Columbia, where Gladys had hoped to see her sister Ida, but unfortunately she was too busy to see them.

Much to the delight of the Governor, Bruce and John Cliffe followed them to England and arrived in time for Christmas. The boys and their grandparents were all invited to spend Christmas day with John and Virginia at The Lammas but at the last moment, Virginia was taken ill and so they joined us in Worcester where Catherine was already a guest. Neither Bruce nor John had experienced Christmas in winter, and they were not used to the traditional English fare of turkey and plum pudding. Christmas crackers were pulled, party hats unfolded and worn, and there was joy on their faces when they saw the turkey, sausages, bacon, stuffing, roast potatoes, sprouts, carrots, cranberry jelly and the other dishes which made up the main course at dinner. Their delight increased when June carried in the plum pudding covered in flaming brandy.

They spent much of their holiday with their grandfather and their uncle, visiting the farm, talking about modern animal feeding methods, studying the workings of the mills and the other activities in which Oldacres were involved. They arrived back in New Zealand well pleased with their experiences in the old country.

Catherine had given up her nursing career and taken the tenancy of Trapp's cottage which she converted into a shop and tea room, using the upper floor as a flat. Here she ran a bread and confectionery business, and a tea shop for ten years. In 1965 she felt that she needed a change, anticipating that she might soon have to give up her freedom in order to look after her ageing parents, so she returned to New Zealand, first for a holiday and then to work for a few years.

During Catherine's absence, Gladys Oldacre's arthritic condition deteriorated quite rapidly, and even though her gallbladder had been removed, the symptoms still caused her trouble. The Governor was liable to panic about his wife's health and often June was called to Bishops Cleeve only to find it was a false alarm. If the calls came when the children were on holiday she took them with her and I was left to fend for myself. In term time Stephen was away at boarding school but Sarah had to stay at home with me. In the summer of

1967 the calls which the Governor made became more regular and were fully justified. June had to spend long periods away from home. She was now trying to look after the bungalow, cook for her father, do the washing and nurse her mother night and day. She moved her father into the spare bedroom and slept in the bed alongside her mother. We went down to Homelands each weekend. Stephen managed to get one afternoon off from school and he arrived at the bungalow to find that June had been unable to leave her mother's side for many hours. The boy volunteered to sit with his grandmother throughout the whole of his break from school, to allow his mother to get some rest. The situation was too much for June to handle alone, so she cabled Catherine in New Zealand.

Catherine was in England within a few days and took command of the situation. She spent the next 16 years keeping house and nursing one or other of her parents. Her return was timely. In May 1968, June moved to Lewes, Sussex where I had obtained a top management appointment. June's mother was pleased at my promotion but the Governor seemed to resent my success in that June was no longer at his beck and call.

Shortly after Catherine left New Zealand she was followed to England by Hilda who understandably was concerned about the health of her mother. She was accompanied by Delwyn and Ian, but her husband remained at home with Bruce and John. Hilda was pleased to see her mother on the way to recovery when she arrived and was able to spend a pleasant holiday with her parents before returning home.

June's mother was the parent about whom we had all been concerned, but it was my mother who was to be the first of the four friends to die. She celebrated her 80th birthday on 2 January 1969. On St Valentine's day she was happy to witness the second marriage of my brother, John, who was a widower. We stayed at my parents' home for the wedding and could see how pleased she was to see John happily married again. We left her in good spirits and apparently in good health but on 23 March she attended communion, cooked the lunch, washed up the dinner things, and after complaining about feeling unwell, died later that evening. My father was deeply shocked and quite unable to look after himself so he went to live permanently with Mary and Ernest.

The Governor's 80th birthday was celebrated on 9 May and because of pressure of work, plus the shock of the sudden death of my mother and my father's despair, I could not find the time nor the energy to make the long journey from Lewes to attend his birthday luncheon. This omission resulted in a number of aggressive and abusive letters addressed to June. We had not experienced this side of him before but we were aware that the Governor had made such sorties against others in the family. June wisely burnt the letters immediately, but the added stress kept me away from work for three weeks. After this experience, I found it extremely difficult to re-establish the close relationships which I had enjoyed with him over the previous 40 years.

After the Governor reached 80 years of age, the bank once again began to show concern about the effect of death duties on the business and the trust in the event of his death. Eventually a decision was reached about the future of the farms and the provision of insurance cover against death duties. William John gave the farm, subject to the company tenancy, to his four daughters, Catherine being unmarried received a two-fifths share against one-fifth each to her married sisters. The farm was then sold on a professional valuation to John, who gave his sisters a mortgage for part of their share, the other part going towards meeting the premium on a decreasing term life assurance policy which John took out on the life of his father. William John was guaranteed an income for life and occupancy of Homelands, the farm house. This complicated arrangement was completed in 1969.

In the same year, Bruce Cliffe the Governor's eldest grandson, came to England from New Zealand with his wife, Jo, and started work with Oldacres. He was 21 years old and a graduate of Auckland University. He joined the salesforce in Somerset before being sent on a management course at Oxford.

The steadily increasing demand for Oldacres feeds necessitated either further extensions to their recently modernised mills or the building of a third unit. The board decided that maximum economy of transport would be achieved if they built a third mill at Calne. The location of the three mills

Three Generations
John Oldacre, William John, Bruce Cliffe

would mean that most of the customers would be within an hour's delivery time, also all were well placed in relation to the expanding motorway network.

John had long believed that it should be possible to build a modern animal feed mill on a virgin site for as little as £100,000. He searched the United States, Japan and the Continent for a mill which would meet his ideal but without success. Meanwhile, as part of his normal work schedule he travelled between his own mills often accompanied by his wife Virginia. At Ducklington mill he had in Frank Chappell his mill manager, a man with similar visions about mill design to his own, and they discussed the possibilities endlessly and at length. It was while John was travelling on a night ferry to Holland, that the concept of a weighbridge

William John digs first turf at Calne

acting as the nerve centre of any new mill was born, and he decided that such a mill should indeed be managed by Frank Chappell.

The new mill at Calne was opened by John Godber MP, Minister of Agriculture, in 1969. It incorporated the latest equipment and feed–milling techniques, and was designed to operate as a satellite unit, micro–ingredients being obtained in pre-mix form from the micro-ingredient mixing plant at Bishops Cleeve. One man only was required in the processing plant. The weighing of ingredients and batch control was fully automatic, and the finished products were conveyed direct to pre-selected bins for bulk loading or bagging-off. Two men were employed in the warehouse to speed up bagging and loading. This kind of efficiency was the basis of Oldacres competitive ability. Output from the three mills at Bishops Cleeve, Witney and Calne now exceeded 50,000 tons and sales were in excess of £1,000,000.

William John resigned as chairman of the company in 1970. His resignation was accompanied by the resignations of his wife and Mary who felt that the time had come for younger executive directors to be appointed. Oldacres were a company of stature in the market. In addition John had played a major role in leading the challenge of country millers against the might of the great port millers. Over the years between 1958 and 1968 the total compound production in Great Britain had remained almost constant, but production at the country mills had increased from 30 percent of the total to over 40 percent. Oldacres claimed 5 percent of the total country mill production in 1958, and 50 percent by the end of the ten year period.

When three members of the family all resigned from the board at the same time, the Governor was concerned that this left John as the only family representative. Mary's husband Ernest Charnock was now elected to serve as a non–executive director on behalf of the family.

In April 1970, my father left the comfort and safety of Ernest and Mary's house and moved himself into an hotel in West Kirby, Cheshire where he believed that he could live his own life without interference from his family. The hotel had a fine view over the estuary of the River Dee but the furnishings were spartan and much below the standards to which my father was accustomed. In the summer after mother's death he had spent three months in Lewes with us and I knew that he was desperately unhappy without his wife beside him. Later when I visited him in West Kirby he was in despair and lacked the will to live. I was distressed and sad to see my father in such a sorry state, throughout his life he had been such a wise and strong support to family and friends alike. When William John saw the plight of his friend he was again angry with us all, but we knew that my father still had a mind of his own and that nothing we said would persuade him to return to the vicarage. Inevitably his condition deteriorated and at the beginning of June, Helen found him in very poor shape indeed. He was now so weak that she was able to take matters into her own hands. Father was moved to the home of my brother, John, where he died on 6 June. William John was outraged and he blamed my brothers for father's death. In his mind, the sale of Thomson and Charnock Ltd., and the treatment which father had suffered at the hands of his sons, had been the cause of death. In fact father was almost 85 years of age and had lost the will to live.

9

THE PACE OF GROWTH INCREASES
1970–1983

(i) The role of the family in the management of the business diminishes

William John believed that he had founded a family and business dynasty which would last for generations to come. His perception was seldom at fault but on this matter he exhibited a blindness which was uncharacteristic of the man. The business was successful and still expanding with remarkable rapidity. John Oldacre as Chairman and Managing Director could not exercise direct management control over every activity, nor did he wish to do so. The bakery had been sold, the retail trade had been closed down, Leslie Aston had taken over the coal business, and Oldacres were now specialising in the manufacture of compound animal feeds and farming. Management responsibility was delegated to each Line Manager and further business growth demanded the dedication of those managers to the company, and such commitment called for men who were financially involved in the company. Also, William John had a large and mainly young family; he had one son and four daughters, five grandsons and five grand-daughters and two great-grandchildren; over the next 12 years a further 12 great-grandchildren would be born. Oldacres was financed mainly from family capital, the overall direction of the company was in the hands of John Oldacre, but successful trading was dependent upon the skills of Executive Directors and Managers outside the family.

W J Oldacre Ltd was moving forward with confidence but under difficult trading conditions. The grain harvest in 1970 was poor. This led to higher feed prices and inevitable business failure for some farmers. An outbreak of fowl pest added further problems to those already being encountered by Oldacre's customers and the company suffered trading losses over the first eight months of the financial year. There was a recovery before the year ended but the holders of ordinary shares received no dividend on their capital.

Bad harvests are often followed by bumper grain crops and this happened in 1971. In anticipation of the likely expansion of livestock production as the nation prepared to enter the European Economic Community, management boldly set about modernising and extending their Ducklington Mill. Over hundreds of years prior to Oldacres purchasing Ducklington Mill, the mill was driven by water power, the River Windrush having been diverted to create a head of water capable of driving the milling machinery. The mill improvements now undertaken by Oldacres involved clearing the old channel of the river so that once again water ran along its original course. Four grain silos were built on the area where the head of water had been held back prior to entering the wheelhouse of the old mill. The output of the newly installed 150 horsepower mill and press at ten tons per

Ducklington Mill, Ducklington, Witney

hour, gave a similar standard of operational efficiency to that achieved at the Calne Mill. The directors felt that they had prepared the company to meet the challenge which was likely to come when Britain entered the EEC. But dangers which could come from over specialisation were apparent to the board and they looked for ways and means of diversification and further improving the management of the company.

The three mills, the scientific branch and the transport department had been largely autonomous under their own Line Managers for some years, but the continuing expansion of the company had over extended lines of communication; lines of responsibility were not clearly defined; many members of the staff particularly at satellite mills were beginning to feel remote with a consequent increase in the rate of staff turn-over and an unwillingness to accept responsibility; and more serious still, some customers were of the opinion that Oldacres were becoming all too akin to their larger and more impersonal competitors.

John Oldacre felt that the time had come for a fundamental change in management style if the company was to achieve its declared objectives of continued growth, and retention of private independent company status. He reviewed the company structure with his senior executive colleagues. It was clear that in order to shorten lines of communication and at the same time to remove a feeling of remoteness amongst the staff, and the growing impersonal image to customers, the company had to break down the organisation into smaller even more autonomous units and to move towards divisionalisation. The resulting formula was to create five divisions and profit centres, plus a headquarters or administrative division. Three divisions were to be based one at each of the three mills, and the transport and technical divisions giving a service to the mills were to be based at Bishops Cleeve. For each division to become largely autonomous it was necessary to provide the managers with a company manual covering organisational and financial controls. In addition there was a need to define company policy.

The Governor disliked the thought of transferring responsibility down the line and he urged John to be cautious, fearing that growth in trade might be coming too quickly. His concern lessened somewhat when he saw the draft of the company policy which was to be passed to all managers; it set out much of his own approach to good practice.

On completion of the company manual and the policy statement, the changeover was effected quite smoothly and simply by line managers becoming divisional managers, the managers previously in charge of sales, production and marketing each took over responsibility for all of these functions, plus part of the transport fleet at one of the mills. The transport division became responsible for hiring on contract those lorries allocated to the mills, running a pool of vehicles for long distance haulage and servicing the fleet. The technical division took over production of the scientific formulation of feeds and offered field services to the customers of each mill.

The new structure was introduced on 1 June 1972 and satisfied that the managers concerned had been properly briefed on their future responsibilities and accountability, John Oldacre set off on a four week tour of compound plants in Japan and the Far East. On his return he saw that the company was functioning well. Before long efficiency had improved and staff morale far exceeded John's expectations.

Divisional managers were now encouraged to suggest extensions of their profit centres with closely allied activities. The transport division came forward with the offer of a Mercedes Benz franchise for commercial vehicles. The technical division started marketing minerals and supplying supplements to other compounders, and the feed division became active in grain marketing.

The offer of a Mercedes Benz franchise was of particular interest to the board. They were aware of the penetration of these vehicles into the Continental market for commercial vehicles and considered that the British might be equally receptive. Within one year of the franchise being granted, the amount of capital needed and the low rate of return anticipated during the initial life of the venture, led to the formation of a separate company W J Oldacre (Services) Ltd so that expansion of the feed company would not be inhibited.

As the Golden Jubilee of the company approached, the board agreed that it would be fitting to celebrate the occasion by changing the name of the family company to W J Oldacre (Holdings) Ltd, and to form three separate wholly owned subsidiaries, W J Oldacre Ltd, Homelands Farm Ltd, and W J Oldacre (Services) Ltd. These changes were accompanied by a further increase in the capital of the company. Each ordinary shareholder received an additional four shares for each share held on the named day, and room was made for a future Share Purchase Scheme for managers.

W J Oldacre (Holdings) Ltd owned all the shares in the subsidiary companies and all freehold land and property. It stood as guarantor to the bank for the individual financial arrangements of the subsidiary companies. John Oldacre became chairman and managing director, and the board included the managing directors of the three subsidiary companies – William John Oldacre, Henry Shouler, and Bruce Cliffe, together with Alan Bartlett, Ernest Charnock who only remained on the board for a short period and Eric Watterson. Ken Talbot became company secretary and group accountant.

Nothing could have pleased the Governor more than to be invited back after only a brief spell away from the board room. He joined the board of the Holding Company as managing director of Homelands Farms Ltd, but there was a snag; he had to retire completely from any role in the active management of the farm. The loss of controlling influence over farming methods and standards was a blow to him, but the board felt that the pace of change in farming technology and economics was too much for the Governor, and following problems with retaining managers, a contract farming agreement was entered into with a neighbouring farmer, R H Baird and Son. The farm was now run as a partnership between R H Baird and Son and Homelands Farms Ltd, the agreement covering an initial period of three years.

The newly constituted W J Oldacre Ltd encompassed the activities of the animal feed production divisions at Bishops Cleeve, Witney and Calne, and of the technical sales division. The chairman of this company was John Oldacre; Henry Shouler was appointed managing director; the executive directors were Herbert Bull (Bishops Cleeve), Eric Bull (Witney), and Bob Phillips (Technical); and David Stevens and Geoffrey Clarkson were appointed as non–executive directors. The four divisions continued to operate autonomously, each with a director in sole charge. The two non-executive directors served a particularly useful function. Standing aside from day-to-day management, they could view the company and its products from the customer's standpoint; David Stevens was a progressive dairy farmer and customer, and Geoffrey Clarkson a former bank director, brought with him knowledge of the operation of successful companies in other spheres.

Bishops Cleeve was still the largest of the three milling divisions with annual sales of 33,000 tons. David Stagg led a team of six salesmen in the field. The mill was managed by Maurice Maizonner and he had ten men in the mill, plus one fitter and eight drivers. The office staff of six maintained contact with customers and kept records and stock control. The total annual sales at Ducklington were 23,000 tons. Don Ford managed this mill with a staff of nine, plus a fitter and four drivers. Pat Bint led the four salesmen and there were four office staff. David Holborow was sales manager at Calne where sales topped 27,000 tons a year. The mill was under the control of Frank Chappell and he had a staff of six, with six drivers; the office staff numbered four.

The technical sales division was led by Bob Phillips. The staff of seven were responsible for the design of the Oldacre range of animal feeds, checking the quality of production and giving advice and guidance to farmers. An important part of their work was undertaken out on customers' farms. Such visits enabled the staff to advise farmers on the best standard rations to meet their requirements, or the special needs of a farmer were assessed before rations were designed back in the laboratory to meet those needs.

The four divisions of W J Oldacre Ltd were served by a central office staff. Under the direction of the company secretary, Graham Hibberd, all financial matters were controlled, sales records, wages, salaries, pensions and accounts records kept.

W J Oldacre Ltd was the most profitable part of the whole group. Henry Shouler as managing director of that company became the most powerful executive after the chairman himself. The Governor watched this development with total confidence in Henry Shouler's abilities but with some concern for the future role of his grandsons in the business.

The late Walter John Oldacre had started trading as a carrier and dealer in horses and oxen. Some 90 years later his great-grandson, Bruce Cliffe, became managing director of W J Oldacre (Services) Ltd, dealing in vans, trailers and lorries.

The nucleus of this new company was the transport division of the original W J Oldacre Ltd, but new horizons were seen beyond that of a service company for Oldacres. Valuable franchises for Mercedes-Benz trucks and York trailers were won for the areas of Gloucestershire, Wiltshire, Oxfordshire, Hampshire, Berkshire and the Isle of Wight. In addition to vehicle and trailer sales and service, contract hire was also undertaken, and a heavy duty service was organised for motorway recovery work. The company expanded into the engineering field in order to undertake heavy duty plant repair, welding, and hydraulic and electrical repairs. Bruce was promoted in his early twenties to the post of managing director of the services company and onto the board of the Holding Company. This was followed by his resignation from the animal feed side of the business, another cause of concern to the Governor.

At the end of the first trading year after the Golden Jubilee, the board were able to recommend a gross dividend of 20 percent for ordinary shareholders. The animal feed production company had increased annual sales to almost £4 million and were showing substantial profits, thus helping to overcome losses which the service company suffered.

In the following year the oil crisis pushed world trade into deep recession. There was galloping inflation and political leaders seemed willing to sacrifice the viability of industry for short term expediency. Trading conditions became much more difficult than at any time since the Second World War. The severe economic pressure forced many farmers into drastic cutbacks in livestock production and this led to a 10 percent drop in the overall market for compound feeds. The market for new commercial vehicles was over-supplied. It was a testing time for every commercial enterprise, but John Oldacre was able to report to his shareholders that the company had experienced another record year for sales and profitability. The success of the company was a remarkable achievement. It was due in large measure to the far-sighted vision of John Oldacre, the management structure which had been adopted, and the excellent team spirit which existed throughout the firm.

The company had been in the forefront of modern commercial practice for many years. The record profits of the past two years allowed the board to activate a Profit Sharing Bonus/Share Purchase Scheme which entitled managerial staff to convert that portion of their bonus in excess of a defined threshold into equity in the operating company. A threshold considered to give a reasonable rate of return for shareholders was to be set and any profits in excess of that figure were then to be divided one third to the staff, one third to shareholders, and one third to be retained. The distribution to the staff was to be based on a percentage of wages or salary varying between 10 percent and 40 percent according to responsibility. The aim of the scheme was to allow participating members to purchase 20 percent of the equity of the subsidiary company over a 20 year period.

The premises at 31 Winchcombe Street, Cheltenham were now sold and the board looked to investing the proceeds of that sale into large office premises in Bishops Cleeve. They wanted a more prestigious headquarters for the company. A successful bid was made for Bishops Cleeve Rectory and after substantial renovation and conversion the company moved into the new office in May 1975. They celebrated the event by inviting customers to view the refurbished and quite magnificent building. 'The Open' as it was called took place on 16 and 17 May when some four hundred lunches, two hundred teas and 750 suppers were served. The invitation included a history of 'Cleeve Hall' as it was now to be called.

> 'Cleeve Hall, formerly known as The Rectory, is described by David Verey in "The Buildings of England – Gloucestershire" as "probably the oldest and most splendid parsonage in the country".
>
> In the 13th century it was a manor house used by the Bishops of Worcester, who held much land in the parish by sequestration of the original grant made in 770 by Offa, King of Mercia, to found a college of canons hence the

Cleeve Hall
HQ, Oldacre plc

prefix Bishop's in the name of the village.

The original manor house built c.1250 consisted of a stone-built hall running north-south, with solar and buttery cross wings projecting on each side. The three blocked doors with chamfered jambs and pointed arches in the present central hall formerly opened from the cross passage into the service wing.

The house was refurbished in 1667 by Bishop Nicholson of Gloucester, the central part being filled in and a huge hipped roof built over the central hall and medieval roofs of the cross wings. The two-storey porch on the east, and the stair turret to the west, were added at the same time.

During the 18th century the alcove on the half-landing of the stairs was made and painted with a classical scene, and c.1810 the first-floor room in the solar wing was covered with mural paintings depicting scenes connected with the Townshend family. One shows the bride arriving at Steanbridge House, Slad, near Stroud.

Several 17th century windows remain, having their original ironwork and catches of Charles II period.

Bishops Cleeve is an historic village founded in the 9th century as a settlement for the monastery at Gloucester. Oldacres have been part and parcel of the village for more than a century, and the family has always been conscious of its local heritage.

It was with some pride, therefore, that W J Oldacre Ltd, acquired the Rectory when it came on the market some months ago. The purchase gave a two-fold opportunity – to restore and preserve this historic building, and at the same time to house the administrative division of this growing company under one roof, in a lovely environment'.

The move to Cleeve Hall was welcomed by William John. He was satisfied that this fine old building with its long history properly reflected the position of the Oldacre family and business in the local community. The solid foundation of the building, the family and the business augured well for the future of the dynasty. The move also meant that Mill House was surplus to requirements and this paved the way for the demolition of the house and of Trapp's Cottage, and the redevelopment of the whole of Oldacre's frontage along Church Road. It was fitting that the last occupant of Mill House (formerly The Pollards), was Bruce Cliffe, the great grandson of Walter John Oldacre who had lived and worked from the house for more than forty years. The house had little architectural merit. Immediately before it was demolished, it stood in a sea of tarmac and served as offices and with one room set aside for use by the board. The demoliton of Mill House caused no heartaches, but did herald the end of an era. The loss of Trapp's Cottage caused much concern in the village. After Catherine Oldacre closed her shop and tea room the cottage was used by Cleeve Motors Ltd, and by Leslie Aston's coal business before being almost destroyed by fire. A long battle ensued between the Company, as owners, and the Council before it was agreed that the listed building could be demolished.

The company was never static. The occupancy of the prestigious headquarters was accompanied by changes in management and other staff, and further growth.

David Carpenter joined W J Oldacre Ltd, as company secretary and George Evans replaced Maurice Maizonnier as

Skeffington Mill

manager of Bishops Cleeve mill. The retirement of Syd and Doris Burnett brought to an end a long chapter of full-time and loyal service to the company and the Governor and Mrs Oldacre in particular. It seemed hardly possible that more than 50 years had passed since Gladys Oldacre had asked the young and delightful daughter of Bill Little, the hay trusser, if she would work for her when she left school. The close ties between William John and Gladys Oldacre with the Burnetts did not end with formal retirement. Doris continued to help at Homelands, and Syd could often be seen cutting the grass for the Governor.

Personalities in and around the firm were changing as new divisions were added to the existing subsidiary companies, and further subsidiary companies were included in the group. By 31 March 1977, Oldacres were trading from five mills. Skeffington Mill, Leicestershire was fully operational under the Oldacre banner by mid-1976, and Haddenham Mill, Buckinghamshire by March 1977. The purchase of these two mills gave the company effective coverage of the country from a line between the River Mersey and The Wash, southwards to the channel coast, but excluding Cornwall and West Devon, and a line east of Cambridge and Brighton. The annual sales exceeded £10 million by the time that Hadden-ham was operational. W J Oldacre Ltd was now the largest animal feed processing company in private ownership in the country.

The services company was not to be outdone. A new depot was opened at Wokingham. This new facility was strategic-ally situated one mile from the M4/A329(M) junction, and covered territory east of Reading and into the western approaches of London. Profitability was always a problem and the activities of the company were reviewed regularly.

A grain and seed division of W J Oldacre Ltd started trading at Bicester in 1974. Alan Hayward was the manager and the division was involved with the purchase of malting barley, milling wheat and milling oats, as well as normal commercial grain. Alan Hayward negotiated contracts with seed houses, enabling Oldacres to offer both cereal and grass seeds to their customers. Four articulated lorries operated from Bishops Cleeve hauling supplies mainly between London and the mills. The division was soon operating successfully.

Cleeve Motors Ltd with its agency for Fiat cars became a part of the group in 1977.

William John's eyesight was failing and he had given up driving his car after a minor incident in Winchcombe Street, Cheltenham. This minor problem did not prevent him from taking an active interest in all the developments. He was driven to the building sites by Catherine or another member of the family, and offered a visiting Clerk of Works service to the company. His eyes may have been weaker than they had been when he was younger, but he seldom missed any mistakes which were being made and he was quick to offer sound advice. He also made regular visits to all the mills and what he saw did not always please him. He was particularly quick to sense the strengths and weaknesses of the managers and the sales staff, the office staff also coming under his careful scrutiny. Nevertheless, the Governor was welcomed on all these visits and much respected. John was willing to let his father continue with these outings providing that he did not attempt to give any instructions to the staff. Against this contingency he advised the senior staff that they should only act on such orders after discussion with their divisional director.

(ii) The frustrations and sorrows of old age

It is seldom easy to cope with old age and it was even more difficult for William John Oldacre whose body could no longer keep pace with his lively mind. William John gained great stimulation from his inspections of the Oldacre premises, but the feeling of elation did not last long. A few days confined inside the walls of Homelands and he could become like a lion trapped in a cage. A coffee break with John might assuage his thirst for knowledge about the wellbeing of his family business. On another occasion, a visit from John might arouse frustration and great anger, ending with John walking away from the encounter, only to return many days later when the atmosphere was more conducive to rational discussion. When John left Homelands, Gladys never knew whether she would hear glowing praise of her son or violent criticism.

In 1945, the Governor had encouraged John to return to the business and he felt that he had offered him excellent terms of employment and a level of opportunity far greater than that offered to him by his father in 1919. He had selflessly handed over the role of managing director of the company to John with the minimum of delay and given him freedom to develop Oldacres in his own way; he had even agreed to the sale of the bakery business in order to provide capital to satisfy John's development programme. The Governor was of the firm belief that had such opportunities been given to him, then he would have discussed every one of his development ideas with his father, listened to his father's views and amended the proposals accordingly. Where had he gone wrong in his dealings with his own son? He could not find an answer. The fact of the matter was that drastic changes had taken place and were still taking place in the business in which Oldacres were engaged. In 1946 there had been 44 members of the Corn and Agricultural Merchants Association in Gloucestershire, and Oldacres was one of the smallest. In the late 1970s, the membership had fallen to single figures and after excluding two national companies, Oldacres was the largest. In order to achieve this position, it had been necessary to demolish many parts of the business which the Governor had built up during the 1930s and 1940s.

Also grandfather, father and son were very different characters and they reacted to situations in very different ways. William John saw life in black and white, there were no shades of grey. The other two men could, in their own way, offer intellectual argument in support of their views and proposals.

In his darkest moods William John felt that his son had stripped him naked. John had taken the business and the farm away from him leaving him with nothing to show for a lifetime of hard work. He had also been let down by his daughters who would not support him against their brother; in fact the girls knew that any criticism of their brother was likely to find them in severe trouble with their father within a short space of time. When the Governor complained about John to his daughters, the only reaction open to them was to follow the wise example set by their mother and to say nothing.

The difficulties in the relationship between father and son stemmed partly from the staunch and disciplined upbringing which William John had received at the hands of his own father. He grew up to accept the virtues of strong patriarchal control, and to work from morning to night in the interest of the family and the business; it was a matter of all for one and one for all.

In spite of a remarkably alert mind, the Governor never came to terms with some aspects of modern business practice. He would not accept that socialising with the customers in golf matches, lunches, dinners and the like were a necessary part of the manager's role. Time which managers and executive directors took away from the office was time wasted, profit lost and presented a poor example to the workforce. Managers who took such liberties were bleeding the life blood from the business and giving nothing back. The Governor also expected managers to show a parental style interest in the men they employed and in their families. He demanded that the mills, warehouses and transport should be scrupulously clean at all times, presenting a caring and efficient image of the company to customers and visitors. These were worthy requirements but they were not wholly conducive to business practice and maximum profit margins in the 1970s.

William John began to believe that he would be happier if he moved away from close proximity to the farm and the business headquarters. Gladys doubted the wisdom of such a move and in any event wished to stay in Bishops Cleeve. The Governor looked for ways to occupy his active nature.

'Mama, there is a 250 acre farm up for auction at Treddington.' He would pass the particulars across to her. 'It is just what I am looking for and it would get me away from the constant worry about the business.'

'Oh John, you have everything that you need already,' she would counter. 'You can't possibly want anything more and you certainly don't want the worry or the ties which a farm would bring.'

'I could manage a small farm like that without any difficulty and it would get me away from this place.'

'No Daddy,' Gladys would quietly point out. 'I'm happy here and I am not fit enough to move again, nor do I wish to do so.'

The Governor would pick up his trilby hat, walk out of the back door and start heavy work in the garden. The job was attacked with great vigour. A short time later he would be back in his chair in front of the fire, and the next day complain about the bad night which he had just spent and how ill he was feeling. The sympathy for which he craved was not forthcoming.

'There you are John,' Gladys would eventually say. 'We really couldn't move away from here and look after a farm at our age.'

The arthritis in Gladys' hands, wrists and knees was painful, but she had been much better in herself since Catherine had returned from New Zealand. The house was managed by Catherine who also did all the cooking and acted as chauffeur for her mother and father, but her mother continued to control the purse strings and to keep detailed household records. Unfortunately her eyesight was no longer good enough to allow her to sew or to read, and so in the evenings she watched the television or played scrabble with the Governor and Catherine; she was fond of nature programmes and sport, particularly show jumping and snooker.

Gladys kept a diary all her life, but as she became older the diary included little more than a brief note of major events. She reached 80 years of age in 1972 and her diary shows that she was seldom alone.

The diary records that in a typical week she went shopping in Cheltenham with Catherine, took lunch or tea with relatives who lived locally and attended some meetings of the Cheltenham Inner Wheel. The doctor made monthly visits to check on her condition and the Rector, Canon Edmunds called. She also managed to get away for holidays with Mary or June. In April she travelled as far as the Yorkshire Moors, Grassington and Filey with Mary, before being taken back to Homelands. She noted that on reaching home:

'We were welcomed by Doris who had a piping hot cup of coffee waiting for us when we arrived.'

The whole family congregated at Homelands for the Governor's birthday on 9 May, and then she went back to Tattenhall for a few days in order to join in the celebration of Christopher Charnock's 21st birthday; she attended the birthday dinner at the Grosvenor Hotel, Aldford; shopped in Chester with Mary; Helen took time off from nursing duties in hospital to see her grandmother; she took tea with Mary's friends; and had dinner engagements before returning to Homelands.

By 8 June she was at June's home in Lewes. On this occasion Catherine had driven her mother and father down to see Sarah Charnock on her birthday. The day after the birthday Catherine left on a holiday cruise and the Governor returned to Bishops Cleeve on his own. Gladys stayed with June for the next three weeks and they had a busy time. She made shopping trips to Eastbourne, Hove and Tunbridge Wells; went to the seaside and watched the ferries moving in and out of Newhaven; was entertained by June's friends; made a point of seeing her grandchildren, Sarah at Goldsmiths College and Stephen at Eastbourne College; and dined out regularly. We took her to see Dick Emery, one of her favourite comedians, at the Palace Pier Theatre in Brighton. She thoroughly enjoyed the show but we had the greatest difficulty in helping her to make the long walk along the pier to the theatre and back again. A few days later she was delighted to see Dick Emery, this time in Mr Bondolfi's shop in Devonshire Place, Eastbourne. Mr Bondolfi was always pleased to welcome the family when they were in Eastbourne.

The Governor and Sarah arrived in Lewes in time for Mother's eightieth birthday on Sunday 18 June, when we had a luncheon party at the Cavendish Hotel, Eastbourne. After an excellent meal we found ourselves the only diners still left in the restaurant. There was a fanfare and the head waiter and the chef entered carrying a large birthday cake; the cake was topped with a mass of lighted candles. It was a memorable occasion and many years later the Governor talked about the pleasure that the day had given to his wife.

Early September saw the arrival in England of Hilda and Mervyn Cliffe. The family were assembling for the wedding of Helen Charnock which was to take place at Tattenhall on 16 September. This celebration was the last gathering to be attended by all the surviving members of William John's generation of the family, all his children and nieces, his English grandchildren and his great-niece and great-nephew, and a number of his great grandchildren. The ceremony was conducted by the bride's father and the reception was held on the lawn at Tattenhall Rectory. The only thing which marred a wonderful day for Helen was that it could not be shared with her Charnock grandparents.

The Governor was now stricken by further prostate trouble. He returned to hospital and had a second operation on 30 October, which he withstood remarkably well but he had to undergo cobalt treatment on five days each week for five weeks starting in mid-November.

The Governor's illness placed an even greater load on Catherine's shoulders. She was a most capable nurse and housekeeper but she needed outside activities to break the monotony of time spent with elderly and infirm parents. She was able to take holidays when Mary or June looked after her parents, but she needed more routine interests to get her away from the house for short periods. She was a member of the National Trust and of the British Legion, and many years earlier she had become a keen archer.

Catherine's interest in archery began when she spent a pre-war holiday in Belgium accompanied by her step-grandmother, Nancy Beckingsale. Auntie Nan as she was known in the family, was keenly perceptive. She realised that Catherine

lacked the confidence of her sisters and believed that she was
the 'black sheep' of the family. Auntie Nan saw that the girl
had a latent strength which would only mature if she was
prised away from the home environment. It was during this
Belgian holiday that Catherine was introduced to archery
and that she gained the courage which eventually led her to
leave home for a nursing career. The war prevented the
development of Catherine's archery skills, but in 1956 she
met the late General Vickers at a British Legion dinner which
she attended with a newly-found friend, Betty Hilltout. The
General, who came from an old established Cheltenham
family, was bored with retirement and decided that the time
had come to revitalise the Cheltenham Archery Club, a club
founded in 1857. In Catherine he found a willing helper. She
served as secretary of the club for many years and later was
elected chairman. But Catherine was not just a willing
administrator, she was an outstanding performer with the
longbow, Robin Hood's weapon. Catherine was the winner
of all the major club trophies for ladies and in the early 1960s
was selected to represent Gloucestershire. Longbow shooting
is the most skilled form of archery. The longbow has no
sights, and it is made from one piece of yew. Catherine was at
her best in the sport before the man-made fibre, Dacron, was
used for the bowstring, and when the tension of the flax or
linen bowstring had to be adjusted depending on the
temperature and humidity. At the time of her parents' illness,
Catherine was a prominent archer in the Cheltenham Club, a
member of the Worcestershire Bow Meeting, the Hereford-
shire Bow Meeting, the Gloucester Club, the Ilkley Club, and
the British Bow Society. More importantly she was a member
of the Royal Toxopholite Society, the leading archery club.
These interests helped her to endure the strains of life at
Homelands.

By June 1973, Catherine had nursed her parents to better
health and they were able to travel to Liverpool for the
wedding of Christopher Charnock. This was followed by
their Diamond Wedding anniversary, held at Prestbury
Court Hotel, Cheltenham. The photographs of that event
clearly portray the changes which were occurring in the
structure of the family. Grandchildren and others of their
generation were in the majority, Enid Beckingsale and her

twin sister Alice Keen were the only members present of the happy couple's generation. The wide gap in age between the principal guests and their family in no way took away from the pleasure of the occasion and the warmth of feeling for the couple was far far greater than they had experienced from the families at their wedding in 1913.

Sarah Charnock was married on 2 August 1975 but neither her grandfather nor her grandmother were fit enough to make the journey to Lewes, although they did visit her at her new home in Wantage a short time afterwards.

In 1976, the Governor was unwell again and re-entered hospital for further surgery. A large growth was removed from his abdomen and he was deeply distressed to find himself almost totally incontinent for many months. Catherine was no longer able to cope with nursing her parents and looking after the house without assistance. She employed a woman helper and May Payne, Jim's widow, who was a trained nurse, acted as relief for Catherine in the sickroom and visited Homelands each day to bath both Mr and Mrs Oldacre.

The Governor was not an easy patient to handle. Immediately his strength improved, he was out of bed expecting to be allowed to work in the garden. But Catherine and May Payne both former hospital sisters, had more than enough experience of difficult patients to keep him under control. By the beginning of 1977 he was out and about again, able to do some gardening and to take short walks around the farm.

On 14 February 1977, William John sat beside his wife's bed while they both drank their morning coffee. He was in a light hearted mood but restless to be outside in the freshness of his garden.

'I'm just going to pick a few sprouts and to do a bit of tidying up', he said as he finished the last of his coffee. He looked back at his wife as he left the room and she managed a nod and a smile.

Shortly after her father had left the room, Catherine returned to find her mother vomiting blood. She did all that she could to make her mother comfortable before running to telephone for the doctor: the number was engaged and Catherine felt that vital minutes had slipped by before she eventually managed to summon him. She now had the delicate task of informing her father of his wife's serious condition, a duty which she had deliberately delayed because she anticipated that he would be highly emotional and a hindrance to her. William John was indeed deeply distressed and extremely angry with Catherine for not calling him earlier.

Gladys seemed to sense that she was dying and pleaded with Catherine to let her die in her own home and in her own bed. The doctor knew immediately that the bleeding came from a perforated stomach ulcer and could only be arrested with surgery. He administered a pain killing injection and called the surgeon and the ambulance. The sadness in her mother's eyes when she heard the ambulance bell ringing as the vehicle approached Homelands and she realised that she was to be moved to hospital, deeply moved Catherine, and the memory still lingers with her. There was nothing that Catherine could do to change the course of events, the doctor was rightly in charge of the situation. When his wife had been lifted into the ambulance, the Governor travelled with her to the hospital and Catherine alerted Enid Beckingsale, who lived close to the hospital, to be ready to meet the ambulance and to look after her father when his wife was taken into the operating theatre. Once Catherine had tidied up at Homelands, she drove to the hospital to be at her father's side when the operation was over.

An operation to stop the haemorrhage from the stomach was performed immediately Gladys Oldacre arrived in hospital and blood transfusions were given. The Governor waited anxiously for news and was much relieved when he was told that his wife had come safely out of the anaesthetic. Exhausted and in a very distraught state he returned to Homelands with Catherine. He was clearly anxious about his wife's condition but he was also angered that she had been taken away from the home which she loved. His attitude did little to help Catherine who was also much distressed. The next morning, John Oldacre visited his mother and in her semi-conscious state she recognised her son, but at 11.30 am on 15 February 1977, shortly after John had left his mother's side, Gladys Oldacre passed peacefully away. She was 85 years of age.

June arrived at Homelands to hear the telephone ringing.

She steeled herself to break the sad news to her father, and held him tightly and did her best to comfort him as he shook and sobbed in anguish. William John had relied on his wife's calm wisdom on family and business matters for more than 60 years. He had been in love with her since 1907 and he could not face the future without her.

William John summoned up the strength to lead the family mourners at the funeral service which was held at Saint Michael and All Angels, Bishops Cleeve. After the service he was taken back to Homelands where Doris Burnett looked after him until the sorrowful family returned from Cheltenham Crematorium.

Gladys Oldacre's will reflected the concern which she had always shown about the preferential treatment which her husband had given to his grandsons over his granddaughters, when placing company shares into trust funds. His original trust, in favour of all his grandchildren, offered possible advantages to any boy who joined the business. Later he made further trusts in favour of his grandsons alone. Gladys Oldacre's will included small legacies of shares to her five granddaughters, before the bulk of her estate was divided between her five children, part on her death and part on the death of her husband. The gesture towards her grand-daughters reflected the fairness which dominated her thinking throughout her long life.

(iii) Modern technology arouses the interest of William John

William John Oldacre was a sad and sick man following the death of his beloved wife and the family wondered if he could survive her for more than a few months in such a depressed physical and mental state. However, he still had a resilient nature and slowly but surely he began to gain strength under the firm and loving ministrations of his daughter Catherine. He came to rely on her totally and to accept her authority in the home. He established a relation-ship with his daughter which was in many ways similar to that which had existed between himself and his father so many years earlier. William John was never to regain the buoyancy of his earlier years, but his mind remained active and he was stimulated by the progress of the family business of which he still considered himself to be the head.

Shortly after the death of Gladys Oldacre, Bruce Cliffe completed eight years with the family business and as agreed, William John released to him a second and final block of shares from the W J Oldacre Discretionary Settlement Trust, which had been formed in favour of all of his grandchildren.

The Governor was now to receive a further blow. John Oldacre and Henry Shouler had both been recommending Bruce to broaden his horizons and possibly take employment for a short period outside the family company. By April 1977, Bruce had made up his mind on what he wished to do, and advised the board that he intended to return to New Zealand on 31 May. Bruce remained as a non–executive director of W J Oldacre (Holdings) Ltd, but resigned from his position as managing director of Oldacre (Services) Ltd. From New Zealand, he worked in a company with overseas markets and familiarised himself with international trade.

Whatever the motives of the board of Oldacres and of Bruce Cliffe may have been the Governor's vision seemed shattered. He had worked and hoped for a grandson to take control when the time came for his son, John, to retire. He had five grandsons. Bruce had gone back home; John Cliffe, an accountant, was working happily in New Zealand; Christopher Charnock, a biology graduate, was in local government; Stephen Charnock, a law graduate, was serving his articles with a firm of solicitors in London; and Ian Cliffe was still a student.

A man who has had boundless energy throughout his long life does not take kindly to the problems of old age. William John was mentally alert but plagued by physical disabilities. He was severely deaf, partially blind in one eye and constantly troubled with his bladder. The effect of these debilitating conditions on his temperament was further aggravated by frustrations stemming from his lack of control over the family and the business. He was not a man who could sit back and enjoy the hard earned fruits of his earlier labours.

By the summer of 1977 he had regained some of his former strength. He missed the company of his wife, but he became fit enough to spend a limited amount of time in his garden where the heavier work was now being done by Syd Burnett. Each enjoyed the other's company in the rather unique relationship which had existed between them over many years; the Governor was still the master but Syd was a friend as well as an employee. They disagreed on many facets of vegetable gardening and they were great rivals when it came to cropping levels and quality, but they shared their produce. Syd and Doris now lived in a property in Oxenton owned by their son-in-law, Trevor Cook; Trevor was the grandson of John Cook who had offered the Governor financial help so many years before. Here Syd helped Trevor on his farm whenever the need arose. This continued practical involvement in farming offered a good basis for discussion with the Governor when they were together.

The Governor was prevented from striding over his farm by the rough and sometimes sticky nature of the ground and by the hedges and fences, all of which now formed obstructions to the old gentleman. He had to content himself with using powerful binoculars to look across the fields from the picture windows of his bungalow. When there was no work for him to do in the garden, or when he wished to make a more thorough inspection of the stock, he might take exercise walking along the narrow and busy Gotherington Lane which led to the farm buildings. The journey was barely more than two hundred yards but despite failing eyesight he missed nothing along the way. He noted the state of the gates and gateposts, any ditches which were silted up and any areas of wet land in the fields, poor hedges or fences, the state of the crops and the health of the animals as they grazed the pastures. Once in the farmyard he examined the cattle or sheep in the stockade at close quarters. He missed the fine Hereford steers which had played such a prominent role in his farming days, but he willingly rubbed the nose of any Fresian beast which came to greet him. If he was fortunate enough to meet one of the farm workers, he would pause and chat about soil conditions, crop and milk yields, feeding policies or any other farming matter.

Gardening and farming were not his sole interests. He was anxious to keep himself abreast of the activities at his mill and of his business generally. It was not long after Bruce had left for New Zealand that Christopher Charnock joined Oldacres

Spalding Mill

firstly as a representative in the Cheshire area, and later as a member of the technical division. There was now an upsurge in the Governor's spirits, and in his eyes Christopher became John's righthand man. The true position was that the company was firmly under the guidance of John Oldacre and Henry Shouler.

In spite of a falling national market in animal feed, W J Oldacre Ltd, the animal feed company continued to prosper and expand. At the beginning of 1977, it was clear that the massive increase in sales of Oldacres animal feeds which had occurred in the previous year following a major drought, would not be repeated. The total number of heifers in calf for replacement of the dairy stock and beef production had reduced, the total numbers of pigs and egg-laying poultry were also down. However, in these more difficult trading conditions, Oldacres sales still increased to a record 160,239 tons, against national consumption of animal feeds which had dropped. The company's share of the national market was higher than ever.

Oldacres were ready to begin their search for a seventh mill and John Oldacre found exactly what he was looking for in Spalding, Lincolnshire. South Holland Mill, Spalding, which had been a mill since the start of the eighteenth century had been purchased by the Plowman family in 1908. The Plowman business had been founded in Moulton Chapel, Lincolnshire in 1849 and the background of the business fitted in well with Oldacres, who were ideally suited to carrying on the traditions built up by the Plowman family over 130 years of trading with the Lincolnshire farming community. The mill had been completely re-equipped with new machinery over the previous five years, and Oldacres planned further modernisation to increase the efficiency of the mill and to improve the quality of the products. They began trading from the mill in 1979/80. It was scheduled to produce 25,000 tons in 1980/81, three quarters of the output would be delivered to customers in bulk and orders would extend over seven counties.

Development in the technical division kept pace with growth in the feed division. The laboratory and computers were still based at Bishops Cleeve and the success of the division was largely due to its close on-farm involvement with customers and its capacity for preparing feeding programmes to meet the individual circumstances of the customers. Bob Phillips and his team spent the majority of their time out on the farms dealing with questions about rations for dairy and beef cattle, and pigs and sheep, while Lesley Silvester who managed the laboratory and computer was called in when needed as the poultry expert. The laboratory was capable of analysing customers samples speedily and similarly of offering speedy decisions on quality control for all the mills. In addition the division advised farmers on the nutritional value of feeds which they had mixed for themselves, and they gave similar advice to the smaller county compound millers even though they were competitors. Oldacres supplied these farmers and smaller millers with premixes and various products and indicators. As the basis of animal feeding became more and more scientific, Oldacres were prepared to analyse the quality of sileage in a farmer's clamp and to recommend the best compounds to supplement that sileage.

Farmers wanted and needed to be kept abreast of the latest developments in animal nutrition. To this end, Oldacres organised conferences, teach–ins, mill visits and farm walks.

On these courses Bob Phillips and his colleagues introduced and explained the benefits of feed formulae which had been designed in the laboratory, the methods and advantages of manual or computerised dairy cost programmes and the calculation of feed conversion factors. While most of the classroom study was centred on the conference room at Cleeve Hall, Bishops Cleeve, larger meetings might attract as many as 150 famers and these were held at local conference centres, speakers being drawn from Agricultural Colleges, Government Departments and the farming community itself, as well as staff from Oldacres. The division also organised visits to the Continent where feeding methods were examined and discussed.

The Governor was proud when he heard from John about new mills coming into production, or about progress in the nutritional field. But best of all, he loved to hear for himself the throb of a mill, to inhale the rich smell of warm meal and molasses and to talk with the staff. A left turn onto Gotherington Lane as he left Homelands would start him on the threequarter mile walk to the mill and Cleeve Hall. His journey took him to the village school. At the kissing-gate opposite the school, he would abandon the highway and cross the churchyard emerging near Beckingsale's shop, from there he walked down Church Road to his mill. He would stand near to the mill weighbridge awaiting the arrival of a bulk grain lorry. Once the weight was recorded, he would follow the vehicle and watch as the load of grain was deposited into an elevator hopper from which it was lifted into one of the tall silos standing beside the mill. Next he would visit the control room where he could watch the movement of grain along feed lines as lights flashed up on the control panel monitoring the operation of the mill. Moving around the mill his hand would slip between an outlet shoot and a paper bag clasping warm pellets before they passed into the bag; he would take a deep draught of the rich aroma from the pellets in his hand as he walked towards the warehouse. Here row upon row of Oldacre bags were stacked on pallets ready for delivery. The stacking of the bags and the movement of the pallets was done by fork–lift trucks; a far cry from humping and trucking hessian sacks of feed which had so often been his task when his father was alive. The

Governor would complete his tour with a quick check on the loading of bulk carrier lorries which now handled most of the animal feed leaving the mill.

The laboratory was fast becoming the nerve centre of the whole compounding operation and was not to be missed. Here the Governor would ask Lesley Silvester for information on the latest feed formulations and on the quality control which was being achieved at each of the mills; he was also interested to learn about the use to which the computer was being put. Most old gentlemen like to dwell upon the past but this was not the way of William John Oldacre. He wanted the staff to tell him about current happenings at his mill and to discuss prospects for the future. It was only after such preliminaries that he might tell the staff quite forcefully where they were going wrong and then how the job should really be approached. Throughout these inspections the Governor was shown great respect.

It was only a short walk from the mill yard to Cleeve Hall, where the ladies would give the Governor a warm welcome and immediately offer him coffee and companionship. News of his arrival at Cleeve Hall would pass around the office like a bush-fire. Henry Shouler was always ready to spend time discussing the progress of the business with him and each held the other in high esteem. But, most of the senior managers would take up defensive positions based on the theory that larger numbers offered greater safety from interrogation by the Governor. By the time he had finished his coffee they were likely to be involved in urgently convened meetings. The Governor may have been welcome and quite easy going on the shop-floor, but managers knew that any one of them could be subjected to detailed and difficult questioning on any aspect of the business; failure to offer an answer satisfactory to the old gentleman could mean that they would have to endure the full force of his wrath. All the Governor's energy would be spent by the time he was ready to leave Cleeve Hall. It was now the task of one of the staff to take him home by car, a service for which he was always grateful.

On his return to Homelands a meal would be ready for him. Catherine now acted as his companion, nurse, house-keeper and chauffeur. They did have quite open disagreements but she did not tolerate his tantrums and did not indulge him in the manner of his mother or his wife. He was happy for her to continue playing archery, taking an active part in club affairs and maintaining her other outside interests, provided he knew where she was going and when she would be back.

Catherine found that her father was openly appreciative of all that she did for him, and was a very much more responsive car passenger than her mother had been. On their regular outings through the Gloucestershire countryside over which he had canvassed and done so much business, he told her the names of his former customers as they passed by the farms; described graphically the appearance of the hay and corn ricks which they used to build in the fields and the quality of the crops and stock which the farmers had kept; recalled which farmers had been good customers and good payers, and those who had been bad payers; commented on any improvements which had been made to the landscape and to the farm buildings. He liked to call on Howard Counsell or Freda Wise, both of whom were friends as well as former employees. They would enjoy a cup of tea or coffee together, remember old times and talk about the growth of the company in which they all had served. Sometimes father and daughter travelled further afield to Oldacres mills at Witney and Calne; the Governor still liked good food and always preferred to take his main meal at mid-day, so when he was out with Catherine they lunched at the best hotels and took a glass of wine together.

The Governor was particularly pleased when John invited him to visit the more distant outposts of the Oldacre empire, but he could only make these longer journeys to Skeffington, and Spalding when he was fully fit. He found it most stimulating to sit beside John in his large Mercedes-Benz and to spend the whole day in the company of the man who had his finger on the pulse of the whole business. At times they disagreed quite violently about the handling of some aspect of the business or the size of the Governor's pension, but he adored his son and was proud of his achievements. And the son respected his father who had unselfishly handed over control of Oldacres when he was only 60 years of age.

John Oldacre reached his own 60th birthday in August

1977. In the past Gladys Oldacre had arranged all the great family gatherings, John now took on that role. The Lammas at Minchinhampton was an ideal setting for the celebration of his birthday and John invited his daughters, grandchildren, sisters, brothers-in-law, nephws, nieces, cousins, aunts and of course his father.

Once the party was over it was business as usual. William John's main interest was the feed company, but Cleeve Motors was showing a healthy return on capital. The eventual demolition of Mill House and Trapp's Cottage in Bishops Cleeve made room for a new development by the holdings company along the frontage of Church Road. Cleeve Motors had taken over the Bishops Cleeve garage in December 1978 along with the Fiat franchise. The Church Road development offered an excellent site for a new car sales showroom. The company began operating from this more prestigious show-room late in 1978. Four other retail premises formed part of the same development, and these were soon occupied, giving a much tidier frontage to the mill and the garage. By 1980, Cleeve Motors had leased additional premises on Eastern Avenue, Gloucester where a Volkswagen/Audi franchise was operational in the following year. The Governor took a keen interest in both developments and made regular inspections before the showrooms and workshops were opened.

John Oldacre was under constant attack from his father over the trading position of the service company. Sales of Mercedes-Benz commercial vehicles were rather slower than anticipated and output from the workshops was disappoint-ing. As a result, the company was giving a rather poor rate of return on capital and the holdings company board decided on major management changes. The necessary changes were made towards the end of 1979 and they pleased the Governor. Among those appointed were Stephen Charnock, then a qualified solicitor working as group solicitor with a public company. He became a non-executive director. The new management felt that efficiency in the workshops at Tewkesbury and Wokingham could be improved, but that larger premises were needed at Calne if real changes were to be effected. The holdings company now looked at the possibility of extending the land holding at Calne for the further extension both of the feed company mill and of the services company workshops. Six acres of land was bought adjacent to the existing mill but it was decided to close the Calne workshops and to move the business to a new and larger site in Swindon. Later, Christopher Charnock became a non-executive director of Cleeve Motors so three of the Governor's grandsons now had some involvement in the family business at board level.

The profitability and market activities of all the subsidiary companies came under close scrutiny by the holdings board. They kept a tight rein on capital expenditure, company and personnel policies, looked for and examined opportunities for further diversification and kept a close eye on government legislation. In turn the Governor watched the activities of the board most carefully, and on more than one occasion was moved to turn up at a meeting; John was not pleased and refused to start on the agenda until the 'intruder' had left.

The Wider Share Ownership Scheme which had been introduced by government became effective on 6 April 1979, and gave companies the opportunity to introduce Profit Sharing/Share Purchase Schemes which could take advantage of tax savings. This fitted in well with John Oldacre's ambition that the company should stay in the ownership of the family and the management personnel actively engaged in building the business. Under the new scheme, the board agreed that a proportion of the profit should be allocated to a staff bonus account each year and after distribution of cash bonuses, the balance should be paid to the trustees of the Share Purchase Scheme. The trustees, all employees of the company, were to use that money to buy shares in the company for eligible members and provided that the recipients held those shares for at least ten years, they would gain from the fact that no tax would be incurred on capital appreciation. The long serving members of the staff could in this way build up a personal stake in the company and benefit from any company growth.

John was pleased to use the grain and seed enterprise to explain to his father, the benefits which came from encouraging staff to build up a stake in the company. Oldacres had always purchased large amounts of feed cereals from their customers, but when mill requirements were met the customer had to look for other and often less advantageous outlets for the remainder of his crop. In 1974 management in the feed division had seen the opportunity to offer a marketing service to farmers whose grain met the necessary quality requirements, on the grounds that Oldacres should be able to obtain better prices for the grain than the farmer was able to obtain for himself. The enterprise was so successful that soon more than 100,000 tons of cereals off farms was being marketed and the scale of the operation warranted the formation of a separate company within the feed division. Oldacre (Grain) was born, with offices in Bicester, Edinburgh and Romsey, trading in milling wheat, milling oats, malting barley, oil seed rape, beans and all classes of home-grown feed grains.

In the late 1970s the Holdings Group results were excellent and shareholders became accustomed to dividends in excess of thirty percent. As the company sales approached £50 million in the 1980s, the authorised capital in the company was increased to £500,000, then to £1,500,000 and shareholders received further scrip issues of shares.

Although William John wished to keep the company in the ownership of the family, this did not prevent John from recommending the board that a change of status to that of a Public Company should be examined. He approached Stockbrokers, Stock Beech and Company of Bristol, who advised that it could well be in the long term interest for the company to apply to the Stock Exchange when proposed new rules for Unlisted Securities had been adopted. Further, they advised that the exact timing for such an approach would have to be determined later. The board asked Stock Beech to prepare a programme for discussion, with a view to an approach being submitted to the Stock Exchange in the autumn of 1980. In the event, no early action was taken.

By this time Bruce Cliffe had returned to England and was acting as a consultant to the group on international trade. His first report on opportunities for expansion overseas came at a time when Henry Shouler was about to embark on a study tour of milling techniques and export potential in North America, Japan, Australia, New Zealand and the Far East. When Henry arrived back in England, it was decided that any export activity should be based on Singapore rather than on Australia or New Zealand, and that such activity should initially concentrate on supplementation and technical expertise to the agricultural industries in South East Asia. Bruce was invited to examine the proposition in detail and to prepare a report basing his findings on a budget of £50,000 per annum over two years.

A new subsidiary company Oldacre (International) was formed in 1981. Hayward Sum Associates of Connaught Road, Hong Kong, were engaged to carry out market research and to look at the development of exporting and international trade in agricultural and related activities, over a trial period from 1 May 1981 to 1 March 1983, terminable by either party on not less than three months' notice in writing. The company also examined the possibility of setting up a small animal feed company in Egypt with The First Arabian Agribusiness. The proposal did not define clearly Oldacres financial liability, but they agreed to consider a royalty arrangement provided their liability was not greater than 42 percent of the total venture. Henry Shouler became a member of the board and Bruce Cliffe was asked to present a paper on a reassessment of the company's activities covering its past, present and future activities, with a view to establishing its place within the Holdings Company.

The incursion onto the international scene did not inhibit Oldacres from making bids for the issued share capital of a number of British companies. In the autumn of 1982, Grainec Ltd was acquired as a wholly owned subsidiary of the Holdings Company. Grainec was involved in business complementary with that of the grain division and their trading area which was adjacent to several of the group's mills, extended the geographical coverage of the company in that field of activity.

Food surpluses were a developing part of the EEC structure and their large stores of butter were soon referred to as the 'butter mountain'. It was clear to all in the farming industry that grain would be the next commodity to be in surplus as production was increasing while consumption was static and likely to fall. Oldacres as grain traders had always had to provide considerable storage capacity and they now saw the opportunity to turn grain storage into a profit making activity. The European Intervention Board for Agricultural Produce became a major customer for the

Chichester Mill

storage of grain by Oldacre (Grain) through the Home Grown Cereals Authority. Trading in these fields was of course much influenced by political decisions as well as market forces, and Oldacres had to watch the political scene most carefully. In September 1978 the company concluded negotiations with Southdown Feeds Ltd for the purchase of Terminus Mill, Chichester. The mill was situated on the Chichester Trading Estate close to the railway station and made an ideal location for the expansion of Oldacres sales into new territory in Hampshire, Sussex, and the Home Counties. The mill and warehouse were also in close proximity to port facilities offering easy access to the Channel Islands and to Europe. The availability of the manufacturing base of a sixth mill for three-quarters of the year, led to an upward adjustment of the company sales target for 1978/79 by 20,000 tons, from 185,000 to 205,000 tons.

Towards the end of the 1970s, the EEC promulgated new hygiene regulations which made it difficult for poultry packers in the United Kingdom. The packers found that they needed to upgrade their premises to meet the regulations and that this was expensive. Hintons Prepacked Poultry Ltd, an old established company and a major customer of Oldacres,

Santa Fé Express

found themselves short of the necessary capital to make the required changes. Oldacres came to their assistance with the offer to convert Hintons feed debt into equity in that company. The offer was readily accepted, Henry Shouler and Bill Wyman joined the board of Hintons and Oldacres effectively controlled the company. The changes stemming from EEC legislation encouraged many of the other compound feed millers to become similarly involved in poultry rearing and packing.

In the autumn of 1982 Santa Fe Express Ltd was acquired by Oldacres. Santa Fe operated a dry goods warehouse and heavy haulage company based at Stoke Orchard, close to Oldacres Bishops Cleeve headquarters. The coming together of the two companies offered maximum utilisation of Sante Fe's vehicle fleet. Their operations were seasonal between April and September each year, whilst Oldacres required more transport for their business between October and March. Santa Fe remained independent of Oldacre Services and Cleeve Motors, but it fitted in well with the transport activities of the Group and offered possibilities for the formation of a new transport and workshop company at a later date.

The 59th annual general meeting of Oldacre (Holdings) took place on 24 September 1982, and proved to be the last meeting at which the Governor was present. He watched as his portrait, which had been commissioned by the directors, was hung in the board room alongside that of his father, Walter John Oldacre Senior, the founder of the company.

(iv) The life of the Patriarch draws to a close

On 9 May 1979, the Governor reached ninety years of age. John arranged a party for the adult members of the family this time at Standish Park Farm. The numbers were swollen by friends of the family, including Howard Counsell and his wife, and Syd and Doris Burnett. The next day, the whole family including the children, attended a birthday lunch at Homelands in his honour. The dining table was moved into the lounge and was opened up to extend over the full length of that large room. More than twenty sat down to lunch, including Hilda and Mervyn who were again on a visit from New Zealand. At tea-time, candles were lighted on the birthday cake and the Governor enlisted the help of the youngest great-grandchild present, Matthew Aylen, to help him blow them out. Many of the family met again in October to celebrate Catherine's sixtieth birthday.

William John Oldacre was generous by nature and after the death of his wife he made two major gifts. In memory of his mother and father he provided new west doors for the parish church of Saint Michael and All Angels, Bishops Cleeve. The Archdeacon of Cheltenham dedicated the doors and the family were present at the service. Later he endowed a room at the Cotswold Cheshire Home in Cheltenham in memory of his wife.

His generosity and unselfishness were further evidenced by the encouragement which he gave to Catherine to take holidays on her own. He never wished to be a burden to her or to prevent her from living a full life. When she was away he preferred to remain at Homelands where May Payne had offered to look after him at any time, but he would not let her come. Twenty four hours after Catherine left Homelands he would be lonely and the telephone might summon Freda

Four Daughters
June, Mary, Hilda, Catherine

Wise to prepare his lunch. More often than not June would receive a telephone call in Lewes, much as she had done when her mother was still alive.

'I'm ill. Come at once', he would say, and put the receiver down.

After a few such abrupt telephone calls which had to be acted upon because he might be genuinely unwell, June did her best to persuade her father to come to Lewes when Catherine was on holiday. When the Governor was with us June acted as substitute factotum for Catherine. Together they made inspections of the mill at Chichester and enjoyed the Sussex coast and countryside. One of his pleasures at Lewes was to go shopping and he particularly liked one of the gentleman's outfitters in the narrow and busy High Street and the expedition tested June's driving ability and her patience to the full. Her father had to be driven to the shop door then she had to find a parking space, help make the purchases, fetch the car, once again park it right outside the shop, and then load her father into the car with all his parcels. The Governor made a number of off-the-peg and bespoke purchases at the tailor's, both for himself and for Syd Burnett who was of similar build. All went well on these visits until he decided to have a full suit of clothes made. It was an unfortunate decision and a great embarrassment to June. The suit did not fit to his satisfaction and although a number of alterations were made, the Governor would not accept the garment. June offered to pay the tailor but the offer was refused.

While the suit was being altered in Lewes, the Governor took another trip to New Zealand. Catherine bravely agreed to escort her ninety year old father on this journey half-way round the world. They travelled first class by air from London Heathrow, via Los Angeles to Auckland, a journey of more than thirty hours' duration. The Governor seemed to have enjoyed the flights and the pampered treatment which he received in the airports where he was taken from the VIP lounge to the plane by motorised wheelchair. The holiday was not a great success as he was expecting too much, and had too many memories of his earlier trips. Once the Governor was safely in Hilda's care, Catherine took the opportunity to cross the Tasman Sea to stay with friends in Sydney. The Governor was totally lost without her, even though he was well looked after by Hilda and her family. His poor eyesight and his inability to walk more than a short distance meant that his freedom of movement was restricted. When Catherine returned to Auckland, in the hope of improving his humour, she arranged to take him to see some of his old friends in other parts of the country. They travelled by an internal flight and hired a car at the airport. Their first port of call was with Reg and Ethel Coleman at Palmerston North. He was pleased to see Reg and Ethel, to swap family news and to walk around the small farm again. Later they moved on to the home of George and Ann Redman. George had retired from farming and while they had much to talk about, the Governor missed the freedom which he had experienced on earlier visits when they spent much time riding horses across the open range. The Governor stayed in New Zealand for a total of two months from 19 December 1979 to 10 February 1980, and made the return journey by air via Los Angeles.

The Governor was at last beginning to realise that his

dream of all his grandsons working in the business was unlikely to become a reality. He accepted that all the young men had spirit, were capable of reaching senior management posts on their own initiative and of commanding salaries which it would be difficult for Oldacres to match. He was pleased with the drive his grandsons exhibited, but he accepted the hard facts about Oldacres reluctantly. However, he still hoped that the business dynasty which his father had founded 100 years earlier would continue for many generations to come.

The Governor was deeply disturbed by the sudden deaths of Arthur Pears, the husband of his niece Lucy, and of John Charnock, both in their early sixties. But a further shock was in store for him. Syd Burnett was killed in a tractor accident on the farm of his son-in-law, Trevor Cook. It seemed impossible to the Governor that Syd should have died before him and in such tragic circumstances. The funeral took place at Oxenton church, Catherine was away from home and June travelled to Gloucestershire to stand by her father at the service. Howard Counsell was also present and the two men were white-faced and drawn as they moved slowly towards their cars after the service. Howard Counsell returned to Homelands with his old friend and they sat together silently over a cup of coffee whilst Howard Counsell gained the strength to drive himself home to Tewkesbury. Syd's death left yet another great void in the Governor's life.

Many of the Oldacre family seem to have been overseas whenever illness struck one of their number at home. Mary and Ernest were with their daughter Helen in South Africa for Christmas and New Year 1983, and we were staying with Hilda in Auckland. When we left England, the Governor was having some difficulty in swallowing his food and he spent some part of each day in bed, but he seemed to be reasonably strong for a man of his age, but as the New Year approached the Governor spent more and more time in bed. Catherine wrote to the families in South Africa and New Zealand alerting them to their father's condition; and within three days he was unable to eat any food and so she had no alternative but to move him to the Nuffield Hospital in Cheltenham. She again wrote to her sisters warning that their father's life was slowly drawing to a close. Hilda and June were shocked by the news and after a hurried telephone call to England, made immediate plans to return home. Mary was making similar plans in South Africa.

During these anxious days Catherine, John, his daughter Jill and the Governor's three grandsons, Christopher, Stephen and Ian who happened to be within a reasonable distance of Cheltenham visited the hospital. On the afternoon of 20 January John arrived at the Nuffield to find his father asleep so he settled himself in the chair beside the bed. Later his father opened his eyes and they talked for a few minutes before the Governor said:

'I've had a good life John and I'm ready to go.' He paused, 'I don't know what I would have done without you and Cath, thank you both.' He then dropped off to sleep.

Catherine spent most of the next afternoon at her father's bedside but he was in a coma, and at 7 pm on 21 January 1983, he passed away peacefully. Ian Cliffe, on holiday in England from his home in New Zealand, was at the hospital and it was he who broke the news to Catherine.

Hilda and Mervyn arrived in England on 21 January, but June was stranded with me at Sydney airport where our plane was grounded with engine trouble. We arrived the next day. Mary and Ernest also arrived home too late to see the Governor before he died.

The funeral service was held at Saint Michael and All Angels, Bishops Cleeve, the church where he had been baptised more than 90 years earlier. John was unwell and unable to attend so Mary led the family mourners. Later the Governor's ashes were taken to join those of his beloved wife in the grave in which their daughter Mildred had been laid almost 38 years earlier.

10

FLOTATION ON THE STOCK EXCHANGE
1983–1986

The death of William John Oldacre at the age of 93 marked the end of an era. He had dominated the family and the business through the strength of his character and the power of his personality. It was inevitable that his death would be followed by changes in the nature of the family which at that time numbered 28 children, grandchildren and great-grandchildren, and in the status of the business.

The Governor prepared and signed his last will only a few months before he died. It was quite straightforward. He left the whole of his estate to his daughter Catherine, who had devoted so many years of her life to the care of her parents. The family readily accepted the action of the Governor During his lifetime William John Oldacre had transferred almost seven times the probate value of his estate to his children and grandchildren, and had made numerous charitable gifts.

In the 90 years of William John's life Oldacres had grown from a small corn merchants' business serving farmers local to Bishops Cleeve by horse and dray, into the largest privately owned animal feed compounder in the country, trading over the whole of the Midlands and South of England, and Wales. Seventy seven percent of the ordinary capital in the company was held by 15 members of the family, of whom four controlled the majority of the shares directly or indirectly. The demands on the business of the various members of the family were diverse. The death of William John in 1983, posed very different problems for the management of the company from those which followed the death 50 years earlier of Walter John Oldacre Senior, the founder of the business.

William John had made a very major contribution to the success of the business. In particular, he had devoted the whole of his boundless energy to the business from the time when he left school in 1904, until he resigned from the role of Chairman in 1970. He had fought without respite to rectify the situation in which he found himself on the death of his father in 1933. At that time he had been the major shareholder controlling the business goodwill, the plant and the stock, but his mother and sisters owned the majority of the property from which the business functioned, and he had been desperately short of capital. He had vowed that he would never leave his son with the same financial problems and had later made good that pledge. When at 60 years of age he had handed over control to his son all the buildings used by the company were in their ownership and he had been prepared to use his land as collateral when Oldacres needed extra capital. Although his son did not directly control the majority of the ordinary shares at the time of his father's death, he did have effective control; the value of the capital of the other members of the family and the rate of return on that capital were in the hands of the Board of the Holding Company.

At the 60th annual general meeting of the company in September 1983, the board of Oldacre (Holdings) Ltd included two members of the family, John Oldacre (chairman), and Bruce Cliffe, as well as Henry Shouler (chief executive), A F Bartlett and W Wyman. Shortly after William John's death the board was strengthened by the addition of Stephen Charnock (non-executive); David Carpenter (financial director), and A Wignall (group accountant). Changes were also made to the boards of the subsidiary companies, at which time Christopher Charnock joined the board of Oldacre (Services) Ltd as company secretary.

Oldacre (Holdings) continued to prosper and there was a further capitalisation of reserves in February 1983, when shareholders received two additional shares of £1 each for every £1 share which they held at the close of business on 15 February; at the same time an interim dividend of 7.5 percent was declared on the increased issued capital. A second interim dividend of 7.5 percent was paid in May of that year

Oldacres Board Members
Erick Watterson, John Oldacre, Henry Shouler
Bill Wyman, Bruce Cliffe
Herbert and Eric Bull

and a final dividend of ten percent was recommended at the annual general meeting in September 1983.

Oldacres entered the new financial year of 1983/84 full of confidence. The group anticipated a profit of £3.1 million on a turnover of £87 million and the feed company was again expected to contribute the major proportion of that profit. The feed company budgeted on sales of £39 million, representing an increased market share and profits in the order of £2.5 million; profits for the other subsidiaries were expected to vary between £130,000 for Santa Fe Express downwards to £2,600 for Oldacre (International). In the event, the feed company failed to achieve the budgeted margin notwithstanding the fact that the volume sales budget was exceeded. The principal factors leading to the disappointing performance stemmed from the unexpected rise in raw material prices, unprofitable term contracts and to a higher proportion of the less profitable pig feed sales. The other subsidiaries achieved satisfactory results.

The Holdings Board still had in mind the possibility of applying to the Stock Exchange for dealings in the company's shares on the unlisted securities market. They chose that market because they believed that dealings on the listed market would require 25 percent of the ordinary shares to be made available on the first day of trading, and that this would not be acceptable to the shareholders. They agreed to prepare a five year profit projection bearing in mind the possible need to change the articles of incorporation, the revaluation of the land and buildings, and the level of dividend that should be paid on the increased capital which had been agreed in February 1983. Meanwhile the board continued to look for further milling outlets and warehouse premises, and to investigate other businesses which might fit in with the activities of the broader based Group.

A new mill was planned at Cullompton, Devon, and the board considered the possibility of increasing their activities in poultry rearing and packing. Hintons Prepacked Poultry had experienced further financial difficulties in 1980 because the majority of the shareholders would not put more cash into the business. Oldacres had been given the option to purchase the company and Henry Shouler had strongly supported the suggestion, but the directors had other more pressing demands on their capital. Hintons was sold. Swifts, the American meat packing company, took a 50 percent share, Henry Shouler remained on the board of Hintons and Oldacres continued to supply their poultry feeds. In 1983 the other shareholders offered to sell their stake in Hintons to Oldacres who were very anxious to protect their proportion of the rapidly expanding poultry feed market. In the event Swifts were taken over by another American firm and negotiations with Oldacres were ended abruptly, with the additional loss of Hintons as a customer. Oldacres could not afford to be squeezed out of the packaged food market and turned their attention to another poultry packing firm, Wiltsdown Ltd, which they later acquired.

The village of Bishops Cleeve had expanded rapidly and the Local Plan for the village involved further substantial development. It envisaged a new bypass to the west of the village, with housing and industry being located between the bypass and the existing Evesham Road; a local distributor road was planned to pass through the garden of Cleeve Hall. The site of the mill on the opposite side of the Evesham Road was also affected and zoned for housing and retail use. The latter proposal offered the opportunity for Oldacres to realise their capital and to relocate the mill on a site at Stoke Orchard either adjacent to Santa Fe, or in the buildings of the old aerodrome. In May 1983, while all these matters were under consideration, the answers to the earlier questions raised about flotation came back onto the agenda. The board still felt that an application to the Stock Exchange was not in the best interest of shareholders and employees, but they decided that they must reconsider the matter at regular intervals.

Shortly after the board's decision had been made, a letter was received from Messrs Taylor Garrett, a firm of Solicitors, acting on behalf of unnamed clients. Their clients were shareholders in the company who apparently felt that problems existed in the lack of freedom in the marketability of their shares and the market value of those shares. John Oldacre met Taylor Garrett's representative with Mr E D Watterson, Oldacres' solicitor. They were told that Taylor Garrett were acting for shareholders who held in excess of 25 percent of the issued capital of the company, but that they were not in a position to give the names of the shareholders. Taylor Garrett suggested that their clients should be allowed to sell their shares freely at a 'reasonable' price and one which was not controlled by the board of directors, or the company should be listed on the Stock Exchange.

The directors believed that there were two possible courses open to them. They could challenge the position in which they found themselves for they believed that they could by retaining the best legal advice, hold off the challenge; or they could agree to seek a flotation. It was realised that the prospects for the feed company were of paramount import-ance if the latter course was to be adopted and they reviewed the 1984/85 budget closely in the light of that possibility. After much deliberation they advised shareholders and employees that in the best interest of all concerned, they were considering a listing.

By July 1984, Stock Beech and Company, Bristol had made representations to the Stock Exchange on behalf of

Oldacres and the necessary work was put in hand to meet the flotation requirements. The name of the company was changed to Oldacre (Holdings) PLC; it was re–registered as a public company; the land and buildings were revalued by professional valuers; the authorised capital was increased to £5 million; the existing ordinary shares of £1 each were subdivided into shares of 20p each; further reserves were capitalised on the basis of a one-for-one bonus issue; and the articles of association were amended to meet the requirements of a public company. An introduction timetable was prepared for a full listing, and this indicated that dealings could start on 4 October 1984 provided admission was granted. The earlier investigations had revealed that a full listing was indeed possible, since 23 percent of the shares were held outside the family by existing and retired staff, and these could be considered to constitute the major part of the necessary 25 percent of the equity which the market would require at the start of trading.

When the listing took place, Oldacres sales of animal feed had increased to more than £45 million, and showed higher profitability than in the previous year. During the year, the new mill at Cullompton, Devon had been brought into production, the company had invested £1.2 million in updating and expanding the facilities at their other mills and were confident that their production per man hour was one of the best in the industry. The areas of Cheshire and Wales were now served from two new stores opened during the year at Carmarthen and Buckley, Clwyd. A national survey into the feed industry in the United Kingdom indicated that Oldacres was the leader for return on capital employed, and that this had been accomplished by their continuing investment in modern feed milling technology.

The grain trading and storage activities of the company had also increased to £28 million, again with higher profitability. But, following the large surplus of Common Market grain, the board warned of likely political and economic pressures on the grain market. The majority of the grain which Oldacres handled was stored on behalf of the Intervention Board of Agricultural Produce, with the balance being for an International Trader on a long term contract. The effective utilisation of their grain stores was dependent

Walter John Oldacre Junior
Chairman, Oldacre plc

upon the ability to handle large volumes of grain in the short period immediately following harvest and the company were planning capital expenditure to improve their efficiency in that field.

Vehicle sales and servicing were both beginning to move out of recession and Oldacres sales were showing a healthy increase. Mercedes Benz commercial vehicles were finding favour with operators and their tractors were slowly being accepted. The registration of new cars was increasing and the new Audi/Volkswagen dealership at Gloucester and the change to Volvo at Bishops Cleeve meant that Cleeve Motors Ltd was returning to profitability. The other subsidiary companies showed similar good returns and the dividend payable in 1984 was 35 percent against a dividend of 25 percent in 1983.

At an extraordinary general meeting of the company held on 14 September 1984, special resolutions relating to the status of the company as a public limited company were approved. Trading in Oldacres shares began on 4 October, at a figure of 92p.

John Oldacre remained as chairman and Henry Shouler as chief executive of the public company. The first year of trading showed continued growth and development in all activities. John and Henry had worked together for 25 years and had formed an outstanding management partnership. On demobilisation from the Royal Air Force, John Oldacre had been single-minded in his determination to make Oldacres a major and respected force in the agricultural industry. He was urged on by the belief that anything which his grandfather and his father could do, he could do better. Against strong initial opposition from his father, he moved the company out of general corn merchanting and into the manufacture of compound feeds. Throughout his stewardship of the company he remained a master of staff selection and was prepared to delegate responsibility to the men whom he had chosen, but he kept his own finger firmly on the pulse of the whole farming industry. He gave total support to any member of the staff who gave of his best, but he did not suffer fools gladly. John's personality, detailed knowledge of farming and his quietly persuasive approach made him much respected by the farming community. His contribution to the success of the company was immeasurable. Henry Shouler was a shrewd businessman and his insight went far beyond the rather specialised trade in which Oldacres were involved. His judgement on the broader horizons of the business world was always sound.

However, the financial year ending 31 March 1985 proved to be most challenging with perhaps the most difficult trading conditions that the company had faced for more than a decade. National politicians had been exhorting farmers to increase production for a good many years in order to keep back imports. This policy was now reversed by EEC quotas restricting milk production. The change brought a dramatic reduction in cattle food purchases nationally. But Oldacres once again managed to obtain a larger share of the animal feed market, limiting the fall in their sales of dairy feed and increasing their sales of poultry feed, largely offset the worst effect of the reduced market. A dividend of 4.0p per share was paid in 1985 against 3.5p in 1984.

Over the next 12 months the total sales of Oldacres animal feed increased to a new record level of £99.3 million, due mainly to the quality of goods and the service which Oldacres provided to their customers and partly to an increase in their geographical coverage. The company now started construction of another animal feed mill at Wrexham; acquired the grain trading business of Richard Moss (Grain) Ltd and relocated the business to their existing premises at Calne; completed the purchase of 10.6 acres of land at Stoke Orchard for industrial development; and acquired the assets of Wiltsdown Foods Ltd, a duck processing business in Wiltshire, taking their first independent steps into food processing. These developments came at a time of increasing unemployment, but Oldacres were able to report that they had created 35 new jobs in their company through continued investment and expansion. Oldacre (Holdings) PLC was ripe for take over.

A number of multi–national companies had been making overtures to John Oldacre and Henry Shouler about the possible acquisition of their company, but the sums which they talked of offering did not match the valuation which management placed on Oldacres. However, in July 1986 a formal offer of 160p per share was received from Unigate

PLC, the dairy, food and transport company. After much serious discussion by the board, it was decided that in view of the food surpluses being built up in the EEC, and future political considerations likely to adversely affect the farming industry which would make it difficult for the company to match the Unigate offer to shareholders for a considerable number of years, the chairman should open negotiations with the chairman of Unigate. John Oldacre and Henry Shouler had a number of meetings with the board of Unigate and a final offer of 183p per share was agreed, provided that the holders of 50 percent of the shares accepted the offer within 48 hours. John quickly got into touch with shareholders who together controlled a total of just over 50 percent of the issued capital, and asked if they would be prepared to accept a recommendation from himself to sign an irrevocable undertaking to sell their shares to Unigate. The shareholders were sworn to secrecy about the offer and prevented from dealing in Oldacres shares until the matter was resolved. The Unigate offer was worth just under £26 million and 51.6 percent of Oldacres shareholders gave the required undertakings. The bid represented a premium of 75 percent over the price of Oldacres shares immediately prior to the announcement of the bid. The offer became unconditional on 22 August 1986, when Unigate had gained control of 92 percent of the shares.

The zeal and single minded devotion to the business of three men, Walter John Oldacre Senior, William John Oldacre and Walter John Oldacre Junior was at an end. Trading by a company which had been a family concern, or at the very least a company in which the whole family had been involved for more than 100 years, came to an end.

The family found that only large sums of money remained from the business which had so dominated all their lives. At the time of the takeover, not one of the family lived in Bishops Cleeve.